Praise for *Trauma Made Simple*

"In *Trauma Made Simple* Jamie Marich accomplishes exactly what the title implies. Sure, trauma itself is never simple or easy to understand, but there are ways to uncover it, break it down, look at it, and treat it that are, and that is what Jamie presents here. This straightforward, easy to read, wonderfully accessible book will benefit not only treatment professionals, but lay readers seeking to better understand their trauma-related issues."

—Robert Weiss LCSW, CSAT-S
Author, Speaker, Clinical Addiction Media Expert

"Having a solid understanding of trauma is the lynchpin in the health and wellness of our society and Dr. Marich does a phenomenal job of synthesizing decades of divergent and complex thought and practice into an accessible framework cleverly woven together by personal stories and experiences. Trauma can be quite a complex topic but it doesn't have to be and this book proves it! Jamie brings a wonderful combination of personal and professional experience, academic understanding and just the right touch of defiance to provide an excellent, accessible, and heartfelt overview of the critically important topic of trauma."

—Dan Griffin, MA
Author of *A Man's Way Through the Twelve Steps* and *Healing Men Recover*

"*Trauma Made Simple* by Dr. Jamie Marich, is an articulate and accessible guide to the experience and the healing of trauma. Using stories and first-hand accounts, Dr. Marich beautifully conveys the human aspect of trauma. With its clear presentation of the technical aspects of trauma treatment, the book is a valuable resource for anyone working with trauma. Moreover, its user-friendly language is a gift to trauma survivors who seek to more fully understand both what has happened to them and how to move toward healing. Dr. Marich certainly knows the field of trauma. Whether you are a mental health professional or a person who has experienced the wound of trauma, *Trauma Made Simple* offers information, insights and a sense of caring that will be very helpful to you."

—Terry Fralich, LCPC, JD
Author of *The Five Core Skills of Mindfulness: A Direct
Path to More Confidence, Joy, and Love* and *Cultivating Lasting
Happiness: A Seven Step Gr* ⋯

"Dr. Marich's book is a beautiful, "common sense" guide to working with tr
type of therapist who gets weighed down by research, science, and the ov
need to pick up Dr. Marich's book. *Trauma Made Simple* breaks things dow
best be described as practical, human, and relevant."

—Sł
Author of
Psychotherapist/Contributor to VH-1's

"In *Trauma Made Simple*, Dr. Marich has provided an indispensable tool for all clinicians and caregivers. Her integration of personal and professional experience, research into trauma studies and trauma treatment, and the wisdom of others in the trauma community literally has resulted in a handbook for trauma treatment. Whether you are a trauma trained professional seeking additional helpful foundational materials for your work, or a clinician new to the world of trauma focused therapy, you will find the answers and guidance you seek along the way. Clinicians will benefit so much from this book, and even more importantly, so will their clients."

—Stephen Dansiger, Ph.D.
Private Practice, Los Angeles, CA
StartAgain Publishing

"Dr. Marich's personal style of writing is engaging, This is a "must read" for all clinicians dealing with diverse forms of trauma today. The title: *Trauma Made Simple*, is well chosen. She writes to her strength. Five stars."

—Paschal Baute, Ed. D.
Author of *Win-Win Finesse* and *Resilience of a Dreamcatcher*

Trauma Made Simple has heightened my ability to judge therapeutic timing . . . the extreme value of "the work before the work!!" Great clarification and practical thought about the sometimes nerve-wracking transition from DSM IV to the DSM-5, and about the role of the brain in trauma work. Thanks, Jamie, it really does "unscramble the eggs!"

—Connie Schultz, M.S. LICSW
Private Practice
Avon, MN

"This is a must read for every mental health clinician. Dr. Marich compassionately demystifies trauma by gently reframing the treatment focus on client wounds, with an emphasis on holistic and natural healing processes from the initial assessment and diagnosis through termination. The book thoughtfully and meaningfully clarifies an often murky transition to the current DSM-5. She genuinely listens to others, as evidenced by the inclusion of numerous "In Their Own Words" disclosures. Dr. Marich demonstrates a passionate embrace for a client-centered approach and provides us with not just another clinical read, but a rather moving experience."

—Frank A. DiLallo, M.Ed., LPC, LICDC, OCPS
Author of *Peace Be With You: Christ-Centered Bullying Solution*

"As someone who's meditated their way off of meds and worked with addiction and trauma for nearly 30 years, I'm astounded at the clarity and directness of Dr. Marich's work in this book. This book simplifies trauma etiology, diagnosis and treatment for clinicians and laypeople alike. A must read!"

—Darren Littlejohn, CYT
Author of *The Twelve Step Buddhist* and *The Power of Vow*

Trauma Made Simple

*Competencies in Assessment, Treatment
and Working with Survivors*

by

JAMIE MARICH, PhD, LPCC-S, LICDC-CS

Published by
PESI Publishing & Media, PESI Inc.
3839 White Ave
Eau Claire, WI 54703

Cover Design: Amy Rubenzer
Edited By: Blair Davis

Printed in the United States of America

ISBN: 978-1-936128-92-1

PESI
Publishing
& Media
www.pesipublishing.com

This book is dedicated to the veterans of the Vietnam War
From the bottom of my heart, thank you
Your stories particularly touched my soul as
I prepared this book
With special honor to our Vietnam veterans still
finding their way home . . .

Table of Contents

Acknowledgments

The alternative rock band My Chemical Romance released a song in 2010 called "Sing." This song is nothing short of an anthem for people who have something to say and, after a long period of repression, are finally able to say it. As I wrote this book, their anthem is what I heard in my head, and not just because I felt I had something valuable to share. Rather, it became my wish that survivors of trauma everywhere would be able to embrace the power in this song and be encouraged to feel their feelings, speak their voice, and express their truth:

> *Sing it for the boys*
> *Sing it for the girls*
> *Every time that you lose it sing it for the world*
> *Sing it from the heart*
> *Sing it till you're nuts*
> *Sing it out for the ones that'll hate your guts*
> *Sing it for the deaf*
> *Sing it for the blind*
> *Sing about everyone that you left behind*
> *Sing it for the world*
> *Sing it for the world* (Lanois, Daniel)

My most sincere gratitude, as ever, is to my clients for sharing your lives with me and teaching me so much of what I share in this book. May you sing your songs for the world, always, as you have inspired me to sing!

To my workshop attendees, readers of my previous works, and social media friends who continue to reach out to me in dialogue, I thank you. You all become a part of my support network when you make contact, and please continue to do so!

I wish to thank the people in my personal and professional support system who sustain me in my drive to sing my anthem. Special thanks to Maureen Lauer-Gatta, Mandy Hinkle, Allison Bugzavich, Ramona Skriiko, Kathleen Barreca, Trish Taylor, and Amber Stiles-Bodnar: You are not only collaborators, but soul sisters and the women most responsible for keeping me sane. To all of my *Dancing Mindfulness* facilitators, especially Abbey Carter Logan, I honor your spirits and thank you for your faith in me; you give me faith in the future of our helping professions. To my colleagues and fellow trailblazers all over the country, many of whom served as contributors to this book, namely Dr. Paschal Baute, Dan Griffin, Jeff Zacharias, Susan Pease Banitt, Dr. Earl Grey, and Colleen McKernan: Thank you for your encouragement and showing me that I am not alone. Your anthems ring in my heart every day. To my long-standing mentors, Dr. Doug Darnall, Dr. Amy Donovan, Dr. Howard Lipke, Dr. Scott Miller, Sara Gilman, and Dr. Laurel Parnell, there are no words to thank you for giving me my wings. I may have left the respective nests, but I always fly with you in my heart.

Thank you to those of you who provided invaluable assistance with this book in the form of your help, contributions, and beautiful sharing: Dr. Bruce Merkin, Dr. Wayne Eastlack, Holly Ann Rivera, Heather Bowser, Maridee Costanzo, Nikki Meyers, Lee Tze Hui, David Ferruolo, Paula Bossert, Susan Moffitt, Dr. Eli Mitchell, and Liz Rubino. Of course, thanks to those who contributed and wished to remain unnamed. You gave this book a human touch, and I thank you.

To my family at PESI, Inc./PESI Publishing & Media especially Claire Zelasko and Linda Jackson: THANK YOU!!! Both of you ladies continue to provide a platform for me to share my message with other helpers, and you inspire me in ways I can't put into words. Thanks for believing in this book and through our conversations, willing it into existence! Thanks to Mike Olson for supporting the vision, and for playing a vital role in career development over the years. Special thanks to Blair Davis, my editor; it was an honor and a privilege getting to work with you again.

To my "kids," Niki, Clayton, Kara, Eric, Will, Kayla, John, Amber, Corn, Scrappy, Misty, Joy, Ethan, and Brendan: Words do no justice to explain how your lives touch mine. I am a better person because all of you are in my life.

To my husband, my "Sun and Stars," David Reiter: We prove every day that what makes sense to everyone else about relationships isn't necessarily what works. Thank you for teaching me the meaning of unconditional love and for being my rock, my most steadfast support on this amazing journey.

And, of course, to Janet Leff... this book, my career, and my life all exist because of you and our shared Higher Power. *Hvala Vam lijepa!*

CHAPTER 1

Trauma Matters

The wound is the place where the light enters you.

—Rumi

DEFINING TRAUMA

No topic of social importance was off-limits to the late American comic George Carlin, including the psychiatric diagnosis of Post-Traumatic Stress Disorder. In one of his most famous rants, "Euphemisms" (from *Doin' It Again*, 1990), Carlin presented the evolution of how the psychiatric profession described trauma over the course of the 20th century. In World War I, combat trauma was called *shell shock*. Carlin mused that its two syllables—"simple, honest, direct language"—sounded like a piercing bullet. Then the Second World War ushered in the term *battle fatigue*—four syllables—and softer in Carlin's view. Next came the Korean War, when the term *operational exhaustion* prevailed, and as Carlin posited, with more syllables came less humanity. Finally, in the aftermath of Vietnam, the term *post-traumatic stress disorder*, our current label, emerged. As Carlin quipped, we now have eight syllables, a hyphen, and an even more sterilized, clinical-sounding diagnosis. In perhaps the most brilliant commentary on modern psychiatry and psychology, Carlin declared, "The pain is completely buried under jargon. . . . I'll betcha if we'd still be calling it *shell shock*, some of those Vietnam veterans might have gotten the attention they needed at the time."

As a clinical counselor specializing in the treatment of trauma and stressor-related disorders, I agree with George Carlin. In our attempts to be clinically savvy and medically relevant, we have lost the human touch when it comes to healing wounds. In its simplest form, that's what trauma is—a *wound*. The English word *trauma* is a direct translation of the Greek word for wound. One syllable—simple.

1

The past two decades witnessed increased interest in traumatic stress research. Trainings on PTSD proliferated, multiple organizations came into existence or expanded to address trauma, and clinicians reached out to those in need of care. Yet, so many human service professionals are more lost than ever when it comes to trauma and how to treat it. A central thesis of this book is that the helping professions continue to overcomplicate how we conceptualize and treat trauma. Perhaps we need to go back to the word origin basics for enhanced insight into understanding and healing emotional trauma.

Consider everything that your human experience teaches you about physical wounds and how they heal. Wounds come in a variety of shapes and sizes, resulting from various causes. While some are more serious than others, most wounds require care to heal. A gunshot wound will necessitate a trip to the hospital and may be fatal, especially if proper care is not administered. In contrast, a scrape may require only a simple washing and bandaging. Yet, with proper care and rehabilitation, the gunshot wound survivor may be well on his or her way to health, while the person with an unattended scrape could experience repeated infections.

Wounds can happen quickly and take a very long time to heal. However, if conditions are right, a person can recover from or at least adapt to an injury and lead a relatively full life. Some people are in a better position to heal than others. Perhaps they have access to superior care. Maybe they are given adequate time off from work to recuperate (compared to others who do not receive such accommodation). There are differences in genetics and constitution; for example, a simple scrape on a hemophiliac or someone with vulnerabilities to infection requires a higher level of care. Sometimes, the proverbial X factor in healing is attitude—consider how a person who believes "I am weak" might fare compared with the person who can accept that "I am only human—accidents happen."

Our society encourages us to continue working and navigating daily life while injured. We praise athletes who can muddle through injury, and when we are hurt, we may tell ourselves, "It's just a sprain—it's no big deal." We, like the athletes we admire, may be able to push through the pain—we learn that we can't baby every little injury or sickness. While there may be some truth to this logic, many of us too deeply internalize these "tough it out" scripts and ignore the legitimate warning signs of physical or emotional injury. We ignore our body's cues and cries for help. Like the Black Knight in *Monty Python and the Holy Grail*, we protest, "It's just a flesh wound!," when in reality, we're in bad shape (or in the case of the Black Knight, all of our limbs are falling off).

Veteran psychologist Dr. John Hoover (2010), a trauma expert and retired Marine, renders a useful distinction between being hurt and being injured using the metaphor of a football game:

> During almost every football game, play will be stopped if a player lying on the ground hurt is being attended to by the trainer. The announcer is likely to comment that the trainer is determining whether there is an injury to the player or if the player is just hurt. Injury is defined essentially in physical terms such as a break, tear, separation, sprain, whereas hurt refers essentially to pain. If the player does not have an injury, after waiting one play, he can return to the field of play even if he still feels pain. If the player does have an injury, he will not likely be cleared to play again until the injury has healed. Thus the phrase "you can play the game hurt but not injured" (p. 112)."

Life is like a football game. Because life can be very traumatic, pain is inevitable and it would not be feasible to stop life every time we got bumped. Like Hoover explains, learning the distinction between hurt and injured and knowing how to honor our need for care when we are injured are paramount.

In worst-case scenarios, especially in evaluating injuries that lead to permanent disability, total healing is not biologically realistic. Consider Heather Bowser, a woman whose story I will be telling throughout the book. Heather was born in 1972 with only one leg and severe deformities of both hands, injuries attributed to her father's exposure to Agent Orange during his Army service in South Vietnam. While Heather's gestational injuries are permanent in the medical sense, her ability to adapt to her condition is nothing short of exemplary. A successful counselor, business owner, wife, mother, and advocate for victims of Agent Orange exposure and children of Vietnam Veterans, Heather proves that even with grave, irreversible physical injury, it is possible to live a full and healthy life. That is the power of adaptation and resilience.

The human brain is hard-wired for healing in both a physical and emotional sense. However, quality of the healing conditions can make all of the difference. If a person is given the resources he or she needs for healing (e.g., time, social support, validation, proper care, spiritual guidance), emotional wounds can be healed. As with physical wounding, there may be scars, but if that emotional wound is given proper attention, the part that was hurt can become tougher—just like the skin of a physical scar—a beautiful metaphor for resilience.

I have spent years experiencing trauma, healing from it, helping others heal from it, writing about it, and teaching about it. Informed by these experiences, I contend that the wound concept is the simplest way to conceptualize trauma. Let's keep it simple—*trauma means wound.* If you want to delve into a more nuanced translation of the Greek word *traumatikos*, it means a physical injury that is capable of being closed up. Think back to the time in your life when you felt the most wounded, either physically or emotionally. What did you need to heal?

Being a trauma-sensitive professional and human being is, above all, about acknowledging and honoring woundedness. If the parallels between physical and emotional wounding resonate, this book will make total sense to you. The *wound* is the main motif of the book, and we consider its healing lessons throughout.

The title of the book is not meant to suggest that there is anything simple about traumatic stress and how it can wreak havoc on the human experience. On the contrary, the aftereffects of trauma can entangle survivors in a complex web of distress and complicated living. Untangling these webs can be a very involved process that is anything but simple. However, the title is meant to suggest that as helping professionals, we overcomplicate the study of trauma. It seems that every month someone comes out with a new model or paradigm for treating trauma. While advances in neuroscience continue to give us cutting-edge information on how trauma affects the brain, I see little to suggest that these scientific advances (and their dissemination) are producing more trauma-competent therapists.

Consider this metaphor: You can know everything about how a car works—the intricacies, the mechanics, the operations—but at the end of the day, do you know how to drive a car? More importantly, does your technical knowledge of the car help you drive more effectively in treacherous circumstances? If this answer is yes, that's great. My belief is that experience with working the car and navigating the roads of life is what makes you a skilled driver, not your knowledge of the car itself. Similarly, when scientific or philosophical knowledge takes humanity out of the equation or minimizes the vital role of experience in applying that knowledge, the knowledge fails to be useful.

In 2011, I wrote a book called *EMDR Made Simple: 4 Approaches for Using EMDR With Every Client.* My contention is that many people get tripped up with learning and implementing Eye Movement Desensitization and Reprocessing (EMDR) therapy (a popular modality in treating traumatic stress) because they overcomplicate it. I feel the same way about trauma treatment in general, and I carry that same spirit of *less is more* into this book. I have long embraced the wisdom of Occam's razor—that all things being equal, the simplest explanation tends to be the right one, even with something as complicated as trauma.

> Trauma is wounding.
>
> Wounds need care and time to heal.
>
> A little common sense and human connection go a long way in helping wounded people heal.

Trauma is a subjective human experience, colored by an individual's perception, life experience, and healing style. My general assumption is that if an experience is wounding, to a person, we should validate it as traumatic. This approach, what I call "broadening the definition of trauma," is not without controversy. Many people I've trained and professionals with whom I work get nervous when we start talking about trauma as more than just diagnosable PTSD. As one mentioned, "Well, if we say that everything can count as a trauma, aren't we impugning what people who go through really major stuff, like wars and genocide, experience? I mean, so much of these other things like divorce, and bullying, and losing a job are just life—deal with it!"

My answer to this sort of comment is that life, on the whole, is traumatic. Trauma affects some people more than it affects others. Just like there are various types and styles of physical wounds, so, too, are there different manifestations of emotional traumas. Expanding the clinical scope of trauma to include all human wounding is not meant to minimize the types of life-threatening trauma that may qualify for a PTSD diagnosis. Being *trauma informed* or *trauma sensitive* (I use the terms interchangeably throughout the book) is about recognizing that all wounds deserve attention. Being able to appreciate the subjective nature of wounding and healing is a core component of being trauma informed, and it will help us to be more effective in the delivery of clinical and community-based services.

IN THEIR OWN WORDS

When I give trainings on trauma, I challenge participants to take a few minutes to jot down their working definitions of trauma coming into the workshop. I inevitably find that no two people give me the exact same

(Continued)

definition or wording, which is to be expected when we consider how subjective trauma really is. How would you respond if you were asked, *What does trauma mean to you?* Some people describe a very specific incident, like the death of a loved one, 9-11, or a life-changing injury that, in their view, represents trauma. However, others give a more general or global definition, some of which are worth sharing:

Donna: Trauma means feeling horrible in response to someone or some situation that totally overpowers me. Trauma is like riding my bike, and the chain falls off—I can't get away!!!

Karen: Trauma is living with the aftermath of neglect, physical, mental, emotional, sexual abuse, abandonment, rapes, domestic violence, betrayals.

Vicki: Trauma means a wound that is either inflicted or perceived, which affects either the body or spirit.

Jim*: Trauma dries you out—it takes all of the natural oil and flexibility out of you so you can't bend with life—that's why traumatized people are so defensive. They are so afraid someone can break them at any time.

Nadia*: An event that alters the course of your life forever, a reoccurring nightmare that you have to strive to overcome . . .

Rena*: Trauma is reoccurring fear, paralyzing panic, guilt, shame, based on past life experiences, preprogrammed childhood upbringing.

Holly: Something that has shaken your inner core so badly you have to work through it.

Patty*: I've always viewed trauma as a weakness, not a wound, which is part of why I hated the word *trauma* so much; my therapist helped me redefine my definition.

Colleen: An injury due to a stressful event—affecting body, mind, spirit; I think most Native Americans would also define it as lack of integration from spirit.

Kathleen: Trauma and loss, for me, are interchangeable.

Joseph*: Hell.

Carla: Hell on earth.

*Pseudonym used to protect the contributor's identity.

ABOUT THIS BOOK

Throughout this book I share many stories and first-person accounts. Some stories are my own (both personal and clinical); others I cite from the literature and from the direct words of people who agreed to contribute their experience, strength, and hope to this project. The contributors and their experiences are major informants to this overall work. Some of the voices are friends, others are former clients and colleagues, and others are people who read about the *Trauma Made Simple* project online and agreed to participate for the sake of educating others. In some cases, former clients or contributors did not wish to be named, (when I use a pseudonym, I indicate this with an asterisk). Rest assured, this book addresses issues of technical importance to clinical practice (e.g., diagnosis, treatment planning, billing, agency logistics). However, the experiences of real people are included throughout the book to infuse humanity into the subject matter at hand. Encountering the lived experiences of trauma and recovery is, in my opinion, the best way to learn about trauma and how to treat it. As a clinician and an educator, I fully embrace the wisdom of poet and activist Muriel Rukeyser (1913–1980): "The universe is made of stories, not atoms."

I wrote this book primarily for a professional audience: social workers, counselors, psychologists, medical doctors, nurses, marriage and family therapists, pastoral counselors, and case managers. This book is not intended to teach you how to reinvent the wheel of your practice, but hopefully it will help you become more trauma sensitive in your day-to-day operations. If you already consider yourself to be a trauma-informed professional, I hope this book serves as an affirmation for you! You might be able to take some ideas from the book and blend them with your existing approaches.

Those who work in tandem with helping professionals are also likely to benefit from this book; for instance, 12 Step recovery sponsors, wellness providers (e.g., nutritionists, body workers), yoga or fitness instructors, teachers, and administrators. You are an important part of a client's world, and being trauma informed as a global precaution for all human services is optimal. This book is not meant to be a substitute for professional training, so if at any time you are reading a concept and are unclear about its meaning or appropriateness of application, seek guidance from a clinical professional within your network.

Because I strive to write in user-friendly language, there is a chance that you, the survivors of trauma, may be picking up this book to better understand what's going on with you. If you are in this boat, go for it. We can all stand to educate ourselves on what ails us. However, I strongly advise that you not use this book to replace professional diagnosis and treatment; only a licensed professional in your state can provide these services. If you are not currently under care and the concepts in this book are resonating with you strongly, I encourage you to pursue professional help. Seeking such help doesn't make you sick or flawed; it simply means that you are open to the assistance that might be out there for you. If at any time you feel like material in this book is too much to handle emotionally, put it down and engage in an activity you know will help you to distract in a healthy way (e.g., a hot bath, a cool shower, a brisk walk, prayer, playing with your pet, word puzzles, knitting, calling a trusted friend). If you experience an acute psychiatric emergency, (i.e., you feel like harming yourself or someone else), please call 911 or seek help in your local emergency department immediately.

My disclaimer about self-care applies to all of us—professionals, paraprofessionals, and lay people alike. Reading about trauma can be an intense, even triggering, experience. Thus, if at any time your body's internal cues tell you that you need to put the book down for a while, honor that. Finishing a book is not a race. Reading this material provides a chance to practice honoring your internal cues and treating yourself with kindness and compassion.

Chapters 2 through 4 continue to build on the foundation laid in this opening chapter. In Chapter 2, the new DSM-5® category of Trauma- and Stressor-Related Disorders, including updates to the DSM-5® diagnosis of PTSD, is thoroughly explained. These diagnoses are discussed with consideration to biopsychosocial-spiritual elements. In Chapter 3, we consider how grief and loss can be conceptualized as trauma, explain the constructs of grief, bereavement, and mourning, and discuss the broader definition of trauma. Chapter 4 presents the basics of trauma neurology that are most relevant to clinicians.

Chapters 5 through 7 cover important issues regarding assessment and treatment planning. Chapter 5 covers a variety of assessment strategies, quantitative and qualitative, direct and subtle. It is the hope that this chapter will allow professionals in clinical settings to know trauma or grief when they see it and develop an initial plan of action. Chapter 6, "The Addiction Imperative," is included because the comorbidity between trauma-related disorders and addictive disorders is so high. In this chapter, readers get a brief orientation to addiction and how to assess for it, especially when trauma-related disorders are also present. Chapter 6 also helps clinicians develop an initial plan of action for addressing addiction. Chapter 7 examines how empathy and the therapeutic alliance can be established from the first session. The quality of empathy is essential in working with clients on trauma. In this chapter, strategies for building empathy with a client, even very difficult ones, are explored.

Chapter 8 explores the consensus model of trauma treatment and its three stages: stabilization, reprocessing, and reintegration. The three-stage consensus model can be universally implied, regardless of a clinician's therapeutic or theoretical orientation, and it serves as an effective framework for healing trauma. Chapter 9 covers the first stage, stabilization, in greater depth, with Chapters 10 and 11, respectively, delving into reprocessing and reintegration. Chapter 12 is the ultimate wrap-up, challenging you to consider what you absorbed by evaluating what makes a good trauma therapist. The chapter delves into what professionals need to effectively work with trauma in clinical and community settings. Issues of self-care, self-awareness, and personal and professional competencies are explored in depth.

FURTHER READING

Mitchell, E. C., & Hoover, J. E. (2010). *The elders speak: Two psychologists share their lifetimes of experiences.* Knoxville, TN: Authors.

Mollica, R. F. (2006). *Healing invisible wounds: Paths to hope and recovery in a violent world.* Orlando, FL: Harcourt, Inc.

CHAPTER 2

Diagnosing Trauma:
DSM-5® and Beyond

If we can make the correct diagnosis, the healing can begin. If we can't, both our personal health and our economy are doomed.

—Dr. Andrew Weil

ON DIAGNOSIS

After two years of working as an English teacher and humanitarian aid volunteer in post-war Bosnia-Hercegovina, my mentors suggested that I return to graduate school for counseling. I looked at the admissions brochure from the small Catholic university in the United States with ties to my parish in Bosnia-Hercegovina. There was a stack of books on the front of the brochure, artistically staggered texts with titles like *Developmental Psychology* and *Counseling for the Modern World*. One book was thicker than them all, and the spine read *Diagnostic and Statistical Manual of Mental Disorders IV-TR (DSM-IV)*. I remember telling myself, "I don't know if I can do this!"

I learned not to fear the scary tome from the brochure picture, and even though I didn't agree with some of it, I learned how to use it. After all, using it was a necessity in the hospitals and treatment centers, where I completed my internships. My larger frustration was with meeting professionals who, in my view, misused the *DSM-IV*, or at very least, misinterpreted diagnoses. Even at my first clinical internship site, the evidence of unresolved emotional trauma was so apparent in the children and adolescents we treated. The irritability and emotional reactivity they demonstrated, especially when they felt cornered by staff, were all too familiar. Yet, the psychiatrists seemed to know only one diagnosis: Bipolar Disorder. When I transitioned to my second internship

11

site, a drug and alcohol facility, I was told I didn't have to worry about mental health diagnoses when I assessed patients, even though several clearly met criteria for PTSD.

Diagnosis in the treatment of mental and emotional problems is controversial territory. Even the chair of the *DSM-IV* task force, Allen Frances, MD (2013), believes the helping professions have gone too far in pathologizing the ordinary stresses of human life. I generally support the position of psychiatric legend Irvin Yalom, MD (2001), who believes that diagnosis is only really needed to get a patient's treatment to be paid for by third parties. There are so many people in my professional circles, especially expressive therapists and humanistic psychologists, who are adamantly opposed to diagnosis on moral grounds. They have especially raged against the new edition of the *DSM*, the *DSM-5*®, with vehemence! When I submitted an article to one expressive arts publication, the editor responded that he liked what I had to say overall, but he couldn't get past me using labels like *PTSD* or *disorder*. On one hand, I see his point—it would be fantastic if we saw only the person and not the diagnosis. But on the other hand, I have spent my career working in settings where I must diagnose in order to justify treatment and bill insurance companies or the government entities sponsoring treatment. Good luck working in an agency without using diagnosis!

I refrain from obsessing over diagnosis. If you're frustrated at me for already getting into heavy material on the DSM, especially in a book that claims to make something simple, I actually feel your pain. I want the focus to be on the person and not his or her illness, but diagnosing is a necessary evil in American clinical culture. Even the great humanists among us have to play the game, depending on where we work.

Moreover, there are some contexts in which learning about one's diagnosis can be useful and even empowering. Consider those individuals presenting for treatment believing that they are just "crazy" or "nuts." While labeling can, no doubt, be stigmatizing for some, for others it can be a relief to hear that their troubled behavior can be explained. I do not advocate using a diagnosis as an excuse for poor behavior (e.g., "I go off on my children because they trigger me—the PTSD makes me do it!"). When clients say this to me, I challenge them with, "Okay, so it's the PTSD. What can we do to help you with it?"

For other clients misdiagnosed or over-medicated by previous providers, learning about PTSD as an explanation of their behavior can be life changing. Consider Helen,* referred to me for a trauma assessment after two and a half years of largely unsuccessful hospitalizations, group treatments, and individual sessions with a variety of therapists. All previous providers labeled her as bipolar because of her "moodiness," lashing out, and intermittent suicidal ideation. Yet after 10 minutes of sharing, it was so clear to me that Helen, in her early thirties, suffered intensely due to a legacy of unresolved trauma.

During her early adolescence, a close family member sexually assaulted Helen over a period of several years. She never dreamt of saying anything to her beloved mother because she knew her disclosure would cause unrest in the family. Helen entered adulthood carrying her pain in silence. She was successful at her job and got married. Although she struggled emotionally, she did not present the full-blown picture of PTSD, at least on the surface, through her early adulthood. Then, a family member close to the original abuse situation died just before her 30th birthday, and Helen's grief reaction sent her into a tailspin. She no longer felt she had to carry the family secret, so it all came flooding out, even to her mother. After this death, Helen began experiencing the classic symptoms of PTSD with what DSM-5® now calls *delayed expression*. She vividly dreamt about being sexually violated, and her intrusive thoughts about possibly being attacked again, even by random strangers, were intense.

Helen could no longer be intimate with her husband and found that she couldn't leave the house without major effort. When she did leave the house, it was to go shopping at 3 am at a 24-hour megastore, and only if her husband accompanied her. The most social contact she experienced was online, where she spent hours zoning out, engaged in a fantasy life. She could no longer work because being out in public made her jumpy and caused her to react inappropriately with customers at her place of employment. Above all, she lived her life colored by the belief "I am powerless," mired in negativity and paralyzing depressed moods.

As soon as I mentioned PTSD as a possibility, Helen lit up. She said that all the providers she saw before me seemed so uncomfortable discussing her trauma, with one group counselor in a hospital even telling her, "That's the past, you need to forget about it." They kept telling her she was bipolar, yet the medications psychiatrists prescribed her numbed some of the symptoms without helping her to really feel any better. For Helen, the PTSD diagnosis, which I like to view as more of an explanation than a label, offered her a new hope and a new plan of action.

Diagnosing the Impacts of Trauma: DSM-IV-TR *Versus* DSM-5®

Released by the American Psychiatric Association in May 2013, the fifth and latest version of the *DSM* is a major overhaul. Even the shift to an Arabic numeral instead of a Roman numeral was a big change. The American Psychiatric Association wants to allow for smaller revisions, like with computer software updates (5.1, 5.2, etc.), before having to publish the *DSM-6*.

The release of *DSM-5*® was wrought with controversy, with certain major clinical organizations threatening to boycott it, and many other organizations writing strongly worded letters of protest to the American Psychiatric Association. Every clinician in my sphere of contacts has a pretty strong opinion about some element of it being inaccurate or misrepresentational. My general feelings about *DSM-5*® are summed up in a recovery slogan: Consider the source. The workgroups that wrote *DSM-5*® were composed primarily of psychiatrists writing for other psychiatrists, so there is naturally going to be a medical model bias. Although there was some effort to include non-psychiatrists in the field trials (one of my clinical mentors participated in these), the process of training to participate in these trials was time prohibitive to the average clinician, especially those working in agency settings.

My main objection to the process of assembling a diagnostic manual is the workgroup's picking and choosing of relevant research. There are numerous inconsistencies in the research justifications throughout the new *DSM*. Certain diagnoses seem very well supported, whereas others have relatively little substantive support. This so-called cherry picking of studies that support a pre-determined position occurs in the helping professions, which is why I approach positions that claim to be research-based with healthy skepticism. Although I do not agree with most of his views on mental illness, I was very interested in psychiatrist Joel Paris' (2013) description of the politically charged process that went into creating the *DSM-5*® in his book *The Intelligent Clinician's Guide to the DSM-5*®. If you are interested in reading more about this process, I recommend Paris' book.

Several of the controversies about the *DSM-5*® PTSD diagnosis and the new category of Trauma- and Stressor-Related Disorders are worth mentioning. For instance, many clinicians who work with trauma are upset that Complex Traumatic Stress Disorder, a construct introduced by Judith Herman, MD, in 1992 to account for more complicated manifestations of traumatic stress, is not directly named. Bessel van der Kolk, MD (2005) and his team proposed a diagnosis called Developmental Trauma Disorder that specifically describes the intensity of affective and behavioral symptoms that result from complicated and prolonged experiences of early childhood trauma. For many months, it seemed like this diagnosis would be included in *DSM-5*®, but ultimately, it was not. The strongest protest I hear from trauma-informed colleagues about the *DSM-5®* is that Developmental Trauma is not included as a diagnosis. Others continue to protest the use of the word *disorder* connected with trauma, believing that it shifts responsibility onto the patient and away from dysfunctional systems (e.g., military culture, the alcoholic home) or people who inflict the violence that leads to trauma. Although the humanitarian in me appreciates this perspective, the pragmatist in me views the word *disorder* as another one of those necessary evils of working in a medical model. *Disorder* means that the symptoms are intense enough to interfere with day-to-day, healthy life functioning. For me, this distinction means that I can justify treatment for my clients who need it, so I work with the term.

Perhaps the most significant shift from *DSM-IV-TR* to *DSM-5®* is that trauma gets it own chapter. *DSM-III, DSM-IV,* and *DSM-IV-TR,* PTSD categorized PTSD as an anxiety disorder. *DSM-5®* introduced the category, Trauma- and Stressor-Related Disorders, which includes the following diagnoses:

- Reactive Attachment Disorder
- Disinhibited Social Engagement Disorder
- Acute Stress Disorder
- Posttraumatic Stress Disorder
- Adjustment Disorders
- Trauma- or Stressor-Related Disorders Not Elsewhere Classified

This chapter of *Trauma Made Simple* discusses all of these diagnoses as part of the larger issue of diagnosing the impact of trauma.

PTSD, PTSD Specifiers, and Acute Stress Disorder

In my years of teaching on the PTSD diagnosis, I've found the following "nutshell" definition to be a useful summary (*DSM-IV-TR,* American Psychiatric Association, 2000):

A: Actual or perceived threat of injury or death—response of hopelessness or horror

B: *Re-experiencing* of the trauma (Criterion B)—one symptom required

C: *Avoidance* of stimuli associated with the trauma—three symptoms required

D: *Heightened arousal* symptoms (Criterion D)—two symptoms required

E: Duration of symptoms longer than one month

F: Functional impairment due to disturbances

Nutshell means that these are the key phrases you need to consider, and the underlined words describe the major theme of that criterion.

Let's take a look at the nutshell definition for PTSD in *DSM-5®* (American Psychiatric Association, 2013):

A: Exposure to actual or threatened a) death, b) serious injury, or c) sexual violation: direct experiencing, witnessing under certain conditions qualifies

B: *Intrusion* symptoms—one symptom required

C: *Avoidance* of stimuli associated with the trauma—one symptom required

D: *Cognitions and mood:* negative alterations—two symptoms required

E: *Arousal and reactivity* symptoms—two symptoms required

F: Duration of symptoms longer than one month

G: Functional impairment due to disturbances

H: Not attributed to another medical condition

At first glance, there are noticeable differences between the two nutshell definitions. In the following subsections, I break down each of the criteria (A–F) of the PTSD diagnosis as it appears in *DSM-5®*, examine the key changes between *DSM-IV-TR* and *DSM-5®* for that criterion, and discuss the symptoms, keeping in mind what to look for in clinical assessment. The potential specifiers that can be ascribed to the PTSD diagnosis are also described.

Criterion A. In *DSM-IV-TR,* criterion-A traumas were those events that carried an actual or perceived threat to physical life or limb. Criterion-A traumas are those more likely to make the news: combat, genocide, wartime atrocities against civilians, natural disasters, major accidents, rape, terrorist attacks, and other life-threatening violence. "Perceived" threat is an important component, although *DSM-5®* uses the word *threatened* (a semantic change that many do not like).

In *DSM-5®*, there are three categories of trauma: actual or threatened threat of (a) death, (b) physical injury, or (c) sexual violation. This is more specific than the categorization in *DSM-IV-TR*. It also acknowledges that not all forms of sexual violation are life-threatening, yet they can be frightening, paralyzing, or otherwise life altering. In the new breakdown, all forms of sexual violation, regardless of threat of death or physical injury, can qualify for a PTSD diagnosis if the other symptomatic criteria are met.

In the *DSM-IV-TR* era, many people couldn't wrap their heads around the notion that witnessing a trauma was not considered a cause of PTSD unless the witness' life was also in jeopardy. It seems like common sense that watching something terrible happen to someone else could be traumatic. In *DSM-5*®, more direct attention is given to the role of witnessing trauma in the PTSD diagnosis. There are three major ways in which witnessing is covered. First is witnessing, in person, the traumatic experience as it occurs to someone else. For instance, let's say your partner is being raped, and part of the torture that the perpetrators inflict is to have you watch (a common tactic in wartime torture). Witnessing, in that circumstance, now clearly counts as a Criterion A trauma.

Second is learning that a family member or close friend has been killed or injured in a violent or accidental way. Thus, if you get the news that your son was gunned down in Afghanistan or you learn that your niece was injured in a devastating tornado, the criterion is met. The third way *DSM-5*® accounts for witnessing relates to compassion fatigue. The full sub-criterion reads as follows (American Psychiatric Association, 2013):

> Experiencing repeated or extreme exposure to aversive details of the traumatic event(s) (e.g., first responders collecting human remains; police officers repeatedly exposed to details of child abuse); this does not apply to exposure through electronic media, television, movies, or pictures, unless this exposure is work related.

Although exposure to traumatic material in the helping professions is not directly listed as an example in the sub-criterion, it clearly counts here, especially if the individual encounters the details of trauma on a regular basis. The aim of this new sub-criterion is to account for work-related issues and thus give credence to the reality of compassion fatigue and vicarious trauma. The media exclusion is somewhat controversial. It is common knowledge that watching things on the news or in movies, especially out of context, traumatizes many ordinary people.

Criterion B.   The occurrence of a trauma as described in Criterion A is not enough to make a diagnosis of PTSD. A series of symptoms in four distinct clusters must be present for diagnosis. Criterion B, formerly labeled *re-experiencing symptoms*, is called *intrusion symptoms* in *DSM-5®*. The two most common symptoms that professionals associate with this criterion are flashbacks and nightmares. In *DSM-5®*, the description of these symptoms is fine tuned, with flashbacks identified as a dissociative reaction. Dissociative reactions, manifesting as a result of the intrusion phenomenon, are further described as occurring on a continuum, with "the most extreme expression being a complete loss of awareness of present surroundings" (American Psychiatric Association, 2013). *DSM-IV-TR* was clearer in stating that these reactions could also include hallucinations or illusions: These symptoms are not directly described in *DSM-5®*. It must be stated that intrusion distress can include symptoms that come across as psychotic in nature, with a fine line existing between visual flashback and a visual hallucination. My biggest challenge to clinicians in discussing symptom presentation is to always look deeper if a client complains about hearing voices or seeing things. If the client has not shown much improvement after trying the whole gamut of anti-psychotic medications, PTSD must be considered as a possible explanation for the symptoms. This is where the clinician's professional judgment becomes imperative in assessing symptoms.

The term *nightmares* is not used in *DSM-IV-TR* or *DSM-5®*; this is more of a colloquial term that clinicians tend to use because our clients use it. In the diagnostic manuals, the term *recurrent distressing dream* is favored. Similarly, we may use the term *intrusive thoughts* to describe the symptom of recurrent cognitions that do not necessarily have a visual flashback or dissociative component to them. In *DSM-5®*, these are described as "spontaneous or cued recurrent, involuntary, and intrusive distressing memories of the traumatic event." In describing other PTSD symptoms, both *DSM-IV-TR* and *DSM-5®* use the phrase *intense or prolonged psychological distress* when faced with a cue connected to the trauma, which can include symptoms that resemble depression, anxiety, and psychotic disorders (e.g., hallucinations, illusions, stress-induced catatonia). Both *DSM-IV-TR* and *DSM-5®* leave it open to clinician interpretation how to assess whether distress is intense or prolonged.

Another potential re-experiencing or intrusion symptom described in both *DSM-IV-TR* and *DSM-5®* relates to what we call *body memory*. *DSM-5®* specifically states, "marked physiological reactions to reminders of the traumatic event(s)." There is an intensely somatic component to the way that trauma manifests in the body, with gastrointestinal pain, chest pain, light-headedness, unspecified muscle pain, and many other unexplained physical symptoms clearly linked to emotional triggers. Book and article titles like *The Body Keeps the Score* (van der Kolk, 1994), *The Body Bears the Burden* (Scaer, 2007), and *The Body Never Lies* (Miller, 2006) offer apt descriptions of this link. However, so many medical professionals and other helping professionals tend to either dismiss many of these complaints, or write them off as *somaticizing*.

Let's put the symptom descriptions of *DSM-5®* Criterion B, *intrusion*, in a nutshell for general overview:

- Distressing memories (spontaneous or cued)
- Recurrent distressing themes (content connected to event)
- Dissociative reactions/flashbacks
- Intense or prolonged psychological distress (when cued)
- Physiological distress/body memory

To recap, at least one or more of the symptoms needs to be met after the event in Criterion A occurred and must be connected to the event. Variations that may manifest specifically in children, related to this criterion, are discussed later in the section along with an exploration of the subtypes of PTSD and how *DSM-5®* accounts for the experiences of childhood trauma.

Criterion C.   Criterion C is perhaps the most commonsensical of all the PTSD criteria: When people are dealing with unresolved trauma, the potential for distress, especially at the body level, is great. Thus, it is natural to seek out behaviors, many of which are maladaptive or unhealthy, to quell the distress. Common avoidance behaviors seen with PTSD are isolation, be it physical (e.g., not wanting to leave the house) or emotional (e.g., avoiding healthy intimacy and connection with people). Others include substance use, behavioral or process addictions (e.g., gambling, shopping, over-working), dissociation, and direct withdrawal from places or people reminiscent of the original injury (e.g., not wanting to go back to work if the incident happened at or near work).

DSM-5® continues to call this category *avoidance*, although the description is different from that in *DSM-IV-TR*. In *DSM-IV-TR*, an attempt was made to specifically list symptoms of avoidance, which included:

1. Efforts to avoid thoughts, feelings, or conversations associated with the trauma
2. Efforts to avoid activities, places, or people that arouse recollections of the trauma
3. Inability to recall an important aspect of the trauma
4. Markedly diminished interest or participation in significant activities

5. Feeling of detachment or estrangement from others

6. Restricted range of affect (e.g., unable to have loving feelings)

7. Sense of a foreshortened future (e.g., does not expect to have a career, marriage, children, or a normal life span)

Many of these symptoms are included in the new *DSM-5*® Criterion D, which describes negative impact on mood and affect. The *DSM-IV-TR* description was rather limited; for instance, the obvious substance abuse link is not directly described. *DSM-5*® leaves the actual symptoms of avoidance open to clinical interpretation—it does not describe specific symptoms, but instead, indicates that avoidance behaviors (e.g., substance use, maladaptive behaviors, isolation, withdrawal, dissociation, steering clear of reminders) occur in an attempt to avoid:

- Distressing memories, thoughts, or feelings about or closely associated with the traumatic event(s)

- External reminders (i.e., people, places, conversations, activities, objects, situations) that arouse distressing memories, thoughts, or feelings about, or that are closely associated with, the traumatic event(s)

These external reminders can include sounds, smells, physical symbols, exposure to people, places, or things connected to the traumatic event; or many of the intrusion symptoms described in Criterion B.

Criterion D.   Negative alterations in cognitions and mood associated with the traumatic event, is the "new" criterion. In reality, this criterion is not new, because there is carryover from the old Criterion C in *DSM-IV-TR*. Moreover, those of us working with trauma have long understood that the symptoms described in Criterion D are par for the course in treating PTSD. This new criterion essentially posits that the presence of unresolved trauma can significantly alter a person's mood and the way that he or she sees himself or herself in the world—it describes the phenomenon of seeing the word as a glass that is half empty instead of half full. To formally check off this criterion, you need at least two of seven potential symptoms, described here in the nutshell format:

- Blocking out/not remembering important aspects of trauma

- Negative beliefs about oneself, others, or the world

- Distorted blame of self or others (related to trauma)
- Persistent negative emotional state
- Diminished interest in/participation in activities
- Feeling detached or estranged from others
- Persistent inability to experience positive emotions

Unresolved trauma can significantly alter your mood and how you participate in life, specifically how you engage with other people. These realities are captured in the spirit of this new criterion. Negative beliefs about oneself or others imprinted by the traumatic event, such as "I'm bad," and "My nervous system is permanently ruined" (American Psychiatric Association, 2013), are a powerful indicator of the impact of trauma on an individual. (See Chapter 4.)

Criterion E. The old criterion D, *heightened arousal,* is now Criterion E, carrying the general categorical name of *arousal and reactivity.* This renaming is apt, since often, people who "overreact" get mislabeled as bipolar or having other mood or personality disorders. However, on further investigation, it is clear that an individual "overreacting" to a stimulus clearly rooted in past wounding may be more clearly explained by PTSD.

The most commonly referenced symptoms of this criterion are hypervigilance (always being on guard for something bad to happen) and the exaggerated startle response (being "jumpy"). Both symptoms continue to be listed in *DSM-5®*. Although these symptoms frequently occur with PTSD, there are several others that even many professionals tend to overlook. The first, listed in both *DSM-IV-TR* and *DSM-5®* are sleep disturbance, which can include problems falling or staying asleep and restless sleep. This does not include vivid dreaming or nightmares. Rather, it is simple insomnia. Insomnia often gets treated with medication only (the majority of which are highly addictive) without looking at the larger diagnostic picture.

The second of these overlooked symptoms is described as "irritable or aggressive behavior" in *DSM-5®*. (The term *outbursts of anger* appeared in *DSM-IV-TR*.) In many cases, these reactive behaviors are mislabeled as bipolar disorder. Several of these clients are given voice in a later section of this chapter called "Misdiagnosis." If a person with unresolved trauma feels cornered or trapped, reactivity in the form of aggression many result. It sounds like common sense, yet it remains an area of confusion for many professionals struggling to understand PTSD.

The third commonly overlooked symptom under Criterion E is problems with concentration. In my initial education on PTSD in Bosnia-Hercegovina, this symptom was one of the most obvious. The children I taught had clear difficulty concentrating, and it seemed obvious to associate these difficulties with the massive amounts of stress they were trying to accommodate. I think back to my mentor, Janet, saying, "If you were abandoned in Mostar by your parents during the height of bombing and then moved from place to place during the formative years of your childhood, you would have a hard time concentrating in school too, wouldn't you?" Yet, when I returned to the States I was amazed at how many psychiatrists and other clinicians used the diagnosis of ADD or ADHD to explain what was, in my view, concentration difficulties related to traumatic stress. I am not discounting that traditional ADHD exists, nor am I dismissing bipolar disorder as a diagnosis. However, I strongly believe that both conditions are horribly over-diagnosed in many cases of PTSD. If a person has been minimally or virtually nonresponsive to the pharmacotherapies prescribed for either ADHD or bipolar and a history of trauma is present, there is a good chance you are dealing with PTSD.

The new symptom added to *DSM-5*®'s Criterion E is reckless or self-destructive behavior. This can include self-injury, hypersexuality, compulsive overeating, binging and purging, restricting food, and continuing to put oneself into dangerous situations reminiscent of the original trauma or other risky situations. We may even see some overlap here with other disorders in the *DSM*, such as substance use disorders and eating disorders, and there are clear parallels with the avoidance tendencies as well. These issues are discussed more fully in Chapter 6.

Let's recap Criterion E in nutshell format. Remember that you need at least two of the following six symptoms to meet this criterion (American Psychiatric Association, 2013):

- Irritable or aggressive behavior
- Reckless or self-destructive behavior
- Hypervigilence
- Exaggerated startle response
- Concentration problems
- Sleep disturbance

Clearly, many people present to clinical settings with these symptoms, but there may be little recognition that they are part of a PTSD diagnosis. Thus, our clinical interviewing skills are imperative in helping clients explore and identify the origin and large context of these problematic symptoms, which is covered more fully in Chapter 5.

Criteria F, G, and H.   These three criteria further specify what must be present to diagnose PTSD. Criterion F, the time qualifier indicates that the symptoms must be present for at least a month or more. Symptoms lasting three days to a month following a traumatic experience point to an Acute Stress Disorder diagnosis. In *DSM-5*®, the symptoms of acute stress disorder symptoms and PTSD are the same—it's just the number of symptoms and the timeframe that differ. Fourteen potential symptoms are listed within five categories (intrusion symptoms, negative mood, dissociative symptoms, avoidance symptoms, and arousal symptoms), and any nine have to be met, causing clinically significant impairment, to qualify for a diagnosis of Acute Stress Disorder. With PTSD, a specified amount of symptoms must be met within each symptom category, as discussed in earlier sections.

Criterion G is the classic *functional impairment* statement: "The disturbance causes clinically significant distress or impairment in social, occupational, or other important areas of functioning" (American Psychiatric Association, 2013). In other words, the symptoms described get in the way of the person's life in one or more domains. The term *clinically significant* is familiar to many of us in the helping professions. We must be able to justify in our documentation that the symptoms presented are causing problems with the patient's functioning. It is important to emphasize that having experienced a trauma does not make a person pathological or in need of clinical treatment. However, in some cases, the functional impairment is great enough that treatment is warranted, and we, as clinicians, must determine this as part of our assessment. In my experience, if a person presents with symptoms that meet all the criteria to qualify for a PTSD diagnosis, establishing functional impairment is not going to be difficult.

Criterion H also calls for clinical judgment to determine whether the symptoms being described in Criteria B through E are best explained by the trauma or another condition, such as drug intoxication or a medical problem. In many traumatized populations, especially veterans, both PTSD and traumatic brain injury may be present, sometimes acquired during the same incident but sometimes not. Although the *DSM-5*® doesn't offer any hard and fast guidelines on how to make the decision, Criterion H simply calls for all factors to be considered in making the best possible diagnosis.

Specifier: With Predominant Dissociative Symptoms.   If you have worked in clinical settings for any amount of time, you have likely learned that dissociative disorders typically point to a history of trauma. In my view, dissociative disorders are so closely related to trauma, they really ought to be included in "Trauma- and Stressor-Related Disorders." Updated versions of the *DSM-5®* may reflect this change. For now, the category of dissociative disorders appears right after the trauma- and stressor-related disorders category, and clinicians have the option to notate (through use of the specifier "With Predominant Dissociative Symptoms") when dissociative symptoms, such as depersonalization or derealization, are the predominant features of the PTSD. Because dissociation can play out in all four major symptom clusters, this makes reasonable sense.

In *DSM-5®*, *depersonalization* is defined as "Persistent or recurrent experiences of feeling detached from, as if one were an outside observer of, one's mental process or body" (potentially an avoidance or negative mood/cognition manifestation). *Derealization* is defined as "Persistent or recurrent experiences of unreality of surroundings" (potentially a part of intrusion symptoms, avoidance, or negative mood/cognitions); American Psychiatric Association, 2013). Although depersonalization and derealization still appear as their own diagnoses in the dissociative disorders category, those diagnoses should be ruled out if PTSD is the better explanation. Dissociation issues are further discussed in Chapter 4.

Specifier: With Delayed Expression. A major change between *DSM-IV-TR* and *DSM-5®* was the exclusion of the phrase "the person's response [to the trauma] involved intense fear, helplessness, or horror" (American Psychiatric Association, 2000) in Criterion A. *DSM-5®* does not include this statement, recognizing that not all survivors of a major trauma necessarily experience intense fear, helplessness, or horror at the time of the trauma. Rather, these responses may lay dormant for months or even years. The qualifier *With Delayed Expression* further validates this possibility, indicating that full diagnostic criteria for the PTSD diagnosis may not be met until at least six months after the original trauma.

I see many manifestations of this delayed expression in clinical practice. It is not uncommon for a person to experience a major traumatic event and push through life on sheer survival drive for several months to several years. Then, another incident may happen that doesn't necessarily meet Criterion A for PTSD, but that incident can trigger reactions from the original trauma, and symptoms may manifest that will qualify a person for a PTSD diagnosis.

Many of my colleagues who work with veterans describe this phenomenon frequently manifesting in combat survivors from World War II, the Korean War, and Vietnam. The survivors are largely functional for decades, and then the grief that comes with a major life transition like retirement or death of a spouse can bring out PTSD symptoms from their combat experiences. The following text box provides insights from trauma survivor Lily Burana, whose story is a classic case of delayed expression PTSD.

In Their Own Words

Lily

In my years of training as a trauma specialist, I've had the opportunity to hear the great trauma scholars of the world lecture. I don't think any of them can describe trauma and its impacts, or the PTSD diagnosis, as well as Lily Burana (2009), a former stripper from New Jersey. Burana was the survivor of childhood sexual abuse, and by the age of 16, she was working in the sex industry on a fake ID. After dancing for the better part of a decade, she made a decision to leave that lifestyle. Shortly after that, she married an Army officer, and adapting to his world came with its own series of adjustments. He was deployed shortly after the start of the Iraq war, later returning to the States with a serious case of PTSD. Then, Lily's father died. Although he did not play a role in her childhood abuse, the intense grief she experienced in the wake of his death brought up so much emotion from the past that she qualified for a PTSD diagnosis connected to her childhood abuse, even though any manifestations were previously at a subclinical level. Through doing work separately and then together, Lily and her husband were able to find healing individually and as a couple.

I teach Lily's case in all courses I give on PTSD, not only because it is a classic portrait of delayed expression, but also because of the personal power of her words in explaining the PTSD diagnosis:

> PTSD means, in "talking over beer" terms, that you've got some crossed wires in your brain due to the traumatic event. The overload of stress makes your panic button touchier than most people's, so certain things trigger a stress reaction— or more candidly—an overreaction. Sometimes, the panic

(Continued)

button gets stuck altogether and you're in a state of constant alert, buzzing and twitchy and aggressive. Your amygdala—the instinctive flight, fight, or freeze part of your brain—reacts to a trigger before your rational mind can deter it. You can tell yourself, "It's okay," but your wily brain is already 10 steps ahead of the game, registering danger and sounding the alarm. So, you might say once again, in a calm, reasoned cognitive-behavioral–therapy kind of way, "Brain, it's okay." But your brain yells back, "Bullshit, kid, how dumb do you think I am? I'm not falling for that one again." By then, you're hiding in the closet, hiding in a bottle, and/or hiding from life, crying, raging, or ignoring the phone and watching the counter on the answering machine go up, up, up, and up. You can't relax, and you can't concentrate because the demons are still pulling at your strings. The long-range result is that the peace of mind you deserve in the present is held hostage by the terror of your past.

Trauma, Children, and DSM-5®

A common misconception is that PTSD diagnosis is a veteran's diagnosis. We must forever be indebted to the brave men and women who served and drew more widespread attention to the role that unresolved trauma plays in mental health. However, one does not have to survive combat to acquire PTSD. For many of our youngest citizens, combat occurs in their family of origin.

There was widespread discussion in preparing the *DSM-5*® on how to more directly acknowledge that young children can develop PTSD, especially given the epidemic of Bipolar Disorder and ADHD diagnoses in children. As I prepared this book, a workshop attendee complained about the psychiatrist at her agency, who routinely fights with her because he believes it biologically impossible for children to get PTSD. He asserts that children are resilient, and that when their brains grow, they outgrow early childhood trauma. Sadly, I wasn't surprised to hear her story because I've encountered similar attitudes about kids and trauma from professionals.

Several proposals on how to account for the reality of childhood trauma were put forth. This section focuses on what was ultimately decided for *DSM-5*®. In the PTSD diagnosis of *DSM-5*®, notes are given under each major criterion for how variations in symptoms may manifest in children. Under Criterion B (intrusion), it's indicated that children may exhibit repetitive play themes connected to the original trauma, and that trauma-specific reenactment may occur. Also called *trauma recapitulation*, this phenomenon is often used to describe the behaviors of children who act out sexually or violently. These behaviors are part of the repetition compulsion cycle of survivors acting out traumas that resemble those that were acted out on them, in a maladaptive attempt at resolution. Criterion B also describes that disturbing dreams with unrecognizable content may be connected to traumatic experiences in children.

DSM-5® includes a separate subset of the PTSD diagnosis, "PTSD for Children 6 Years and Under." The diagnosis is similar to PTSD in adults, although fewer criteria need to be met because fewer symptom options are given. For instance, Criterion A looks basically the same (the media exclusion of the main PTSD diagnosis remains), although the sub-criterion connected to work is not included. Criterion B is the same as in the main diagnosis, with one symptom required to qualify. Criteria C and D from the main diagnosis are combined for children (as Criterion C), with only one symptom needed to qualify. Criterion E from the main diagnosis is Criterion D in the child diagnosis, with two of the symptoms needing to be met. Although reckless and self-destructive behavior is not contained here, the irritability and anger symptom contains a more detailed description to account for behaviors like extreme temper tantrums and outbursts toward people or objects.

In sum, fewer symptoms are needed to diagnose PTSD in children when you consider *DSM-5®*'s combination of Criteria C and D. From my perspective, the presence of this subset in the new *DSM* makes a strong sociopolitical statement, although it remains to be seen whether diagnosticians, especially psychiatrists, will take its presence seriously. Diagnostic manuals do not bring about change; it's the people who use them that do. It is vitally important that we, as a field and as a culture, recognize that children can be seriously affected by trauma.

I once treated a client who repeatedly referred to her children, all under the age of 14, as "Bipolar-ADHDs," as if all of their behavior was explained by that combined diagnosis. Not only did this imply that treatment meant finding the right combination of medications, it put the responsibility on the children for being organically flawed. These diagnoses kept her from taking responsibility for the extreme trauma to which she and her lifestyle choices exposed her children. Despite the use of the word *disorder*, giving children a PTSD diagnosis puts the responsibility on the caregivers to recognize the impact of trauma and provide an environment that is conducive to healing and less likely to exacerbate the aftereffects of trauma, a challenge that many adults in this culture do not want to embrace.

Two diagnoses associated with children that are included in the new category of Trauma- and Stressor-Related Disorders are Reactive Attachment Disorder and Disinhibited Social Engagement Disorder. In *DSM-IV-TR*, these diagnoses were two different manifestations of attachment injuries in childhood. In *DSM-5*®, the diagnoses are being used to describe two potentially different manifestations of trauma. Attachment injuries, described in both diagnoses, are defined as follows (American Psychiatric Association, 2013):

- Social neglect or deprivation in the form of persistent lack of having basic emotional needs for comfort, stimulation, and affection met by caregiving adults
- Repeated changes in primary caregivers that limit opportunities to form stable attachments
- Rearing in unusual settings that severely limit opportunities to form selective attachments

These conditions, which clearly meet the definition of trauma explored in Chapter 1, are offered as the causes for Reactive Attachment and Disinhibited Social Engagement.

Reactive Attachment, in *DSM-5*® is conceptualized as under-engagement. Criterion A covers emotionally withdrawn behavior symptoms, and Criterion B describes symptoms of emotional disturbance, which can include minimal responsiveness to others. Disinhibited Social Engagement, also stemming from attachment injury, contains symptoms of over-engagement. For example, think of children who may inappropriately approach adults and start to share all of the details of their life with minimal social restraint, a behavior that can clearly be a safety issue and open the child up to further victimization. Impulsive behaviors can fall under this diagnosis, in addition to the overly needy or clingy behaviors that are not better explained by culturally appropriate norms. A note is given in this diagnosis to indicate that some behaviors normally associated with the hyperactivity component of ADHD may be better categorized as Disinhibited Social Engagement, especially if an attachment injury is present. Some of the social awkwardness or inability to read social cues that we might associate with the autism spectrum might also be explained in this new category, especially if clear evidence of a trauma history exists.

When a person's history is seasoned with trauma, it can be virtually impossible to tell which event led to the PTSD diagnosis. Children who grow up with an extensive history of trauma connected to primary caregivers are susceptible to what Dr. Judith Herman (1992) first introduced as *complex PTSD*. Courtis and Ford (2009) explained that *complex PTSD* manifests from conditions that are repetitive or prolonged; involve direct harm and/or neglect or abandonment by caregivers or ostensibly responsible adults; occur at developmentally vulnerable times in the victim's life, such as early childhood; and have great potential to severely compromise a child's development. One of the core principles in Dr. Allan Schore's cannon of work on attachment and trauma is that if a child continually enters the "freeze" response early in life, especially in infancy, the child will be prone to stay frozen or get frozen throughout life. This sense of learned helplessness sets the stage for complex trauma and physical ramifications, including vulnerability to illnesses.

IN THEIR OWN WORDS

Paula

When a person's early history is peppered with trauma, it can be very difficult to determine where to begin with assessment. You may ask yourself questions like, "Which trauma exactly would qualify for the diagnosis?" and resultantly get caught up in technicalities. In meeting a client and forging a solid therapeutic relationship, it typically becomes clear which issues have had the most pervasive impact. From what I have encountered over the years, Paula's experience is very common, in that what we think would be the most significant trauma is not always the most paralyzing to the person in question. For Paula, the injury inflicted by her primary parental figure was paramount, a common experience for clients with a complex history:

> My first trauma came when I was a small infant and unable to defend myself. As I lay in my crib with no clean diapers and no formula, my mother decided it was better to leave her husband (not my father—I was the product of an affair) for another man out of state. [I was] a ward of the court, [and] another family was traumatized when my mother would not allow them to adopt me. Some days you wonder what your life would have been if you were not around the traumatized you in the first place. Fast forward years later and as a teenager I decided I needed to live my own life . . . forget rules and

(Continued)

how others may have felt about my actions. During one of my stupid episodes, I was in a bad place at a bad time and became the victim of a gang rape. It was sad because the person I was with, I thought they loved me and I trusted them. But they were the one to initiate the assault. These two bad times in life do not define and nor do they continue to hurt me. I look at it this way, I survived the absolute worst pain in the world . . . my mother rejected me, she abandoned me, she never took me back into her life. Although another tried and even others have tried to hurt me, no pain can be any worse than the initial pain and trauma of my mother walking away.

Diagnosing Small "t"

Trauma does not necessarily need to fit PTSD Criterion A for it to be life changing or even clinically significant. Shapiro (2001) labeled this concept as small "t" trauma: the upsetting events life sends our way that may prove difficult to heal and integrate into our larger experience. In more recent lectures and writing, Shapiro favors the term adverse life experience instead of small "t" trauma. Many clients get tripped up with the small "t" traumas, believing that if they didn't survive a major disaster, than their trauma is somehow less legitimate or significant. Sadly, I have seen many professionals and family members reinforce this devastating belief when they say things like, "Well, you didn't have it as bad as your brother. He went to Iraq—you just had a hard time with the kids at school."

Small "t" traumas can include a variety of experiences: racial or ethnic discrimination, verbal abuse, bullying, surviving divorce, experiencing a medical crisis, spiritual abuse, mind control, emotional blackmail, or losing a pet. The list can go on indefinitely. Small "t" traumas may not have the life-threatening connotation of Criterion A or the big "T" traumas, but they can be just as life altering. If a person is not able to process or make sense of that experience due to a variety of reasons, small "t" trauma can be just as damaging.

There will always be critics who say that small "t" trauma events are "just life" and should not be regarded as traumatic. I fully recognize that many people can muster their own resources and support networks to heal life wounds without professional care, but many cannot. To recap a point covered in Chapter 1, just experiencing a trauma is not pathological. It's when traumas go unresolved and unhealed that problems can ensue. People whose lives are affected by unprocessed small "t" traumas have every right to access treatment, especially psychotherapy and other psychosocial interventions that can fill the missing gaps in their lives and help them to heal.

Several mental health conditions may be explained by unresolved small "t" traumas or at least exacerbated by them. The links between depressive disorders, dysthymia (called Persistent Depressive Disorder in *DSM-5*®), and various anxiety disorders, and earlier unprocessed life experiences are apparent to anyone who has ever helped a client with these issues. Even personality disorders, long regarded as incredibly frustrating to treat, can become easier to conceptualize when we consider the pervasive impact of unresolved trauma on childhood development. In his landmark book, *The Angry Heart: Overcoming Borderline and Addictive Disorders*, Joseph Santoro (1997) suggests that borderline personality disorder is a manifestation of complex PTSD. If you think about it, many of the Cluster B personality disorders (a distinction that remains in *DSM-5*® for now) develop in individuals who experienced profound trauma in childhood, usually a combination of Criterion A/big "T" traumas and small "t" traumas.

Perhaps the most obvious diagnosis that we associate with small "t" trauma is Adjustment Disorder. In *DSM-5*®, adjustment disorders are now listed in the new Trauma- and Stressor-Related Disorders category which, to me, gives credence to the impact of small "t" trauma on the human experience. To diagnose an adjustment disorder, emotional or behavioral symptoms in response to a stressor occurring within three months of that stressor's onset must be present. Again, that key phrase *clinically significant* is important. There must be marked distress that is out of proportion to the intensity of the stressor (taking contextual issues like culture and development into account) and/or significant impairment in life functioning. Another mental disorder must not better explain these problematic symptoms, must not represent *normal* bereavement (even though *DSM-5*® does not define that), and must not persist for more than six months after the stressor and its consequences have terminated. If the symptoms do persist, another diagnosis should be considered. Like in *DSM-IV-TR*, the qualifiers of the Adjustment Disorder diagnosis include *With Depressed Mood, With Anxiety, With Mixed Anxiety and Depressed Mood, With Disturbance of Conduct, With Mixed Disturbance of Emotions and Conduct,* and *Unspecified.*

I diagnose adjustment disorder a great deal in my clinical practice. Although the diagnosis will inevitably be criticized for pathologizing the highs and lows of life, my belief is that many people are so affected by these stressors, they simply need some outside help to heal. If diagnosing an obvious adjustment disorder is the way to get such people help, the diagnosis is very useful. Small "t" traumas, especially if left untreated or unaddressed, can be just as valid and just as clinically significant as the large "T" traumas.

In *DSM-5*®, two new, catchall diagnoses are introduced: Other Specified Trauma- and Stressor-Related Disorders and Unspecified Trauma- and Stressor-Related Disorder. Examples of the former include adjustment-like disorders, in which onset is more than 3 months after the stressor, prolonged duration past 6 months, certain conditions that are better explained by cultural norms of a given society, and persistent complex bereavement disorder (which is covered in Chapter 3). This diagnosis can also include evidence of a traumatic experience affecting functional impairment when full criteria for any of the other diagnoses are not met. Unspecified Trauma- and Stressor-Related Disorder also includes instances in which the impacts of trauma are clear, but the diagnostician has insufficient evidence to name the trauma in question. For instance, this diagnosis could be used in an emergency room setting, or when there is symptomatic evidence of preverbal or prenatal trauma (covered further in Chapter 5).

There are instances throughout the *DSM-5*® of these not elsewhere classified or unspecified disorders. These diagnoses are receiving criticism in many circles from practitioners and laypeople who say that broadening the scope qualifies just about everyone as having a mental disorder. I can understand and largely agree with this criticism. I also maintain that diagnosis is only useful if it is being applied competently, and even if certain symptoms are met, ultimately, clinicians must make a judgment call about functional impairment. I see both of these diagnoses as having utility if they will allow a suffering person to access the psychosocial and/or medical treatment he or she needs to obtain, restore, or maintain healthier functioning in life.

MISDIAGNOSIS

Many trauma survivors seek out psychiatric help and get labeled as having ADHD and/or bipolar disorder. Prior to the Vietnam War era, countless traumatized veterans received diagnoses of schizophrenia or other psychotic disorders, even within the VA system. The diagnoses of Schizophrenia, Schizoaffective Disorder, and Bipolar Disorder with Psychotic Features are still erroneously given to people whose symptoms are better explained by PTSD. Why does this happen? Is it because the medical model is threatened by the

PTSD diagnosis, one that cannot be as easily *medicated* as other diagnoses? Or, is it still because we, as a field, misunderstand and fear trauma?

There are so many cases of these misdiagnoses, I could probably fill an entire book with such stories alone. Misdiagnosis directly affected one of my most trusted professional colleagues, yoga teacher Mandy Hinkle. Mandy received an ADHD diagnosis at age 16 and was promptly medicated. At the height of her active cocaine addiction in her mid-twenties, a prominent West Coast psychiatrist labeled her as bipolar and put her on a cocktail of five psychotropic medications, including two benzodiazepines. Mandy continues to suffer chronic nerve damage that she believes resulted from being overmedicated for so long. None of the medical treatments helped to quiet her mind and usher in her recovery from both addiction and the wounds of her trauma quite like the practice of yoga, a definite sign that the overmedication resulted from a poor diagnosis that did not take her trauma history or related symptomology into account.

Holly Ann Rivera, a psychology student and trauma survivor, moderates one of the largest EMDR networking groups on Facebook. Holly agreed to be interviewed for this book and candidly shared her story, which appears in several chapters to illustrate various concepts. Holly was a "change-of-life baby," and her entry into this world took both of her parents by surprise. Holly's father suffered from chronic, largely untreated depression, and her mother was completely blind by the time Holly was born. Holly indicates that her mother was frustrated managing her as an infant and toddler, so her mother resorted to hitting her to keep her in line. By the age of 4, Holly made the connection, "If that's what Mom does to me, that's what I need to do to me," and by the age of 10, Holly was cutting herself and beginning to experience suicidal ideation.

Holly first sought out help from a school counselor at age 14 and was further traumatized by a system that was supposed to help her. She describes a series of "horrible" clinicians who seemed overwhelmed by the nature of her issues, and at the age of 16, during one of her hospitalizations, a therapist with no concept of how to deal with adolescents or sexuality forced her to come out as a bisexual to her parents.

A psychiatrist first misdiagnosed Holly with Bipolar Disorder at 15. Psychiatrists placed Holly on a cocktail of medications for a 3- to 4-year period. Holly shares that these years of her life are essentially blocked because she was in such an unnecessary haze. During this haze, several people sexually assaulted Holly, compounding the impact of her existing trauma. Many a psychiatrist wrote off Holly's aggression, which she now identifies as arousal and reactivity (within the PTSD explanation), as hypomania. In recent years,

Holly consulted with a new psychiatrist, who was reticent to diagnose PTSD in place of Bipolar Disorder. When Holly began to defend herself and the relevance of the PTSD diagnosis to her experience, that psychiatrist even challenged Holly's justified defensiveness as hypomania.

It remains to be seen whether the increased awareness of Trauma- and Stressor-Related Disorders within *DSM-5®* will have any significant impact in the field, especially with psychiatrists, who are the most likely to label trauma as something else. I will never forget a comment that a 14-year-old patient made during my clinical internship at an inpatient adolescent treatment center. He was a young African-American male with an IQ of 68 and a history of trauma and neglect detailed enough to fill a chapter in this book. He bravely spoke up during a psychotherapy group I had the privilege to observe. The young man said, "I'm mad. Dr. Reynolds* [the hospital's psychiatric director] walked into the room, talked to me for 30 seconds, and said I was Bipolar I . . . now that's messed up."

Wiser words were never spoken. His observation reflected the sad reality of that particular hospital and of the general state of adolescent psychiatry. It seemed that every child passing through that hospital, most of whom had extensive trauma histories, received some variation of a bipolar diagnosis because that was the hospital's frame of reference and it was the diagnosis most likely to get reimbursement by third parties. Sadly, even the children at the hospital made comments about their doctors being bought off by the drug companies. I will never forget the words of another child, who said, "There's gotta be something in this for them writing all of these prescriptions." This is an ethical issue now being addressed by many brave writers and investigators in the helping professions (Frances, 2013; Olfman & Robbins, 2012).

I hope that those of us who are trauma informed do not become like those we criticize in seeing *everything* as PTSD. When you are trauma aware, it can become easy to view everything through the trauma lens. I am the first to admit that I do. My Bosnia experience taught me to ask, "What role is trauma playing in this presentation?" As this chapter has hopefully established, the manifestations of trauma are more than just diagnosable PTSD. Other diagnoses or nonclinical conditions that require support rather than more intensive treatment may be a better fit to help a person define their problems of presentation. These other avenues of explanation will reveal themselves if we keep an open mind and do a thorough assessment. Let us not become like Dr. Reynolds,* the psychiatrist who labeled the wise young patient after only 30 seconds of contact time. Being trauma informed requires us to operate at a higher standard.

IN THEIR OWN WORDS

Donna

Donna is a 57-year-old woman who identifies as being clean from psychiatric medications for 2.5 years. After reading a little bit about her journey with misdiagnosis, it's clear to see why she identifies as such:

> I was diagnosed by a psychiatrist with rapid-cycling bipolar disorder. Placed on meds like Depakote (a mood stabilizer), Klonopin (an anti-anxiety drug), and at times Wellbutrin. I was told by a clinical psychologist that I would have to be on these meds the rest of my life. Five years into the diagnosis, a new psychiatrist placed me on Neurontin, Effexor, Wellbutrin, and Klonopin. I stayed on the meds 11 more years. After 16 years, I found mindful meditation through a marriage and family therapist.
>
> I stopped each medication one at a time. This took me six months. I made medication sheets to keep track of the decreases, one medication at a time. I lost 20 pounds in 3 months. My blood cholesterol went from 340 to 191. I voluntarily tested at a local college of professional psychology. I did not even have a diagnosis on Axis I. The real diagnosis, I discovered, is preverbal childhood trauma, including enduring abuse. Meaning, I triggered in anger, which brought up trauma responses like not being able to sleep or calm myself. I experienced a series of situational stresses or small "t" traumas that anyone would have difficulty with: not getting the promotion after graduate school, being told to work every weekend, and pm shifts. Being terminated and losing a four-year relationship. Financial problems.
>
> A trauma is an emotional block. When triggered in the present moment, functioning becomes impaired and looks irrational because it's coming from a history of trauma. I numbed myself and became addicted to the psych meds to deal with everyday problems, which was not dealing with them at all. My healing paths have been mindful psychotherapy and coaching, meditation, dream work (Jungian), qi gong/tai chi, yoga, massage, mindful poetry and writing, energy healing, spiritual community, reading, friendships, and volunteering,

(Continued)

to name a few. At this point, I am working with a therapist trained in Sensorimotor® Psychotherapy. There are layers to my trauma. Medications were worthless. A maintenance at best. I spent 16 years on the medications. I saw different psychiatrists and therapists. No one understood. It was not until I took control of my own healing and life that I started to heal. I have a dependent personality—because I learned to survive in an emotionally unsupportive environment. Trauma stole my life. Don't be blind to what is at the root of mental illness. Trauma is stored in the body memory, in the unconscious, and takes the spirit. There is recovery. There is healing for trauma.

FURTHER READING

Courtois, C. A., & Ford, J. D. (2009). *Treating complex traumatic stress disorders: An evidence-based guide.* New York: The Guilford Press.

Herman, J. L. (1992). *Trauma and recovery.* New York: Basic Books.

van der Kolk, B. A. (2005). *Developmental trauma disorder: Towards a rational diagnosis for children with complex trauma histories.* Retrieved from http://www.traumacenter.org/products/pdf_files/preprint_dev_trauma_disorder.pdf.

CHAPTER 3

Grief, Bereavement, and Mourning

I would rock my soul, in the bosom of Abraham,
I would hold my life in his saving grace.
I would walk all the way from Boulder to Birmingham,
If I thought I could see, I could see your face.

—Emmylou Harris (singing about her musical partner,
the late Gram Parsons)

THE GRIEF WOUND

The biopsychosocial model of mental health posits that disease is about more than just the physical body. Mental and contextual factors must also be considered in evaluating etiology, predicting the course of progression, and evaluating the best possible options for treatment. The biopsychosocial model is well known to many professionals in the helping fields. What people may not realize is that the psychiatrist who wrote up the concept and coined the term, Dr. George Engel, was an incredibly prolific writer on the topics of grief and loss. In his seminal 1961 essay, "Is Grief a Disease," Engel beautifully connected the experience of mourning after death to the healing of physical wounds, implying that loss of a loved one is psychologically traumatic to the same extent that being severely wounded or burned is physiologically traumatic.

Few of us who have lost someone to death would disagree.

How do the constructs of grief and loss fit into a discussion about trauma? Are they traumas? Should loss be evaluated separately from traumatic stress disorders, in a clinical sense? You may have asked yourself such questions in your clinical work, or even along your own personal journey. Some of my colleagues have strong opinions that grief and trauma are distinct constructs. Engel's passage answers all of these questions in the context of understanding human wounding, this book's primer for demystifying trauma. Any loss, no

37

matter how it may manifest in one's life (e.g., death, divorce, financial/job loss), qualifies as a trauma. As discussed in Chapter 1, the trauma itself does not necessarily breed problems—it's whether the wound is allowed to heal that must be evaluated. If the wound has not been allowed to heal, problems will result.

The same can be said for recovery following a major loss: If a person is given the time, space, and resources needed to heal, it is likely he or she will come out relatively unscathed on the other end. But, think of how many people are not allowed to heal following a loss? How many times are job losses or foreclosures written off as "just life?" How often are people going through a divorce or major relationship break-up placated with banalities like "Time heals everything?" How often is death, after a certain period of bereavement, met with "You just need to get on with your life?" How many people who've experienced the death of a beloved pet hear comments like "It was just an animal, not a person?"

In the United States, the average length of paid bereavement leave is three days. This reality gives the message of "Time to get on with it" and seems reflective of a larger cultural belief that people should just deal with things without any time or support. The attitudes that people encounter after a loss are very similar to those after any other trauma: "Get on with it."

This chapter examines some of the core terminology of grief and loss and explores its place in the spectrum of trauma. It also evaluates how grief and loss are accounted for in *DSM-5*®. The chapter wraps up with a discussion of the relevance of models for grief recovery and the development of a framework for healing after a loss.

We tend to use the terms *grief*, *bereavement*, and *mourning* interchangeably, although they have distinct meanings. According to J. James Worden (2008), a leader in the field of grief counseling and bereavement:

- **Grief** is the experience of loss in one's life.
- **Bereavement** is the state of living with and adapting to a loss.
- **Mourning** is the process of adaption to the loss.

Examining these distinctions elucidates the similarities between grief and trauma. Like with trauma, grief is simply a part of life. Grief comes from the Latin root *gravas*, meaning heavy.

Grief is an experience that is in and of itself not problematic, especially if the person experiencing the grief is allotted the time, space, and resources needed to grieve, to lighten the load of his or her emotional weight. Just like trauma can be processed adaptively or maladaptively, so it is with grief. To revisit the wound parallel with trauma, the wound of loss can take a short time to occur, but it usually takes a long time to heal.

Worden disagreed slightly with his mentor, George Engel, on some of the semantics about the end result of mourning. Engel consistently used the terms *restoration* and *recovery* in his writing as the goal of the mourning process, although he fully acknowledged and normalized that instances of incomplete healing may manifest throughout a person's life, even if he or she identified as restored following the mourning. Anniversary reactions or other triggers are classic examples of how incomplete healing may manifest, and Engel asserted that such experiences are not to be overanalyzed or pathologized—they are just part of being human. Hence, Worden prefers the term *adaptation* in his writings; for instance, some people may *adapt* better to grief or loss than others. *Adaptation* suggests that a person will never be the same following a loss.

Both Worden and Engel agree that some people adapt better to grief or loss than others, and the quality of this adaptation is usually determined by many situational, contextual, and individual variables. Hence, the grief wound is not the same for any two people, even if they are mourning the same loss. One of the most ignorant things people may be told after a death is, "I don't know what you're so worked up about . . . I lost my mother too!" There are too many variables in the equation for us to make such blanket statements following a death, loss, or trauma.

Let's say that two sisters are grieving the loss of their mother. One sibling may have been closer to her mother in her day-to-day relationship, and the other may have enjoyed a very loving relationship yet remained more distant. The two sisters may have different conceptualizations about the meaning of love and family. They may have different sets of values, not to mention different sets of beliefs about the divine and eternity. One sibling may be subjectively more sensitive than the other, and the two sisters, even if raised in the same environment, might have two completely different sets of coping and adaptation skills.

I offer an example from my own family. My mother adored both of her parents with vigor while they were alive. She never really left home. When the house behind her parents' home went on the market shortly before my mother's marriage to my father, my grandfather bought it for her, so growing up we had our own Croatian village experience right here in the States. I witnessed two completely different grief experiences in my mother when each of her parents died. When her mother died in 1995, it was unexpected. My 81-year-old grandmother was a spitfire who literally worked as a waitress at our local Croatian Fraternal home until the day she experienced the chest pains that landed her in the hospital. She didn't look a day over 65. Within three weeks of being taken to the hospital, she was dead following a failed bypass surgery.

My mother was absolutely devastated—it was as though part of her died with my grandmother. One of the most significant variables in the equation was the loss of security that came with my grandmother's death. Another factor is that my parents' marriage was spiraling toward the end of its course after a decade or more of problems. My mother felt that my grandmother was the only person who really supported her and listened to her about these marital difficulties. Suddenly, my mom felt like she was bearing the weight of the world alone. It was one of the deepest depressions I ever witnessed.

When my grandfather died a decade later, I was expecting more of the same, since my mother was the ultimate "daddy's girl." His death was much different and came at a very different time in my mother's life, as she and my dad had been divorced for several years. We found out that my grandfather had terminal colon and liver cancer in the summer of 2003. After his diagnosis and ultimate decision not to pursue chemotherapy at the age of 90, he lived for nine more months in a nursing home, and finally hospice care made it possible for him to come home to the house he loved.

I know that for me, and for my mother as well, the last nine months of my grandfather's life involved a grief process even though he was still with us. Yet this grief process was ultimately a celebration. We got to say what we needed to say and work through some very difficult feelings and even sort out some old family garbage as my mother, her siblings, and me rotated through the house to help take care of him. During the last week of his life when we knew he was at the end, our family had the chance to surround his bed, a great American hero of the World War II generation, and celebrate his life. My mother made sure that she got the words and music to his favorite Croatian folk song and asked me to re-learn it so we could sing it to him. Unlike my grandmother, who died in a cold, sterile hospital, my grandfather died in the house where he lived in most of his adult life, after we spent a week singing to him. For all of us, it was a truly spiritual experience.

My mother told me later that his death affected her much less than my grandmother's, and considering all of the variables, it makes sense why. Nonetheless, everyone grieves differently, and having a lengthy period to say goodbye can come with its share of difficulties for many. I once treated a client who continued to have nightmares about watching her father deteriorate from chemotherapy, long after he passed away. She felt she said everything she needed to say to him, and she was pleased with how well hospice helped her through his illness, but seeing the man who raised her, her hero, literally change shape before her eyes was the greatest trauma of her life. She had no framework for processing or healing it. Her father had raised her, as her mother had abandoned the family when she was very young. Her father was the only parent with whom she'd made a secure connection.

I could probably fill another several pages with the variables and variable combinations that determine how a person grieves and what complications arise. The key is that, as professionals, we recognize that variability in the human condition colors the impact of grief and/or trauma on an individual's lived experience. Hence, case-by-case rapport building, assessment, and conceptualization are imperative.

One of the wisest lessons I ever got in being a helping professional came from my preschool teacher, Mrs. White. During that Ohio winter, she gave us our first lesson about snow. In looking out the window over a landscape, snow just seems like a blanket, a mass. Yet, she explained, in examining each individual flake under a microscope, you can see that no two snowflakes are ever formed the same way; there is inevitably variation. As a four-year-old child, this concept simply blew my mind. As an adult practicing therapy, the notion makes so much sense. It is easy to herd people through the doors of helping institutions with a "patients are patients" or "customers are customers" mentality, offering them generalized or highly manualized treatment with the attitude of "snow is snow." Or, we can take the time to examine the beauty of each individual being coming into our care with the same wonder that a child may experience when looking through a microscope at the individual variability.

In Their Own Words

Dr. Mitchell

Dr. Ellison "Eli" Mitchell is this northern girl's picture of a real southern gentleman. A trauma expert, U.S. Navy veteran, and all around humanitarian (he worked in critical incident debriefing near Ground Zero in the days after 9-11), Dr. Mitchell shared some of his experiences on trauma and grief recovery with me when we met in 2013. He impressed

(Continued)

me as an elder of our field who has truly done his work and practices for himself what he teaches to his clients about emotional healing. Dr. Mitchell's own path was defined by complicated mourning from a very early age, as his mother died when he was six years old. Dr. Mitchell shares about that experience, and the painful context that made healing difficult, in his 2010 book, *The Elders Speak*:

> Mom had been bedridden at home for months suffering from an enlarged heart caused by rheumatic fever. Three weeks after my sixth birthday, I walked into her bedroom, saw her empty bed, and knew something was terribly wrong. Overwhelmed, I couldn't hear what the adults in the room were saying. However, later that morning, I was taken for a ride in a convertible by a woman in the neighborhood that I didn't know very well. During this ride, my neighbor seemed to be telling me, "Don't feel sad about the death of your mother, just enjoy the ride." I bought into that injunction, and I didn't grieve until many years later.
>
> After this heart-breaking blow, I evidently decided, "If I get close to somebody, they will die." Furthermore, I remember that many times as a child, I would crawl on my mother's bed to be beside her only to be told by an adult [to get off the bed] because my mother needed to rest. This repeated scene probably led me to draw an even more dramatic conclusion: "My love kills."

As Dr. Mitchell's case demonstrates, death, grief, or any loss experience can create a powerful, internalized message, usually one that is false but nonetheless valid to the person because he or she perceived it that way. Eli was not allowed to grieve the death of his mother the way that he needed to, and no one ever corrected his learned negative belief, "My love kills," a core belief that would haunt him for years, impacting his ability to connect intimately with his loved ones. Until he did the grief work and processed the pain, the driving, negative cognition kept him stuck. The unprocessed negative cognition resulting from the loss can be one of the key variables in what makes grief turn into complicated mourning. Some beliefs, like "My love kills," "It's my fault," or "I should have done something more to help," can take on that particularly paralyzing element of blame. Other beliefs may relate to the core self; for instance, "I can't handle this," or "There's something wrong with me because I can't get over it." The negative cognitions associated with a grief, bereavement, or mourning experience are the prime reasons why unresolved trauma and complicated mourning look so much alike. Thus, these negative cognitions must be carefully assessed. (See Chapter 4.)

GRIEF: TO DIAGNOSE OR NOT TO DIAGNOSE?

Since I entered this field, I've heard professionals spar with each other on whether human grief should ever be given a diagnosis. On one side, you usually hear the argument that grief is a normal part of the human experience, and if a person is struggling and seeks care, he or she shouldn't be labeled as mentally ill because that is pathologizing humanity. On the other side of the debate is the argument that a person won't be able to access third-party funding for treatment unless there's a solid Axis I diagnosis. So in this *DSM-5®* era, in which Axis I no longer exists and there's a plethora of psychiatrically imposed changes on how to view diagnosis, who wins the debate? In this section, some of the changes between *DSM-IV* and *DSM-5®* are examined in an attempt to shed some light on whether grief can or should be diagnosed.

In the shift from *DSM-IV* to *DSM-5®*, perhaps the biggest change is the elimination of the bereavement exclusion from the Major Depressive Disorder criteria. In *DSM-IV*, Major Depressive Disorder could not be diagnosed, according to Criterion E of that diagnosis, if a bereavement reaction better described the symptoms. Of course, bereavement appeared in *DSM-IV* as a V code (and continues to appear as one in *DSM-5®* even though there was some talk about its elimination). While V codes can be useful for describing a clinical situation, no third-party payer I ever worked with would fund treatment for a V code alone. *DSM-5®* clearly states, as a note following the Major Depressive Disorder description, that careful clinical judgment must be exercised, acknowledging that the symptoms of a major depression may be better explained by bereavement or responses following other major losses. However, if five of the nine criteria in the diagnostic description are met following a loss, and functional impairment is present, then Major Depressive Disorder can be diagnosed.

On the positive side, many professionals support the elimination of this bereavement exclusion, because it acknowledges that complicated mourning can lead to clinical depression. As I stated in Chapter 2, if having a technical diagnosis can help a person access much needed treatment, especially counseling, the diagnosis serves a noble purpose. In my view, a positive counseling experience following a major loss, even if complicated mourning is not present, can help with anyone's overall healing. It seems so unjust that in most systems within the United States, if a person wants to access such services, he or she needs to self-pay or go to general support groups for grief to avoid being pathologized. Some clients with whom I've worked had no problem having a Major Depressive Diagnosis reported to their insurance company and on their record, yet for other clients, it is an issue. Clearly, this "labeling" conundrum is something that must be handled case by case.

The obvious negative of bereavement's eligibility is the time variable described in the depression diagnosis. Only a two-week period of change in mood, leading to five of nine criteria being present, is required to make the diagnosis. Although *DSM-5®* calls for careful clinical judgment when adding bereavement into the equation, many therapists fear that those going through the bereavement process will be prematurely put on antidepressants or potentially addictive benzodiazepines or sleep medications. While many psychiatrists and family doctors may write these prescriptions with good intentions, it is possible that such psychotropic interventions may stymie our natural mourning process and actually cause more harm in the long run. To reiterate a point made in Chapter 2, diagnostic manuals are only as ethical and as useful as the hands they are in. Hence, education about the natural processes of grief, bereavement, and mourning needs to be more widespread within medical communities. Simple validation and the space and time to do the emotional work following a loss are usually the most helpful interventions.

GRIEVING THE WORLD OVER

There is healing in ritual and in the power of community. Cultures around the globe can teach us a great deal about giving the bereaved necessary time, support, and space to heal. Here is a short list of examples. As you read about these customs, think about what lessons we professional helpers can derive from their power, especially in Western culture, where grieving so often happens in isolation.

Sitting Shiva: In Judaism, *shiva* comes from the word for seven. For a period of seven days, mourners visit the home of the deceased's immediate family. While it is considered a great blessing to bring food for the family, it is an even greater blessing to share stories

---

(Continued)

and remembrances about the deceased. While many close to the deceased simply find comfort in the supportive distraction, others use the time to actively, publicly work through their grief.

40 Days of Mourning: In Eastern Orthodoxy, a traditional period of 40 days after the death of a person is highly regarded; this period is seen as the time when the soul wanders the earth. Special prayers are traditionally cited at the grave of the deceased, a custom that goes back to the pagan rituals of Eastern Europe in the time before Slavic occupation.

Iddah: In Islamic tradition, *iddah* is the extended period of mourning, four months and 10 days to be precise, for a widow or a divorced woman. During this time, the woman cannot remarry, as four months and 10 days is considered to be the amount of time needed to determine with certainty whether she is pregnant. *Iddah* is seen as a way to protect a woman from scandal or public scrutiny.

Wailing: Many African cultures believe that the deceased cannot be carried to the afterlife, to his or her ancestors, without sailing on a river of tears. In African funeral rites, emotion is not held back; public wailing and anguish are shared amidst the elaborate celebration of dancing, drumming, and singing. Those in the community not participating in the specific rites hold space for the mourning.

Season of Ashes: In ancient Scandinavian cultures, the bereaved spent up to a year sitting by the fires, watching them reduce to ashes, until they move through the darkest emotions. Little is expected of the bereaved during this period, as the community understands this is a time to do deep work. Those who undertake the work seriously return from the ashes with a new wisdom that allows them to more effectively support the rest of the community during times of peril (Weller, 2012).

The bereavement exclusion remains in *DSM-5®* for adjustment disorders. This exclusion baffles many professionals. Because bereavement is ultimately about adaptation to a loss, functional impairment during bereavement seems like the ultimate "adjustment" disorder. Several options were offered by the *DSM-5®* work groups for naming the functional impairment that can arise following a major loss, especially a death. What the *DSM-5®* work groups ultimately agreed on is a new diagnosis called Persistent Complex Bereavement Disorder. At present, this diagnosis appears in Section III of *DSM-5*®. Section I is the introduction, Section II contains the diagnoses, and Section III describes issues that may be the focus of clinical attention and further study but are not considered by the American Psychiatric Association to have enough research supporting them to make them stand-alone diagnoses. Section III, in my view, is like an elaborate V code section. There are some good ideas here about what may present clinically, but ultimately, I don't see third-party payers funding treatment for these diagnoses.

Because Persistent Complex Bereavement Disorder appears in a diagnostic manual in the medical professions, time parameters are assigned. This upsets many trauma-informed professionals and humanitarians, since there is a subtle implication that the manual puts a time limit on grief. Although I don't interpret the new diagnosis that way, inevitably there will be those that will. In order to meet this new diagnosis, after 12 months in adults or 6 months in children the person must be experiencing a set number of symptoms on more days than not during a week in a way that produces functional impairment. The language used suggests that qualifying for this disorder only applies to bereavement related to death and not other losses (e.g., job, marriage). To meet criteria, at least one of the following symptoms must be met:

- Persistent yearning/longing for the deceased. In young children, yearning may be expressed in play and behavior, including separation-reunion behavior with caregivers.
- Intense sorrow and emotional pain in response to the death.
- Preoccupation with the deceased.
- Preoccupation with the circumstances of the death. In children, this preoccupation with the deceased may be expressed through the themes of play and behavior and may extend to preoccupation with possible death of others close to them.

In addition, any 6 of these 12 symptoms must be met:

- Marked difficulty accepting the death. In children, this is dependent on the child's capacity to comprehend the meaning and permanence of death.
- Feeling shocked, stunned, or emotionally numb over the loss.
- Difficulty with positive reminiscing about the deceased.

- Bitterness or anger related to the loss.
- Maladaptive appraisals about oneself in relation to the deceased or the death (e.g., self-blame).
- Excessive avoidance of reminders of the loss (e.g., avoidance of individuals, places, or situations associated with the deceased). In children, this may include avoidance of thoughts and feelings regarding the deceased.
- A desire to die in order to be with the deceased.
- Difficulty trusting other individuals since the death.
- Feeling alone or detached from other individuals since the death.
- Feeling that life is meaningless or empty without the deceased or the belief that one cannot function without the deceased.
- Confusion about one's role in life or a diminished sense of one's identity (e.g., feeling that a part of oneself died with the deceased).
- Difficulty or reluctance to pursue interests since the loss or to plan for the future (e.g., friendships, activities).

To reiterate, having any or most of these symptoms in the immediate day or months (as the DSM-5® would allow) is to be expected. What makes these symptoms *disordered* is if they are happening in combination, causing functional impairment, on more days than not, for longer than one year. Essentially, these are people whose mourning has not allowed for sufficient adaptation, with problems of living resulting. *DSM-5®* lists some exceptions: The bereavement reaction must be out of proportion or inconsistent with cultural, religious, or age-appropriate norms, which is why assessing for how one's culture frames death and bereavement is imperative. As an example, in many Native American cultures, altered states of consciousness achieved through ritual soul-searching, prayers, and meditation are necessary to discover the meaning of the loss (Cacciatore, 2008). Mystical experiences that many Western psychiatrists would label as "psychotic" are also very common in many paths of Buddhism to help a mourner accommodate the grief experience into the larger, cosmic consciousness.

The specifier that can be applied to Persistent Complex Bereavement is a phrase that the field has used colloquially for years, *traumatic bereavement*. To meet the specifier of traumatic bereavement, as defined by *DSM-5®*:

- The death must have occurred under traumatic circumstances (e.g., homicide, suicide, disaster, or accident).

• There are persistent, frequent, and distressing thoughts, images, or feelings related to traumatic features of the death (e.g., the deceased's degree of suffering, gruesome injury, blame of self or others for the death), including in response to reminders of the loss.

In essence, when the death is uniquely traumatic, with homicide, suicide, disasters, and accidents being the most widely recognized examples, and the person has strongly disturbing thoughts or feelings about the death, the mourning process can be further complicated. Traumatic bereavement often looks like classic PTSD. The way a person died serves as the ultimate complicating variable to adaptation. As a field, we seem to generally recognize that such deaths can be particularly painful to process and reconcile. In such cases, I typically find that conceptualizing the treatment plan as a PTSD case is the most useful approach.

GRIEF'S BAD TRIP

If you have worked in any facet of the human services, you have likely been exposed to the Kübler-Ross Stages of Grief in a list such as this:

• Denial

• Bargaining

• Anger

• Depression

• Grief

When I was a graduate student, my instructors introduced these to me as a grief model. In the substance abuse field, we talked about how these stages can be used to describe one's grief process after someone says goodbye to his or her drug of choice. Of course, pop culture routinely makes mention of the "stages," with so many movies treating them in a joking manner, and talk show hosts using their knowledge of them to peddle their expertise. When Elin Nordegren, Tiger Woods' ex-wife, gave her first and only interview after her divorce from her notoriously unfaithful husband, she described going through the stages of grief, indicating that she learned about them in her psychology studies.

Let's step back for a moment and examine the context. Dr. Elisabeth Kübler-Ross, the great Swiss-American psychiatrist known for her work in the field of thanatology (death and dying) first published the *themes* that we now know as *stages* in her seminal 1969 book, *On Death and Dying*. Kübler-Ross conducted a phenomenological study with terminally ill patients at the University of Chicago Medical School. In phenomenology, the lived experiences of individuals are collected and examined for the purpose of learning themes about the experience. The five "stages" we reference were simply themes that the patients expressed about their lived experience, and they recognized that there can be an ebb and flow to how they play out. One day you can be perfectly accepting of your fate, and the next day you can be in complete denial.

Although Kübler-Ross continued to give us decades of valuable work in the field of death and dying, she never intended for these original five themes to be a model for bereavement following a death or loss. My contention is that the obsession of our professions to put everything into neat, compact theories turned these five constructs into a stage model. We seem to think that denial is what a person goes through first in the aftermath of a major loss, and once he or she works through denial, he or she will move into bargaining. Once this phase is complete, anger occurs, then he or she enters into depression, a stage that can last a long time. Finally, when this depression is fully experienced, acceptance arrives.

Author and trauma survivor Lily Burana (2009), referenced in Chapter 2, offers such poetic commentary on these "stages of grief" in the style of George Carlin. In describing her feelings following her beloved father's death, Burana wrote, "That whole Kübler-Ross thing? The separate stages of Denial, Anger, Bargaining, Dorothy and Toto, or whatever? TOTAL CRAP. What you get when someone dies is all those feelings ALL AT ONCE, warping and spinning around like grief's bad trip." Lily is not a human service professional, she is writing from a client perspective, and she recognized the flaws in trying to put an experience like grief into a neat package. There's something to be said here: Ordinary people can recognize when our psychobabble doesn't quite cut it in explaining the magnitude of their pain, their experience. So why can't we, as professionals, recognize that so much of what we treat can't be explained in compact, quantitative lists?

Burana's phrase "warping and spinning around like grief's bad trip" is one of the most brilliantly informative concepts I've encountered as a teaching psychotherapist. We try to explain the complicated realties of the human experience in models, and if someone is "stuck" in their symptoms, then they are "stuck" in or on some area of the flow chart. However, Burana's idea of warping and spinning conjures up the image of a circular vortex or perhaps a twisted series of tangles and wires. Feeling stuck in the trip is like not being able to find a way out of the circular, disorganized madness.

Burana's commentary, if we are willing to listen, offers us powerful guidance, whether we are working with trauma, grief, or any painful human experiences. Putting a model on the experience or being overly technical in how we conceptualize our work with a client is counterintuitive to the client's experience. Some of my more regimented colleagues may say that by approaching therapy with structure, we are bringing structure and order to a client's inner chaos. Speaking for myself as a human being, not as a professional, I am not against structure and order, especially when it's needed. However, I've always responded most when a helper or friend has been able to enter my chaos and pain for a while, get to know me and my tangles, go on my "trip," so to speak. By doing that, they build my trust and then help me unravel the mess.

One of my guiding principles as a helper comes from the prolific Dutch priest and writer Fr. Henri Nouwen. Many of us know him from his work *The Wounded Healer* (a label that many of us proudly claim), although one of his most insightful passages on how to make a difference with the wounded comes from his book *Out of Solitude* (1974):

> When we honestly ask ourselves which person in our lives means the most to us, we often find that it is those who, instead of giving advice, solutions, or cures, have chosen rather to share our pain and touch our wounds with a warm and tender hand. The friend who can be silent with us in a moment of despair or confusion, who can stay with us in an hour of grief and bereavement, who can tolerate not knowing, not curing, not healing, and face with us the reality of our powerlessness, that is a friend who cares.

Although penned in 1974, long before his work with the mentally and physically handicapped in one of Canada's *L'Arche* houses, Nouwen's famous words are often associated with his time at *L'Arche*; this quote appears on *L'Arche's* international website. In the late 1980s, Nouwen transitioned out of an academic path, having taught at Notre Dame, Harvard, and Yale. He was one of the most respected divinity professors in the world at the time, yet he found something was lacking in his own internal relationship with the god of his understanding. He followed a call to work at *L'Arche*, spending the past 10 years of his life there. It was there that he finally experienced the true meaning of ministry.

If we take an honest look back at the darkest day of our experience, remember the deepest wounds of trauma or grief that life brought our way, and recall our own struggles to heal, I think that few of us would disagree with Nouwen's wisdom. May we, as helpers, who always feel we should have the answers and know just the right thing to say, recognize that the opposite is often true when it comes to creating a culture of healing for the wounded. May we create a safe, healing space for our clients, informed by our shared humanity.

FURTHER READING

Burana, L. (2009). *I love a man in uniform: A memoir of love, war, and other battles.* New York: Weinstein Books.

Kübler-Ross, E. (1969). *On death and dying.* New York: Simon & Schuster.

Nouwen, H. (1990). *The road to daybreak: A spiritual journey.* New York: Bantam.

Weller, F. (2012). *Entering the healing ground: Grief, ritual and the soul of the world.* Santa Rosa, CA: WisdomBridge Press.

Worden, J. (2008). *Grief counseling and grief therapy: A handbook for the mental health practitioner.* (3nd ed.) New York: Springer Publishing Company.

CHAPTER 4

Trauma and the Human Brain

Oh what a tangled web we weave when first we practice to deceive.

—Sir Walter Scott

AN ENGLISH TEACHER'S GUIDE TO THE HUMAN BRAIN

The 1989 film *National Lampoon's Christmas Vacation* is nothing short of a holiday classic. I have watched this film every year since its release, and I recently realized that Clark Griswold, the film's buffoonish protagonist, was my first teacher on trauma neurology. For those of you who think I'm totally off my rocker, allow me to explain. There is a scene in the film where Clark declares his intention to decorate the house for his old-fashioned family Christmas. When Clark begins to unpack the decorations, he finds that the Christmas lights are all tangled up in tightly wound bundles the size of a beach ball. Clark and his big mess of tangles offer one of the movie's great laughs, especially if you relate to the frustration of having to untangle anything. What is admirable is how this jumble does not discourage Clark. Determined to bring the vision of his perfect Christmas house into fruition, Clark works diligently to untangle the mess. The metaphor is not perfect, because, as those of you who know the movie remember, Clark goes a bit overboard with the decorations! However, the idea is that if we work to unravel an unusable bunch of cords and change the broken lightbulbs, what emerges is something beautiful and useful . . . a string of glowing lights to spread holiday cheer!

Clark's tangled ball of Christmas lights is like the brain of a person affected by unresolved trauma. The more complex the layers of the unresolved trauma, the larger and more intricately wound the ball of tangles. As Lily Burana (2009) said in her description of PTSD (see Chapter 2), you can get some crossed wires in your brain due to the traumatic event. If these crossed wires don't get addressed and reorganized at the time of the trauma or shortly after, they remain crossed, making it more likely that new, incoming information will get caught up in the mess. The tangled ball of crossed wires gets bigger and bigger, continuing to complicate the healing process. This chapter explores how this tangled ball remains stored in a part of the brain (the limbic brain) that was never meant to hold information long term. Thus, the brain works harder than it was intended to just to help the person emotionally survive.

Many survivors of trauma connect with this metaphor of tangles and crossed wires in their head without even realizing it. Abduction and torture survivor Jaycee Dugard viewed her 2011 memoir, *A Stolen Life*, as an attempt to "unravel" the damage that was done to her and to her family (p. viii). A young lady whom I did not treat but had the privilege of interviewing for a major study I conducted (Marich, 2010), shared the following: "Before treatment, my thoughts, feelings, and experiences were all tangled like a ball of yarn; I needed something to untangle them." An Iranian-American survivor of childhood sexual trauma, fundamentalist spiritual abuse, and more than 20 unsuccessful attempts at treating her heroin addiction, she identified the treatment experience that finally allowed her to address her addiction and trauma concurrently as the forum for untangling this yarn. Taking this metaphor a step further, once the yarn was untangled, she was able to knit a beautiful sweater out of it, a demonstration of reintegration or post-traumatic growth. At the time of her recollections, she had three and a half years clean and sober, the longest she'd ever achieved in her adult life.

The metaphor of twists and tangles relates to the notion introduced in Chapter 3: There is nothing neat or linear when it comes to trauma, especially at a neurological level. By nature, it is complicated, messy, and multi-dimensional. However, the presence of the word *untangle* in our vernacular suggests that even the messiest of tangles can be released. Now, if you ever untangled anything, you know that it can be a frustrating process, especially at first. Some tightly wound bundles may take you hours to loosen, and others may necessitate recruiting outside help. "Yes!" you may tell yourself, "I'm getting somewhere!" Then, you may have to go back and do some more detail work until another bunch loosens and falls away. More complicated tangles will require more time and more intensive interventions (which can include the help you recruit) for the transformation to occur.

Keep this metaphor of untangling in mind as you read the material in this chapter on trauma and the human brain. I am much more of an artist and humanitarian than a scientist when it comes to approaching trauma. To me, perfect knowledge about the inner working of the human brain does not necessarily make you a better therapist or helper. Thus, I have chosen to focus on the essentials of what you need to know to provide trauma-informed care. I like to call my approach the "English teacher's guide to the human brain." On one hand, it's overly simplified, especially when compared with the neurological focus of many trauma writers. On the other hand, you may find this simplification helpful, especially if you ask, "What does it all mean in relation to what I do in my office?" whenever you hear presentations on neurology. I start with the basics, and then work in some information you might find relevant to clinical life. If you still want more, check out the recommended reading list at the end of the chapter.

Several years back, I was at a major EMDR conference talking to one of my dear friends and colleagues Dr. Earl Grey (yes, like the tea), a wizard of knowledge when it comes to the brain. Neuroscience research was the buzz at that particular conference, and I felt like a total outsider because of my lack of interest in it. Frustrated, I confided in him, "Unless you can show me how it's going to make me a better therapist, I really find the study of the brain very boring and too complicated to ever master." In his inspiring way, he assured me that understanding the basic premise of the triune brain model is what matters the most: In my view, this gives us the majority of information we need about how to be truly trauma informed in our clinical work.

The triune brain model, originally developed by Paul MacLean, MD (1990), postulates that the human brain is three distinct brains working together as one, each with its own unique sense of time and orientation. If you come from a Christian background, it's similar to the idea of the trinity, or three entities (Father, Son, and Holy Spirit) as one God. The work of psychiatrist Dan Siegel, MD, executive director of the Mindsight Institute and internationally known educator on the human brain, introduced me to "The Hand Model of the Brain," a useful way to understand the triune brain. Let's take a look at a human fist, which resembles a brain in appearance:

The base of the brain, which directly connects to the spinal cord, is called the R-complex, sometimes referred to as the reptilian complex or the "lizard brain." *R-complex* was MacLean's name for the basal ganglia. Essentially, it is the structure that MacLean equated with animal instincts. R-complex includes the brainstem and cerebellum, and it controls reflex behaviors, muscle control, balance, breathing, and heartbeat. It is very reactive to direct stimulation. As a fan of series like *The Walking Dead* and zombie movies, consider this: Our mythical zombie archetype is essentially a human being walking around with only the R-complex working, void of emotion or humanity. Zombies are not

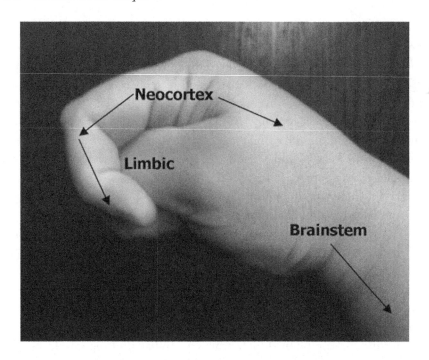

a scientific example by any means, but to my pop culture soul, this idea helps me to better understand this brain.

The paleomammalian complex (limbic system), sometimes called the midbrain, is unique to mammals. This center of emotion and learning, according to MacLean (1990), developed very early in mammalian evolution to regulate the motivations and emotions we now associate with feeding, reproduction, and attachment behaviors. In MacLean's explanation, everything in the limbic system is either agreeable (pleasure) or disagreeable (pain/distress), and survival is based on the avoidance of pain and the reoccurrence of pleasure. The limbic brain contains the amygdala and hypothalamus and does not operate on the same rational sense of time we know as human beings. The limbic brain has no clock, which is why your dog may greet you like you've been gone for 30 years when you just went outside for a few minutes to get the mail. This phenomenon also holds true for people who are stuck in the past, where 50 years ago feels like today. To this part of the brain, where these crossed wires and balls of tangle are housed, 50 years ago *is* today.

When we talk about traumatized people being "stuck," as Lily Burana (2009) worded it, it's as if their panic button is not fully functional. That massive ball of tangled wires gets stuck in the limbic brain. When crossed wires get stuck in the limbic brain, they take on a high level of significance, because material was not meant to be stored here long term. As a high school student of mine once concluded in an oration, "This part of the brain was designed to keep us safe from saber-toothed tigers . . . but it wasn't designed to keep us safe from saber-toothed tigers everyday." When the regulatory capacities of this brain are impaired, it works longer and harder than it was ever intended to, causing the symptoms we associate with traumatic stress. There is a beautiful clip from a CBS news story in which world-renowned psychiatrist Daniel Amen, MD is speaking with a survivor of complex trauma shortly after he completes a brain scan at an Amen clinic. Amen explains to this young man, an adult child of an alcoholic, veteran of the first Gulf War, and recent survivor of an accident, "Your brain's working too hard." That explanation resonated with me as one that is simple and elegant in explaining how the brain, especially the limbic brain, is affected by unresolved trauma.

As one of my dear mentors, Sara Gilman, explained it, the goal of successful trauma processing is to move the charged material out of the limbic brain into a part of the brain that is more efficient in its storage. Gilman was referencing the neomammalian complex (or cerebral neocortex), represented in the hand model by the fingers and top surface of the hand. This brain is unique to primates, and a more highly evolved version of it is unique to humans. The neocortex contains the prefrontal lobes of the brain frequently discussed in explaining human behavior. This brain regulates so much of what makes us human: executive functioning, higher-order thinking skills, reason, speech, meaning making, willpower, and sapience (i.e., wisdom).

Here is the million-dollar question: Have you ever tried to talk reason to someone in crisis?

Most of us working in this field have attempted to, through no fault of our own. Much modern-day training in the human services is so cognitively focused, it is natural for us to confront a person's negative thinking or to get a person to see the silver lining of reason. However, we quickly learn that talking reason to a person in crisis is futile. Cognitive or any reason-based interventions primarily target the prefrontal regions of the brain. However, the limbic region of the brain was activated during the original trauma to help the person survive (through flight, fight, or freeze to submission). Because the left frontal lobe turned off (there is no blood flow) and the right frontal lobe was abandoned (there is awareness but lack of ability to process), the individual was never able to link up that limbic activation with frontal lobe functions during the experience. For a person in crisis or intense emotional distress, this process is playing out in real time, and/or triggers from earlier, unprocessed experiences fuel the distress.

In sum, when the limbic brain is activated, the prefrontal lobes go offline. So, as helpers, why would we appeal to a part of the brain that isn't really "on?"

Our therapeutic interventions, whether used in a crisis or throughout the therapeutic experience, must work with all three brains. For optimal healing to occur, all three brains must be able to work together. Neurologically, unprocessed trauma creates disconnection in the brain. Please don't panic if you think that working with the whole brain will require you to get all kinds of advanced training or special machinery. Consider that breathing is a whole brain intervention. Breath originates in that primal, reptilian region of the brain. Any movement-based, somatic intervention automatically works with the limbic and reptilian brains. Once a person learns to work with regulating distress at those levels or processing their emotional or visceral (e.g., gut level) distress to a more adaptive resolution, the brain can be open to meaning making, reasoning, and the integration of wisdom.

The triune brain concept is criticized by many in the field as being an oversimplification of neurology, especially trauma neurology. In my view, its beauty *is* its simplicity. The triune brain explanation offers great utility in working with clients. You can explain it relatively free of jargon, and people can visualize it if they have the ability to make a fist. More importantly, the concept informs us that words alone do not suffice in helping a person heal from trauma—often words and rational concepts cannot even begin to scratch the surface. As my preschool teacher Mrs. White wisely said, actions speak louder than words. As we will continue to discover in our exploration of the human brain in the healing of trauma, dynamic, relational, action-based interventions typically go much deeper than verbal, rational interventions alone.

In Their Own Words
Jaycee Dugard

Whenever a client seems to lack a basic sense of chronology or sequence in referencing his or her history, it is generally a sign that material is stuck at the limbic level, where the "rational" sense of time we associate with the rational or cerebral brain is missing. Consider this passage, another from the memoir *A Stolen Life* by Jaycee Dugard (2011), written very shortly after her rescue:

> It didn't feel like a sequence of events. Even after I was freed, moments are fragmented and jumbled . . . If you want a less confusing story, come back to me in 10 years from now when I sort it all out!

THE STADIUM METAPHOR OF HUMAN BRAIN PROCESSES

Using metaphors to teach is a key feature of this book, and one of my favorites to help explain the different roles within the brain comes from Earl Grey, PhD. You can read more of his brilliant teaching analogies in his 2010 book, *Unify Your Mind: Connecting the Feelers, Thinkers, and Doers of the Brain*, written for a lay audience.

1. Information enters our system through our senses: seeing, smelling, hearing, tasting, or touching.

2. The brain has a filter that acts like a greeter at a theater saying to new information, "Yes, you can enter" or "No, you cannot enter." This doorman has control over how we perceive information and experiences.

3. The information moves to the ticket taker. The ticket taker (i.e., the amygdala) looks at the information and labels it with an emotion. The first label the ticket taker gives information is "DANGER" or "NO DANGER."

NO DANGER	DANGER
4. Then, the ticket taker sends the information to the lobby (i.e., the hippocampus) before you take your seat. Here, information mixes with other information and is segregated into "useful data" and "useless data," [for example] the body sensations we feel during an event.	4. Then, the ticket taker rushes the information through the lobby (i.e., the hippocampus) and passes it off to the usher (i.e., the thalamus) to the front row of seats (the survival part of the brain; i.e., the hypothalamus). This is where the "show" or event excites us.
5. Next, the information is greeted by the usher (i.e., the thalamus) and led up the steps (i.e., the anterior cingulate gyrus) to the prime second floor stadium seats (i.e., the prefrontal cortex).	5. The excitement of the show incites one of three reactions: The announcer (i.e., the reptilian brain) tells the audience to rage against the information (fight response) or run away as fast as you can (flight response), or stay very still and do what you are told even though you are petrified (freeze and thwart response).

(Continued)

6. Then, the information files into its seats (i.e., the prefrontal cortex) in a very orderly way, and the lobby (i.e., the hippocampus) is cleared out so new information can enter and the brain is calm.	**6.** The crowd (body of the person) does what the Announcer tells them to do with no rational thought.
	7. After the danger is gone, the audience in the front row seats (i.e., the hypothalamus) stays in the seats even after the event is over to make sure that reaction is remembered, just in case the announcer shows up again. This way, the same reaction can happen again faster.
	8. The audience in the front row (i.e., the hypothalamus) and the announcer (i.e., the reptilian brain) work hard to refuel the system and add some extra fuel so they are prepared for the next time. Instead of one hot dog, they will eat five or add extra alcohol while waiting for the show. This refuel process keeps the front row audience and the announcer looking for the substance that will help them numb the system due to the fear that the previous "show" will happen again.

(*Continued*)

9. Once the audience is refueled, they will try to find activities to keep their attention away from what might happen (a repeat of the previous show). Many times, the front row will buy a lot of souvenirs (compulsive shopping) or keep going to the restroom to clean up (compulsive cleaning/washing) or use sexual behavior to get the release of a climax, forcing the system to be very calm (i.e., the parasympathetic response).

Developed by Earl Grey, Ph.D. Reprinted with permission.

ISSUES IN THE TISSUES: USEFUL EXPLANATIONS, MODELS, AND IDEAS

Nikki Myers remembers being a 9-year-old girl watching the news and seeing people of color, people who looked just like her, being hosed and gassed and beaten. Nikki absorbed these images during the social upheaval of the Civil Rights movement, and although she was raised in the northern United States, seeing those images completely shook her sense of authority and self. As Nikki explains,

> Something had to be wrong with me if these people who looked like me were being treated this way. Everything I'd learned in school taught me that government and authority was to be respected, so if government and authority was doing this to children like me, I must be flawed.

Nikki discloses that, to this day, reflecting on that memory brings up a strong visceral reaction in her. The images were imprinted at a cellular level.

Nikki is the founder of a growing program called Y12SR®, the Yoga of 12-Step Recovery. Nikki, a recovering addict and survivor of multiple trauma layers, launched the program about a decade ago. Y12SR® meetings are not affiliated with any one 12-Step fellowship; rather, they are independent gatherings that combine the essence of a 12-Step discussion meeting with a yoga class. The guiding principle of Y12SR® is that *the issues live in our tissues.* As Nikki explains, when you are in the physical posture of a yoga pose or even a simple stretch outside of the context of yoga and you feel those muscles quiver, your body is working something out. Nikki, also a trained Somatic Experiencing® practitioner, heavily channels the work of Dr. Peter Levine in her revolutionary approach. In speaking to human services and wellness professionals, Nikki states, "There has to be a connection between the cognitive and the somatic—the trauma lives in our bodies. Trauma is a stagnated form of energy. It gets stuck in the body. Stuck in our tissues. It must be released on this level."

Robert Scaer, MD, author of the *The Body Bears the Burden: Trauma, Dissociation, and Disease* (2007), specifies that when memories live in the part of the brain that plays out in the theater of the body, that's traumatic stress. The body comes back to the same patterns of self-defense, and the symptoms manifest in body parts that never had a chance to resolve the traumatic injury. Trauma expert Linda Curran (2012) interviewed Scaer and several other leaders in the field of trauma neurology in the documentary *Trauma Treatment for the 21st Century*, and the general consensus was powerful: Talking is not enough, because the trauma is stored in a part of the brain that has nothing to do with talking.

Several key items from these interviews help us further understand relevant teachings from the neurological canon for ordinary clinicians. As trauma expert and Sensorimotor Psychotherapy® trainer Janina Fisher, PhD, explains, in our profession we are all children of Freud and the "talking cure," but we have learned that talking about the trauma can actually be very activating, worsening the experience of distress. Peter Levine, founder of Somatic Experiencing®, explains that body memories need to be completed. Trauma survivors need to feel activation and energy in the muscles. In Somatic Experiencing®, trauma survivors feel gentle vibrating or trembling sensations that represent the letting go; this work is a way to undo maladaptive procedural or body memories.

Holly Ann Rivera, whom we first met in Chapter 2, has struggled with gastrointestinal illness throughout her life, and the connection between unresolved trauma and illness makes complete sense to her. When Heather Bowser, introduced in Chapter 1, was in elementary school getting teased and tortured by her peers about her physical disability, she didn't want to show her emotions at home. She explains that her dad's own illnesses from his exposure to Agent Orange during Vietnam was intensifying at the time, and she didn't want to burden her parents with her problems. She developed enuresis, and going to school smelling like urine added to the torture. In discussing her story, Heather and I agreed that if distress cannot be healthfully processed, the body will get it out somehow, and in her case, her body's response added another layer to her trauma story.

A popular explanation for these body phenomena within the field of traumatic stress studies is the polyvagal theory, developed by Stephen Porges, PhD, of the University of Chicago. Porges (2011) explained the theory and science of the polyvagal theory in his book *The Polyvagal Theory: Neurophysiological Foundations of Emotions, Attachment, Communication, and Self-Regulation*. I admit that the sheer weight of science in this book goes over my head and my qualitative, artistic orientation, so I assume other human services professionals would be equally overwhelmed. Ravi Dykema (2006) of *Nexus*, a Colorado-based holistic health and conscious living magazine, does an excellent job of interviewing Dr. Porges and breaking down the polyvagal theory and its applications in as simple a manner as possible. A link to this article appears in this chapter's Further Reading.

The vagus nerve is the big, long nerve that runs from your brain down the length of your spine, a primary component of the autonomic nervous system. Porges states that it's useful to conceptualize the vagal nerve as a pipeline that contains many other nerve fibers that connect from various areas of the brain to different functions in the body (Dykema, 2006). Porges explains:

> Historically, the autonomic system has been broken into two branches, one called the sympathetic, and the other parasympathetic. It is an organizational model that came into place in the late 1800s and the early 1900s. Over the years, this model has taken on a life of its own, although we know more now. Essentially, it linked the sympathetic system with the "fight or flight" response, and the parasympathetic system with ordinary functioning, when one is calm and collected. This model of the autonomic nervous system has evolved into various "balance theories," because most organs of the body, such as the heart, the lungs and the gut, have both sympathetic and parasympathetic innervation.

While the science behind Porges' work justifies the link between emotional distress and many physical illnesses, you may be wondering, as I did when I first learned about the polyvagal theory, what does this all mean for me as a clinician?

Dykema (2006) created a "Dos" and "Don'ts" list for clients based on the polyvagal theory. This list helps the helpers put the theory into action and thus become more neurologically informed in the delivery of our services:

DOs	DON'Ts
Do make eye contact when you feel safe.	Don't combine intimate conversation with hard exercise; you'll misread all of the other person's cues.
Do express with your face.	Don't always isolate yourself in trying to feel safer; try connecting with others too.
Do modulate your voice (use expression).	Don't push yourself harder to feel social when you feel unsafe; seek safety first.
Do listen to voices; separate them from background sounds.	Don't ignore your gut reactions; adapt to them and learn from them.
Do adjust your circumstances to feel safer (e.g., move to a quieter place).	Don't use fighting or fleeing with loved ones; instead, find a way to get to safety.
Do adjust your focus to things that will make you feel safe (e.g., feel your sensations or focus on something familiar).	Don't adopt a flat, expressionless affect with people whom you want to feel safe with you.
Do play a musical instrument.	Don't substitute Internet relating for face-to-face or phone contact.
Do try moving into social relationships instead of away as a way to reduce slight anxiety.	Don't assume that others' outbursts reveal their "true" attitudes or motivations. Their calmer social capacities (like empathy) are true too.

Developed by R. Dykema. Reprinted with permission.

Dykema's condensation of best practices based on polyvagal theory can give us, as helping professionals, guidance on how we can optimally relate to the people whom we serve. Clients will find some of these tips easier said than done, but it may be worthwhile to build on the skills they can do well (e.g., playing a musical instrument, being able to account for safety) as they work toward skills that may be harder for them (e.g., face-to-face interaction).

The healing power of human connection is a major theme in the literature on trauma neurology. The title of Dr. Daniel Siegel's (2008) classic audiobook *The Neurobiology of "We"* says it all: There is healing in connection. Obviously, many trauma survivors were not able to experience healthy attachment or connection in early life, so relationships can be a part of the larger fear conditioning that defines trauma. However, helping a client to become more comfortable with healthy connections to others can be a phenomenal gateway to healing.

This concept of healing connection informed the field of interpersonal neurobiology, pioneered by scholars like Siegel and Dr. Allan Schore, and continues to be supported by research evidence. However, those of us who have experienced the power of a self-help group or a spiritual fellowship recognize the common sense in this principle. Interaction with others, the very thing that we may fear, is actually the antidote. Healthy, adaptive connectedness is the healing balm that can help to untangle our tangled wires. As is discussed more fully in Chapter 7, the quality of the therapeutic relationship is typically the greatest force for change for a traumatized client. Considering what interpersonal neurobiology teaches us, it makes perfect sense why: There is healing in healthy connection. Restoration is possible through adaptive relationships.

IN THEIR OWN WORDS
Edward Young

Edward Young (1681–1765) was an English poet best known for his free-verse poem *Night Thoughts*. Scholars describe it as long and disconnected, a clue that the author's life was filled with layers of trauma. Perhaps *Night Thoughts* was his way to work through it? Consider this passage, which uses the tangle metaphor, and what we can take from it in the present day as helpers:

> I had looked for happiness in fast living, but it was not there. I tried to find it in money, but it was not there either. But when I placed myself in tune with what I believe to be the fundamental truths of life, when I began to develop my limited ability, to rid my mind of all kinds of tangled thoughts, and fill it with zeal and courage and love, when I gave myself a chance by treating myself decently and sensibly, I began to feel the stimulating, warm glow of happiness.

DEMYSTIFYING DISSOCIATION

When I was two years sober, my therapist (an EMDR-certified trauma specialist) diagnosed me with Dissociative Disorder, NOS. I was always an active daydreamer, and the creative places I went in my head helped me to cope amidst my struggles at home. At a certain point, this daydreaming became so pathological, I was unable to distinguish the fantasy life in my head from reality, and when reality hit me too hard, drinking and drugs became a very appealing outlet for coping. Right around the time of my second sobriety anniversary, I began my clinical internship at an adolescent mental health facility. I handled the practicum part of the internship with little incident, since the hours were limited. However, when the hours escalated, I found myself getting triggered left and right, not so much by the children but by the way I saw staff members treating them at the hospital.

My primary defense mechanism was to dissociate. I rarely did it when I was actively facilitating a treatment group, but when I was doing paperwork or attending to duties on the floor, my mind would just float away—that is the best way to describe the experience. I zoned out to the point that I was numb, almost as if I was floating above myself. Sometimes in the morning when I woke up, knowing I had to go to this awful hospital, I would lie there, awake but immobilized. On the drive to the hospital, I would often blank out; I routinely relied on the music I enjoyed to keep me present in the car after I noticed that zoning was a problem. Looking back on the experience now, I recognize that these reactions were my brain's failsafe to keep me from experiencing a full-on visceral meltdown, since I was quite triggered at the body level. At this time, EMDR came into my life, and my initial exposure to this holistic, somatic work changed me forever.

I share a bit of my story here for one main reason: I know dissociation intimately and personally. It enrages me when I hear professionals, even well-known writers in the field, doubt the existence of the dissociative continuum or challenge whether diagnoses like Dissociative Identity Disorder (DID) are even real. To quote the words of my first client with DID, "People fear what they don't understand." So, let's take some time in this chapter to demystify dissociation. I am not going to go into great neurological detail here, since others, such as Colin Ross, MD, and Onno van der Hart, MD, already do that magnificently in their work. However, it is imperative to know that trauma is typically a major factor in dissociation. Although not all clients with trauma-related diagnoses dissociate to a clinically significant degree, we can safely ascertain that all clients with dissociative symptoms or diagnoses are battling unresolved trauma.

As trauma expert Bessel van der Kolk, MD, shared in *Trauma Treatment for the 21st Century* documentary (Curran, 2012), people tend to cope with trauma by splitting it off. It's too scary to know. The blocking off, shutting down, or separating response of dissociation is essentially a freeze response. It's important to know that dissociation exists on a continuum. News flash: We all dissociate! If you've ever daydreamed, you have dissociated. If you've ever just zoned out to your favorite TV program at the end of a hard day, then you've dissociated. If you've ever been taken into a state of bliss during a guided imagery exercise, then you've dissociated. So much dissociation can be beneficial and not necessarily impairing. For some trauma survivors, the initially very adaptive features of dissociation (e.g., keeping you safe, helping you relax) can eventually backfire if they cross the line into functional impairment. For me, dissociation affected my job performance and could have put people at serious risk on the road, which clearly meets the *DSM* criteria for functional impairment.

What many don't appreciate about dissociation is that the brain functions of freeze and separation that can cause problems leading to *DSM*-defined diagnoses were initially very adaptive. For many survivors, they can still be adaptive. I have treated several DID clients and a few others who, like I once did, carried a diagnosis of Dissociative Disorder, NOS, but there were some clear separation features related to ego state. In my experience, the majority of these clients did not want full integration of the parts, or alters. One of the misconceptions is that successful treatment of DID is about getting all of the different parts to integrate into a cohesive whole. Every individual with DID whom I've either treated or known describes one of their alters as being *the protector*, a completely valid and beautiful alter for a person who experienced unspeakable trauma. No one was there to protect him or her in childhood or infancy, so it was completely natural for the brain to create a protector. When you think about it, it's an amazing example of our brains doing everything in their power to help us survive. So naturally, saying that clinical wellness means taking this alter away is a misguided notion. The best solution seems to be getting the different parts to communicate more effectively with each other.

Clinicians can work with parts, ego states, or separation—however you want to view it—with clients who have diagnoses other than DID. In fact, getting in touch with the different "parts" that are within you, even if you are a pretty high-functioning adult free of *DSM*-style labels, is a major way to understand dissociation. We all have different parts. Think about what yours may be. Here is your gateway to understanding dissociation. Do you have a protective side? An inner child? A raging bitch? A meek lamb? A sexy siren? An old-fashioned prude? A class clown? An artistic streak? These are just some examples—they may not all apply to you. For people who've survived serious traumas, the separation of parts has been more distinct, usually commensurate with the level of distress a survivor had to endure.

After I completed much of my own healing from dissociation, I felt passionately about working with people who dissociate because this protective function of our brains is so misunderstood. That was when I became acquainted with the work of Elizabeth Howell, MD (2008), author of *The Dissociative Mind*. She helped to release the fear I had about treating others who are affected because she validated so much of my common-sense knowledge. We all dissociate—some more than others, some more creatively than others. As Howell wrote:

> The rising tide of trauma and dissociation studies has created a sea change in the way we think about psychopathology. Chronic trauma . . . that occurs early in life has profound effects on personality development and can lead to the development of dissociative identity disorder (DID), other dissociative disorders, personality disorders, psychotic thinking, and a host of symptoms such as anxiety, depression, eating disorders, and substance abuse. In my view, DID is simply an extreme version of the dissociative structure of the psyche that characterizes us all. Dissociation, in a general sense, refers to the rigid separation of parts of experience, including somatic experience, consciousness, affects, perception, identity, and memory.

Howell's words worked for me beautifully, almost like she was validating me. If you are interested in more of the scientific explanations of the neurology of dissociation, I highly recommend the work of Dr. Colin Ross. (See Further Reading at the end of this chapter.) Dr. Robert Scaer also has a wonderful article right on his website called "The Dissociation Capsule" that puts this weighty neurological material into as concise a model as possible. (See Further Reading.)

In Their Own Words

Anna

Anna identifies as a multiple, a survivor of trauma with Dissociative Identify Disorder (DID). She had the chance to receive treatment at one of the world-class hospitals available for healing dissociation, but she found that going back to her part of the country and finding competent follow-up posed a challenge. A survivor of just about every abuse imaginable, including spiritual trauma and mind control, she identifies as having more than a thousand parts making up her being and her experience. Anna is not a client but a reader of one of my earlier books who sought me out to dialogue about the helping profession's view of dissociation. She was gracious enough to share some of her experiences here:

> It's been a painful journey to find one of you to speak to or with, especially one with a degree in the field of trauma recovery who doesn't treat me like a circus freak. I want to address the "us-them" divide. You, the professionals . . . you're "us." You are the ones with the degrees who, like it or not, look down on. . . . "them" . . . those of us who have a trauma disorder and especially one called Dissociative Identity Disorder, which is already mocked and misunderstood by the public and argued within your own realms for the *DSM*.
>
> Don't worry—you don't have to feel oversensitive about my take on "us": It's wholly ingrained in society. Do you see how the media portrays mental illness? I could "come out" as a lesbian (which I'm not) and get no flack about it, but if I "came out" about being a multiple (I'll use that term from now on), I would be ostracized. Instead, I sit alone in my home, politely interact in public, politely excuse myself when I am triggered in public, or have a personality pushing forward to the front of my consciousness . . . and . . . somehow . . . the few people I interact with "on the outside" can think I'm normal.
>
> When I returned from a hospital that specializes in dissociation I needed to find a counselor where I live. I was referred to the nearest local hospital with an inpatient/

(Continued)

outpatient psych center, and I met with the psychiatrist—in society's terms, The Man, only this doctor was female. Here is part of our conversation:

Me: "I need someone who understands my diagnosis."

[Me talking about Judy Herman's *Trauma and Recovery* and other seminal books I've read, in order to gain her respect—which I've found is necessary in getting an "in" to be POSSIBLY treated like a fucking viable human.]

Female White Coat: "Oh. So you're an autodidact."

Me: "Huh . . . what . . .?"

[She "defines" that an autodidact is someone who is self-taught with the haughty, better-than-thou DRIPPING off of her as if she was the evil woman in the movie, *The Devil's Advocate*. I stay calm.]

Me: "Can you . . . just talk to me?" (treat me like a human)

At this point, it got worse, to the point that my protector-gatekeeper personality came out in front, though not speaking. The woman started talking about how I'd be "their first multiple" and "what fun they'd have." Do you see why I don't have a professional working with me?

Now, if you want to know about this disorder, in simple terms, I'll get my protector-part out to calm me down for an hour, and I'll try to let you know. Maybe you can do me a favor in the meantime and get me a drink of water? I'm just calling on the common denominator of humanness and suffering. I just want you to listen.

Dissociation: The past is in present tense; harm is not healed until the memory (and thoughts/beliefs associated with it) are healed.

I worked at a gourmet lunch shop, which used wine in the food. One day, going back in the kitchen, I caught just the wrong and intense inhalation of wine, which hit my olfactory memory, which made my entire BODY feel as if I were actively in the 1980s, trying to separate my large, drunken stepfather's

(Continued)

fists from my brother. My mind, my body all held the belief that I was in THAT time period. At the same time, I could (in this flashback I could) see with my eyes that I was in a kitchen somewhere, some-TIME else, so I fled to a bathroom for the internal screams to subside.

Is that crazy? I think it's immoral and inhumane that my brother and I were not taken away from my "parents." Now I live with a disorder that kept me alive in the past but today takes **away** from functioning and living.

FURTHER READING

Curran, L. (Director). (2012). *Trauma treatment for the 21st century* [Educational Documentary]. United States: Premiere Education & Media.

Dugard, J. (2011). *A stolen life: A memoir.* New York: Simon & Schuster.

Dykema, R. (2006). How your nervous system sabotages your ability to relate: An interview with Stephen Porges about his polyvagal theory. *NexusPub,* March/April 2006. Retrieved from http://www.nexuspub. com/articles_2006/interview_porges_06_ma.php.

Grey, E. (2010). *Unify your mind: Connecting the feelers, thinkers, & doers of your brain.* Pittsburgh, PA: CMH&W, Inc.

Howell, E. (2008). *The dissociative mind.* New York: Routledge.

Levine, P. (1997). *Waking the tiger—Healing trauma.* Berkeley, CA: North Atlantic Books.

Porges, S. (2011). *The polyvagal theory: Neurophysiological foundations of emotions, attachment, communication, and self-regulation.* New York: W.W. Norton.

Ross, C. (2012). *The rape of Eve: The true story behind the three faces of Eve.* Richardson, TX: Manitou Communications.

Ross, C. (2013). *Structural dissociation: A proposed modification of the theory.* Richardson, TX: Manitou Communications.

Scaer, R. (2007). *The body bears the burden: Trauma, dissociation, and disease.* New York: Routledge.

Scaer, R. (n.d.). "The dissociation capsule," In *TraumaSoma: Articles*. Retrieved from http://www.traumasoma.com/excerpt1.html.

Siegel, D. (2008). *The neurobiology of "We": How relationships, the mind, and the brain interact to shape who we are.* Boulder, CO: Sounds True Books.

Siegel, D. (2012). *Pocket guide to interpersonal neurobiology: An integrative handbook of the mind.* New York: W.W. Norton & Co.

CHAPTER 5

Issues in Assessment

There's a phenomenology of being sick, one that depends on temperament, personal history, and the culture which we live in.

—Siri Hustvedt, from *The Shaking Woman, or A History of My Nerves*

In my travels across the country, I have a chance to meet some really neat people. People who are on the front lines to help survivors of trauma heal, and people fighting to make their agencies, their communities, and even government organizations more widely recognize the impact of traumatic stress on human beings. Timothy,* a retired administrator in the insurance industry, now offers community presentations on the role that trauma plays in altering human development. Timothy's mission is to get government organizations everywhere, especially those in a position to influence public health policies, to recognize trauma as a global pandemic. By definition, a pandemic is a disease or illness that is prevalent throughout an entire country or area of the globe; it's much broader in scope than an epidemic.

Although I've heard the word *epidemic* associated with traumatic stress before, Timothy's mention of *pandemic* really gave me pause. Now, to those in the field who think that people like Timothy and I blow trauma out of proportion and exaggerate its prevalence and effects, this idea is patently ridiculous. However, if you are practicing in this field and living in our modern society with at least one eye open, you know that *pandemic* is not an exaggeration. As we've established in earlier chapters, life can potentially be very traumatic, and the impairments we tend to see in society arise from these traumas of life not being addressed or healed. A plethora of peer-reviewed research articles stemming from the landmark Adverse Childhood Experiences

73

(ACE) collaboration between Kaiser Permanente and the Centers for Disease Control (CDC) continue to demonstrate a clear correlation between early childhood distress (e.g., abuse, neglect, and household dysfunction) and the following problems (Center for Disease Control, 2013):

- Alcoholism and alcohol abuse
- Chronic obstructive pulmonary disease (COPD)
- Depression
- Fetal death
- Health-related quality of life
- Illicit drug use
- Ischemic heart disease (IHD)
- Liver disease
- Risk for intimate partner violence
- Multiple sexual partners
- Sexually transmitted diseases (STDs)
- Smoking
- Suicide attempts
- Unintended pregnancies
- Early initiation of smoking
- Early initiation of sexual activity
- Adolescent pregnancy

The findings from the ACE study raise a major red flag to which those of us in the human services need to pay attention: If you see any of these symptoms in your clients, which is extremely likely today, you ought to be assessing for trauma. Let's delve into our examination of how to assess for trauma and its impacts.

DO NOT RETRAUMATIZE

The cardinal rule of ethics in the human services is "do no harm." This general principle of nonmaleficence is a given for the professions, but it takes on another level of significance if you are committed to being trauma sensitive. Part of doing no harm is taking extra care not to retraumatize an individual presenting for services. Retraumatizing actions can span the range of harm—anything from salting a wound to ripping it wide open. Although some amount of discomfort is generally expected in the healing of any wound, and even the wisest professionals make their share of mistakes, our general mission must be to keep the people in our care safe. Safety and flexibility are the two primary qualities of what defines trauma-sensitive care. Creating a safe space and being flexible (as opposed to being rigid) prevent against rewounding, and in trauma-informed care, we must begin practicing these qualities from the first meeting.

First, we must recognize that *assessment* has a double meaning. On one hand, an assessment is the first time meeting between a person and a professional or human service worker. The clinician gathers as much data as possible to ascribe a working diagnosis and/or make the best recommendation possible about care. However, assessment is also an ongoing process. You are not going to get the whole story from clients in a first meeting, nor should you. Part of being trauma informed in your approach to assessment is realizing that if you don't get everything in the first session, that's okay. The depth of pain that a person may need to share should only come out in the context of a trusting therapeutic relationship, so why would we expect a person to get it all out in the first session?

The idea of not retraumatizing during an assessment may seem incredibly oversimplified—maybe even a "duh" is coming up in your mind. However, I continue to hear horror stories from people about how they were handled by an assessing professional. (Refer to "In Their Own Words: Anna" in Chapter 4.) I know that at earlier times in my own career, I probably pushed a client to reveal too much information too soon. Pushing a client for details or prodding him or her about things he or she is not quite ready to discuss is one of the major ways that professionals can retraumatize, especially in assessment or early sessions when a client may have few skills for regulating affect or somatic distress. I've also made the mistake of trying to get a client to see the silver lining before he or she is ready to go there. So often we, as counselors, want to utilize all of our brilliant reframing skills before we get to know a person; this also may retraumatize the client in a very subtle way by minimizing his or her struggle.

The process of assessment itself, especially in mainstream hospitals, is incredibly stressful, especially if a client goes to a hospital in a suicidal or homicidal state. Think about it: We usually ask clients to sit in a waiting room and fill out a big stack of paperwork. In hospitals, emergency rooms are anything but comfortable. In agency settings, the waiting rooms are often loud, crowded, dirty, and overstimulating. Then, we go out to the waiting room to get a client, perhaps shaking his or her hand, even if he or she is aversive to touch (especially by strangers) and then walk the client down a hallway to an office. On entering a room that the client has probably never seen before, we may give a general introduction but then quickly jump in to asking this vulnerable person a bunch of questions about himself or herself (a process that can feel like interrogation), usually documenting our answers on a form or computer. For people who have been in the mental health system for a long time, they've likely had to tell their story over and over, usually without resolve. Even during one admission to a hospital or treatment center, a client maybe asked to re-answer questions over and over for no apparent reason. When I was a new counselor working in my first treatment center, during a counseling assessment, the client asked me, "I've had to answer these questions on the phone to the screening person, to the nurse, to the doctor. Don't you all talk to each other? Why do I have to keep answering these?"

This client made an excellent point.

As a graduate student whom I mentor shared with me upon starting her internship, "The assessment process in the agency I work at is just one long exercise in shaming a person."

Our systems of care are so fragmented, and with each new department or set of services, we are asked, usually for the sake of insurance or accreditation standards, to document the whole interview again. And God forbid if you don't finish the assessment in the hour or hour and a half that you're given to do it! When I teach trauma-sensitive assessment, one of the biggest concerns I hear is that if the form assessment doesn't get done, the clinician or trainee could be nailed by the powers that be for a deficiency in the chart. Another great flaw in our system is how many of these assessment questions are written. They tend to be full of interrogatory, closed questions (e.g., "Have you ever been sexually abused?"), when the healthiest questions in counseling are generally open ended (e.g., "What were things like for you growing up?" or "How did that affect you?"). The *what* and the *how* questions are optimal for trauma-informed assessments, because they invite a client to give as much or a little detail as he or she is ready to give.

Although I recognize that each agency has its own culture of rules to adhere to, my guidance to you is this: Wherever possible, let your conversation with a new client unfold organically. Jump around your form as best as possible. Check with the standards of your agency if you are concerned about leaving items blank. Very often, a line like, "defer to further assessment" will suffice. Another option is that before you start, orient the client to the assessment process and give him or her an idea of why you'll be asking the questions you're asking. When I worked in community dual diagnosis treatment, many mandated clients would ask me, "Why are you asking me that?" Being able to answer such questions is imperative if you are serious about being trauma informed.

A guiding principle of the International Association of Trauma Professionals (IATP) is that assessment *is* an intervention. I couldn't agree more. The initial assessment is a time to plant seeds, to help assuage a client's trepidations about the treatment process, and to begin teaching the client that it's okay to say "No." I like to preface all of my assessments by telling clients that if we've delved into an area that they're not ready to talk about yet, it's okay to tell me so. The other part of this is to be attuned to the clients and their nonverbal or subtle energetic signals (e.g., that "vibe" they give off). The client may not feel like he or she can say no, especially if he or she wants to please you or "pass the assessment." If you sense any level of discomfort in a client's answering a question or talking about a difficult matter, you can make the observation and give the client permission to say no, a powerful teaching technique.

The initial assessment is also a valuable time to begin building rapport and forging a healthy alliance. Although issues about empathy and therapeutic alliance are more fully explored in Chapter 7, there are a few points to mention here. Rapport building does not mean that you have to be fake or phony—it requires genuineness. My working definition of being genuine is being the most compassionate version of you. An approach that advocates for trauma-informed care recommend is to go into assessment with a spirit of "What happened to you?" not "What's wrong with you?" This approach represents a paradigm shift for many, and it highlights the importance of being nonjudgmental with our clients. Being nonjudgmental does not mean that you have to endorse certain behaviors that a client may disclose to you during an assessment. Let's face it, especially if you work with perpetrators or people who have put their children in harm's way as the result of their addiction, you may hear some things that make your skin crawl. Being nonjudgmental means that you respect and honor the dignity of the person at all times, even if he or she has done horrible things.

Let me share a story that represents the difference in paradigm. An old friend from high school is now a police officer, proudly identifying with his work. A few years back, we had occasion to reconnect, and we naturally started talking about our professions. When he listened to me talk about my work with trauma he was respectful but a little skeptical, declaring, "You know, I'm sick of hearing these vets use PTSD as an excuse, like they're beating on their wives because of the PTSD. Some people just beat on their wives because they're assholes." He has a point to a degree—many times people will use their clinically valid diagnosis to justify poor behavior, sometimes holding onto the diagnosis as their great excuse. In response, I validated my friend's concern and then offered, "Have you ever stopped to think that they're assholes for a reason?"

People come into our offices with a great deal of shame. In the addiction field, we say that guilt is when you feel bad about things you've done, but shame is when you feel bad about who you are, at your core. As Anaïs Nin, the French-Cuban writer expressed, "Shame is the lie someone told you about yourself." The paralyzing shame that people carry with them usually results because they've internalized and believed the lie. As professionals, whether we realize it or not, we are in a position of power—the power to keep driving this lie into people's psyches or the power to begin, very gently, to help them realize new, valid truths about themselves. Assessment is prime time to begin this process. Even if you are in a system where you only do assessments and then hand the care off to another counselor, you are still in a powerful position to impart hope by practicing some of the simple, humanistic skills covered in this section.

One of the simplest yet most effective humanistic skills that can be used during assessment is validation. I've worked with so many people over the years whose pain is minimized by family members, society, or even other therapists. Some clinicians seem afraid to validate because they don't want the client to get into a rut of self-pity. This attitude arises time and time again in many traditional addiction treatment facilities. Clients get told things like, "You're here to deal with your addiction, not all of those trauma issues." Even if the treatment center is not set up to work with clients for long periods of time at an intensive level, simple recognition of the history and of their pain enhances treatment (Evans & Sullivan, 1995). Think of how much more validating and less shaming it is for a person to hear, "You know, our center is pretty limited in what we can do with the time we have, but I want you to know that I hear that this happened to you, and I honor that this is part of your story." Holly Ann Rivera (introduced in Chapter 2), after having several "horrible" experiences with counseling, finally felt that she found the right fit with a therapist who used and validated the terms *abuse* and *trauma*.

Consider William, the father of Heather Bowser (introduced in Chapter 1). After serving one tour in Vietnam in the U.S. Army, he was a changed man, both mentally and physically. Heather's mother recognized that he was different but felt powerless to do anything about it, adding to the complexity of the family trauma. William, who used a fair amount of humor to deflect his emotional pain, would sleep with one foot hanging off the bed and touching the floor. He sometimes slept outside of their rural Ohio home with a gun, doing "perimeter watches." When he learned about Agent Orange and made the connection between his physical exposure and Heather's disabilities, he blamed himself for harming his child. He lived the last 12 years of his life in a great deal of physical distress, requiring quintuple bypass surgery at the age of 38, contracting diabetes at the age of 40, having a stroke at age 48, and finally succumbing to a fatal heart attack at age 50.

As Heather remembers, the last decade of her father's life was very hard, not only because of the physical distress, but also because he didn't have any resolution. When I asked her what would have helped him get that resolution, her answer was simple: validation. At no point did he ever experience validation of his injuries, emotional and physical, from the VA, from the government, or even from the outcome of the first Agent Orange class action lawsuit. Acknowledging and validating painful experiences is central to Heather's work with children of Vietnam veterans.

Validation—why is it so simple yet so hard for people to come by? Is it because we live in a world where people and agencies don't want to take responsibility for the pain that they cause each other? Is it because even helping professionals still get squeamish around certain topics, maybe because they haven't addressed their own issues? These deeply philosophical questions are likely the topic of exploration for another book. Thus, I challenge you to think about your own life. Can you remember a time when someone validating or normalizing your feelings made all the difference in the world to you and to your healing? I would venture to guess that most of us could come up with several examples. Think of how you translate some of your own experiences to your work with clients, bearing in mind that *validate* comes from the Latin root *validus*, to be strong.

Suicidality and Other Threats to Harm

Every helping professional has concerns about the suicidal or homicidal client. Sometimes this concern comes from a genuine place of caring; other times it stems from a fear of liability. From my experience, it's usually both. Of course, I would never tell a therapist I train to do (or not do) anything that makes him or her uncomfortable in conducting a standard safety assessment for risk factors. Of course, we have a

(Continued)

duty to report in cases where viable intent to harm oneself or others is expressed. However, I want to put this point out there for consideration: Suicidal ideation can be part of the daily experience for someone dealing with complex trauma. As I disclosed in *EMDR Made Simple*, I struggled with suicidal ideation from the age of 9 to age 25. At one point, during my darkest days of depression and addiction, I entertained homicidal thoughts, and truly, many survivors of trauma often think about getting revenge this way. I offer these examples to show that suicidal and homicidal thoughts can be normal, and if a client feels like you are going to ship him or her off to the hospital every time he or she has one, it will seriously inhibit the therapeutic process. Many therapists have approached survivors I know with an overly protective "You can't be too careful" demeanor, and it ends up alienating many, especially in communities where inpatient psychiatric care is substandard and uninformed about trauma. Of course, you want to assess for plan and intent. I also recommend consulting with a colleague or supervisor, and then you can make your decisions about reporting or hospital admittance.

It is wise to know what resources are available in your community. Many cities have crisis beds as part of mental health facilities that can provide watch services to those that are in crisis but may not require full hospitalization. Also, for clients with long-term struggles in terms of self-harm, suicidal ideation, or homicidal ideation, it is wise to have a plan in place for what to do when they are triggered (e.g., have a list of support people to call, keep a list of viable coping skills somewhere visible, use the therapist's on-call service or a local crisis line). Linda Curran's (2010) manual *Trauma Competency* contains some excellent templates that clinicians can use for safety planning.

VARIABLES AND CONTEXT

As author Siri Hustvedt articulated in the quote that opened this chapter, illness does not develop in a vacuum. It sounds like common sense that for professionals to assess a client, we must get to know him or her as a person, not as a presenting problem. However, in striving to make our professions medically relevant, we often miss these simple guideposts of common sense. Get to know the person, and what ails the person will reveal itself. Even what we may consider to be the PTSD-level traumas—war, rape, major accidents, natural disasters—are likely to be discussed when the person is ready, as long as getting to know the *person* is your top priority. Getting a sense of context must be another major priority in conducting trauma-informed assessment. As Engel (1961) expressed, how much impairment may result from a complicated mourning experience is a manner of degree, based on individual and situational variables. The same idea holds true for trauma. Thus, it becomes our task as assessors to learn about those individual and situational variables to help us best serve our clients.

In this section, we take a look at some of the major variables that can play into the trauma equation: culture, gender, family, sexuality, oppression, spirituality, human development, and of course, protective factors, or the positives in a person's life. As we briefly explore each domain, consider that some of these factors may be major in a person's story, and others may be subtle. For some, the trauma may have occurred in one area (e.g., family), but lessons they learned in another area (e.g., spirituality) blocked them from optimal healing. Yet, it's possible that elements from another area, specifically the protective factors, helped a person to heal. Sometimes an element like family, culture, or spirituality can serve as both a protective factor and an impediment, depending on context. Hence, it is important to get to know each person, and his or her unique variables. By appreciating the context of the trauma and its aftereffects, we are generally able to make optimal recommendations for care. It is likely that not all of these areas will be covered in the first session. As established previously, assessment is an ongoing process, so let the process unfold how it will.

Several prime variables to consider are culture, gender, and the family system, recognizing, of course, that there is usually tremendous interplay among the three. I find that the open-ended question "What were things like for you growing up?" or "What messages did you learn about yourself (e.g., from your home life, from society, from your culture) growing up?" can begin a dynamic conversation about these variables. For instance, Asian cultures are generally collectivistic—the self is not as important as the family or the community. As my colleague Kim (Lee Tze Hui), a Malaysian national, shared:

> To understand an Asian client with a suspected history of trauma, one has to be sure which key values mentioned are actually their own, and which are those that have been drilled into them from childhood. It is also not surprising to find that many Asians do not have their own values and do not know how to think for themselves. When trying to help such a client, a lot of family

objections can be expected should the family be brought into the therapy.

Still, it is important not to make assumptions. For instance, I took a multicultural studies class, and naturally I learned about collectivism in Asian, Hispanic, and African-American cultures. However, going into an assessment and assuming that a person is all about their family can be equally damaging. As Kim explained:

> With Western influence, the new generation of Asians would have more self-esteem, despite whatever trauma they have experienced, as opposed to the traditional communal concept of thought. Thus, in some cases, they can be treated almost as individualistically as a Westerner who has experienced similar trauma. As well, there are different degrees of collectivism among the different types of Asians. For instance, there's a lot of variability between Japanese and Chinese people about speaking their minds: A Japanese person is more likely to believe that he or she should keep the peace at all cost, whereas the Chinese tend to be more open about speaking their minds.

We must also be mindful of our assumptions surrounding gender. Typically, we learn that women are socialized to be emotional, caretaking creatures and that men, as a group, are socialized not to show their feelings and to "tough it out." Although this universal profile has merit in a general sense, it is still worth asking, "What messages did you learn about being a man as you developed?" or "What messages did you learn about being a woman as you developed?" The answers give valuable information about where the person stands in terms of showing emotion and asking for help.

A significant problem in our field is minimizing the impact that trauma can have on a male client. I tend to laugh when I see statistics from the addiction professions specifically, showing spiked rates of traumatic stress symptoms in women as compared with men. I've heard several explanations for these numbers over the years; namely, that women are hardwired to be more emotional so they absorb more emotion, and because men are still viewed as the dominant gender, women are more likely to be perpetrated upon or oppressed. These explanations never quite resonated with my experiences. In working with my fair share of male clients over the years, it seems that just as many men have been abused and traumatized as women, but the stigma of disclosing the abuse is much greater in men ("The Eight Agreements," text box).

THE EIGHT AGREEMENTS ABOUT MEN AND TRAUMA

Recently, there has been a major push in the addictions field to further understand the development of trauma in men and discuss the roadblocks to men getting proper treatment. At the 2013 West Coast Symposium on Addictive Disorders, a "Males, Trauma, and Addiction Summit" took place. Dan Griffin gathered 20 leaders in the addiction field to discuss traditional ineffectiveness in working with men and trauma. They composed this list of "Eight Agreements" about this issue, which serve as a valuable blueprint for all of us in the helping professions:

1. While progress has been made in the understanding of trauma, there remains a myth that trauma is not a major issue for males.
2. Trauma is a significant issue for males with substance and/or process addictive disorders.
3. Males are biologically and culturally influenced to minimize or deny traumatic life experiences.
4. Addiction treatment has been negatively influenced by cultural myths about males.
5. Males are often assumed to be the perpetrator, which has negatively biased our concepts of trauma and models for addiction treatment and often results in the retraumatization of males.
6. Male trauma must be assessed and treated throughout the continuum of addiction services.
7. Male-responsive services will improve addiction treatment outcomes.
8. Effective treatment of male trauma will help to interrupt cycles of violence, abuse, neglect, and addiction.

It is also important to ascertain what role the family system played in development, bearing in mind that each family is its own culture. One of the great jokes of our field is that therapists are in business because of families. I don't mean to come across as anti-family, yet I acknowledge a great deal of truth in this statement. The cycles of unhealed wounds in earlier generations tend to play out in current generations and will likely play out in future generations unless a new culture of healing develops and gets promoted within the family. Culture, in a most general sense, is simply a group of people's way of life.

While it is not usually necessary for a person to recount all of his or her family drama (because contrary to popular belief, conducting a good trauma assessment does not mean that the patient has to recount every single detail of his or her life story), it is necessary to figure out the themes. For instance, "In my house, children were seen and not heard," or, "In my house, I learned that boys don't cry, or else Mom would really give me something to cry about." As taught in the addiction field, the three unwritten rules of the alcoholic home, "don't talk," "don't trust," and "don't feel," are often powerful impediments to healing trauma. Other themes learned in the home, such as "Loyalty to the family at all costs," or "You don't tell anyone else what goes on here!" can also get in the way of a person seeking or accepting the help he or she needs to heal.

If you have ever treated a client who identifies as LGBTQI (the field's adopted abbreviation of lesbian, gay, bisexual, transgender, queer or questioning, and intersex), or identify as such yourself, you know that messages received in the family or society can color a person's acceptance of his or her sexuality. Asking clients about sexuality can be challenging for therapists, even with straight clients who may have internalized their own sets of maladaptive messages about sex and sexuality from their abusers, their homes of origin, their churches, or society. Yet sexuality is a powerful component of the human person that we must honor. Because the sex drive and drive to eat are our two most primal as humans, they are the two most significant gateways for us to really get to know a person. Learning about a client's personal beliefs on sex and sexuality and ascertaining their source is very important to the entire context of assessment.

There are several major issues connected to the LGBTQI community and trauma that we must consider, especially because the shame quotient can be so high in those presenting for services. According to my colleague Jeff Zacharias, the owner and director of New Hope Treatment Center, an addiction treatment program that specializes in treating the LGBTQI community of Chicago, every client in their care has some sort of trauma. This trauma can manifest in multiple layers, from dealing with homophobia, to bullying, to HIV infection and diseases, to dealing with unkindness from other gay people. Jeff, who is openly gay, admits, "Gay men can be very catty." However, the most intense layers of trauma that he tends to see with the LGBTQI population relates to dynamics surrounding family rejection and ostracism.

Interestingly, Jeff discloses that he never felt much shame around being gay as a young man. His biggest protective factor was that he moved to a big city where there was more tolerance shortly after finishing college, a condition that he experienced as a breath of fresh air. Drama therapist and performer Liz Rubino, a self-identified bisexual married to a female, shared that professionals must know that LGBTQI youth go through the same experiences that all kids do. However, they usually reach an impenetrable state of feeling that they can't get out of an oppressive environment, adding another degree of complexity to trauma. In her teenage years, Liz had the arts as a major protective factor, but life was not pleasant for her at home, which she attributes to her parents' own legacy of unresolved trauma. Liz believes that the most important things a parent can do for their children is to always impart the message that it's okay to be who you are; this is the safeguard against causing further traumatic damage. Yet, think of how many children, gay or straight, do not get this in their homes.

Sadly, the oppression of various peoples is a constant throughout the annals of human history. The world today is full of populations that could politically be labeled *minority*, but I tend to prefer the term *oppressed*. An oppressed person, by definition, is cut off from reaching the fullness of his or her potential and wellness as a human being due to sociopolitical factors that are out of his or her control. We talk a great deal at conferences about the role that historical trauma can play in shaping the collective, as well as the individual. For instance, when we think of groups that have historically suffered generations of oppression: the Irish, Jews, African-Americans, and Native Americans, just to name a few, we must stop and consider how unresolved trauma of previous generations has manifested a state of being "stuck," either culturally or organically. The field of epigenetics, or changes in genetic structure over time due to factors like stress, continues to study the biological impact of historical trauma. If cell biologists are interested in this phenomenon, we as helpers should be too.

Through the mustering of protective factors and other resources of resilience, some people have found ways to more fully cope with their societally ascribed status in life and ultimately not see themselves as oppressed. For instance, as a woman, I have never personally identified as oppressed, but I know many of my female peers who do. Other people are faced with the challenge of being multiple minorities and having to negotiate the layers of trauma that that can bring. In the spirit of "make no assumptions," we cannot jump to the conclusion that a client is traumatized just because let's say, she's an overweight African-American lesbian in poverty. The key in assessing for the impact is to examine what messages the person has received as a result of the oppression (e.g., racial, ethnic, gender, poverty). For instance, if a person got the message from some source that "I'm less than because I'm a woman," "I'm less than because I'm black," or "Society sets me up to fail—there's no way I can dig myself out," then we will need to address these issues within the trauma spectrum.

Messages of being less than or not good enough can come from many spiritual systems, whether they be churches, mosques, synagogues, other spiritual communities, yoga schools, cults, or even devout homes. Spiritual abuse, defined as the use of God or religion as a tool to gain power and control by the abuser, is a form of abuse that we usually ascribe to cults or damaging forms of ritualistic practices. I do not want to impugn the trauma that goes on in these systems; however, we must also recognize that spiritual abuse occurs in the "mainstream," in places of worship, spiritual groups, and homes around the world. Any time a person is made to feel like he or she does not matter or is not good enough in the eyes of God, spirit, or the universe and internalizes that message as shaming, we must consider whether the origin of those messages qualifies as a traumatic experience for the person (Marich, in press).

It is very important during the assessment process to figure out where a client is coming from spiritually. Some secular counselors get nervous because they are uncomfortable with spirituality or they don't want their clients to think that they are shoving God down their throats. However, it is imperative that we assess for the spirituality variable as a quality of care issue. It may be a source of trauma for some people; it may be a source of great comfort, a protective factor, for others. For some clients, both dynamics may be playing out, adding to the complexity of context. As clinicians, we must bear in mind that appreciating this complexity will better help us to serve our clients.

Development is another contextual component of assessment. If you've had graduate training, you've probably had at least one course in the basics of human growth and development, and much of this elementary knowledge can be helpful in conducting a comprehensive trauma assessment. For example, consider a trauma like a car accident. If an entire family is in the car accident, it is likely that each person will be affected differently, and not just because of where each was seated in the car. In addition to some of these other factors we've discussed in this section, development could play a factor. For instance, my grandmother was in a major car accident at the age of 49, and she had to learn to walk all over again in rehab. Think of what a jolt that would be to an adult! I recently engaged my grandmother, who is now 91, in a conversation about the accident, and she still has a visceral reaction to talking about the experience. I know what you may be thinking—a child who is injured can have his or her own set of issues, too, and you're right: He or she may, depending on where he or she is in the developmental process. In conceptualizing a case, you can ask yourself, "What did it mean for *this* person to experience *this* trauma at *this* point in his or her life?" In thinking of my own life, what affected me at 9 affected me differently at 20, and at this point in my life, a similar experience probably would not have much of an impact. But if it happened at 65, who knows?

Issues of child development come up a lot in the discussion of trauma and attachment injuries. Think about it: It's easier for a child to learn a foreign language or to learn how to play an instrument because the learning brain, the limbic brain, is like a sponge at a young age. Although we don't stop learning new information as we age, the process certainly changes. Speaking personally, it was much easier to learn complex things like playing a violin and figure skating when I was 3 or 5 than if I would start now! Just like the brain is a sponge for the good in these early periods, so too can it be a sponge for negative, distressful learning about the self and the world. Yet, counterbalancing that to a degree is the quality of resilience and fearlessness that may be more abundant in children than in adults. Don't get me wrong—it drives me crazy when I hear people write off the impact of trauma in children by saying, "Don't worry, kids are resilient!" Yet think about it—if conditions are right for healing, it's generally easier for a child to heal from a fall than it is an adult. There are too many possible scenarios and metaphors that I can present; my point is to take all of these factors into consideration.

Preverbal and gestational trauma must also be on our radar at various stages of the assessment process. A person may not even be aware of trauma that occurred before he or she learned how to talk, so if possible, some fact-finding from collaborative sources may need to be employed. If you are dealing with a person with clear trauma-related symptoms, but even after some work, he or she is not able to trace the origin of certain symptoms, there's a good chance that the disturbance happened preverbally or in utero. I once treated a very intelligent woman who came to me for EMDR. She had a pretty good idea about the source of her trauma—issues with her father—and how these issues connected to her struggles with relationships. She did a very good job with processing early traumas connected to her father, but something still felt stuck. I asked her if she knew anything about the circumstances of her birth or conception, and then it clicked for her. She was an unplanned pregnancy; her parents didn't want her! She deduced, "Knowing my parents like I do, they argued about me every day I was in the womb. I had to pick up on that!" Of course, such memories cannot be processed with talking and often need a more somatic intervention, so we continued to address it with EMDR. I also referred her to a bodyworker to help with the material still trapped in the body.

There are so many other variables we can consider. Do not discount any possibility. Physical health and constitution are two other variables that we may associate with trauma. If not addressed, they can be an impediment to healing. We also discuss factors like personality, demeanor, and temperament and whether those come from nature, nurture, or a combination of the two. My general approach is that where they came from is not necessarily as important as whether they are helping or hindering the process.

My husband, David, recently got me thinking about this whole idea of temperament and demeanor. David is truly the cat with nine lives. One time we did a calculation of all of the times he should have died, starting with being thrown from the back of a car at age 3, up until a recent automobile accident, and I believe we tallied 17. When David was 21, he was in a major trucking accident that permanently injured his spine. He continued to work for another four years, but the pressure of millwork and desk jobs on top of the original injury sent him into a series of seven back surgeries over a 10-year period. Of course I'm the nagging wife who wishes that he would start practicing yoga and stop smoking to better take care of himself, but all in all, I am amazed at how well David does in life considering his physical limitations. He shared with me how one of his family members endured similar problems with disability, but she became very bitter and angry and pushed everyone away. David is the poster child for having a good sense of humor in spite of it all, and I asked him one day, "So how come she became bitter and you didn't? What were the factors?" David said, "It's just not in my nature to take things out on people." Of course, I wanted to know if that "nature" was the result of resiliency or how his dad raised him or anything else. He laughed and said, "I don't know, it just is."

In assessing a person, we don't necessarily have to overanalyze those factors like resilience, personality, motivation, and nature. Rather, if they are positives that serve a person's healing and recovery, we see them as part of the context and hopefully use them in the healing process. As part of every initial assessment that I conduct, I ask, "So what are the good things? What have you done that you're proud of? What are the skills or things you have that work for you?" Naturally, it's easier for some people than others to list things, but taking a strengths-based approach is vital in clinical trauma work. Even if a person can't list the things that are good about himself or herself yet, having an external motivation or friends, family members, hobbies, or interests as a source of positive attachment can be the life raft the person needs until he or she comes to shore. For instance, my friend and social networking buddy Susan Moffitt, a visible figure in the addiction treatment field, shared that her motivation for getting to treatment was her dog, Jake. She had rescued Jake half dead off of the street, and he was her motivation for health. She clearly identifies that Jake saved her life. Susan reveals, "Today when I get a recovery chip at a meeting, I get one for me and one for Jake."

Ask about animals. Ask about hobbies and interests. You might be surprised at what emerges as useful. Getting to know the person is such a vital part of being trauma sensitive; it's so much more important than dissecting the problem every which way. If possible, get to know some of the positive beliefs and themes about the client's life that he or she may still posses. In the back of this book, there is an appendix called "The 'Greatest Hits' List of Positive Beliefs." Feel free to use this as an inventory checklist during your assessment process.

QUALITATIVE ASSESSMENT STRATEGIES

In my practice, I've consistently found that asking a person to identify the beliefs about self he or she has picked up along the way is the most powerful gateway through which to assess for trauma. As mentioned, having a patient rehash the whole trauma narrative is generally counterproductive and can potentially cause more harm than good (Naparstek, 2004). Rather, have the client identify two or three significantly negative, driving beliefs about the self that seem to be causing the problems. Tracing the origins of these beliefs will likely give you most, if not all, of the information that you need to begin working with that person in a trauma-sensitive manner.

Some people come into professional services with a clear sense of their blocking negative beliefs: "I'm not good enough," "I'm to blame," or "The world is out to get me" are some of the popular ones. People may have a sense of some but may not recognize others. For instance, many clients I've seen over the years can clearly identify the big ones, like "I'm not good enough" or "I'm not worthy," but until exploration, they may not recognize other negative beliefs like, "I'm not going to amount to anything anyway, so why bother trying to get help?"

For years, I've made use of "The 'Greatest Hits' List of Problematic Beliefs" tool, available in this book's appendix. I've assembled this list based on my EMDR and cognitive behavioral therapy (CBT) work, and it comprises about 30 of the most common negative beliefs that people have about themselves. Although the variations for using such a list are numerous, I generally apply it as a qualitative assessment tool in the following way:

- Give the client the list.

- Advise the client to read through the negative list and to check off any belief that he or she considers a problem belief. Assure the client that there are no wrong answers: One item, 10 items, or all items may be checked.

- If more than one item is checked, ask the client to rank the two or three most problematic beliefs. Go through each of the top items and ask the client:

  ○ "When's the *first* time you ever remember getting that message about yourself?"

  ○ "When's the *worst* time you ever remember getting that message about yourself?"

  ○ "When's the *most recent* time that you received that message about yourself?"

- If a client indicates that there is a grief or loss issue in his or her initial clinical presentation, you can explore:

  ○ "What role did your loss play in giving you this message?"

  ○ "Does this message predate the loss in any way?"

I generally find that using this list and asking these questions give me the information I need about any traumas, whether they are PTSD level or small "t," and the contexts surrounding them. You can use clients' answers to open up more dialogue if appropriate. Moreover, it is up to your discretion when to use this strategy. Sometimes, I determine that the client is sufficiently stable and we have enough rapport built within an initial session, so I may do this exercise at that time. Other times, I wait until the second to fourth session to make sure the client has obtained at least some basic affect regulation skills in our work to be able to handle the intensity that doing such an exercise might elicit.

Using such an assessment strategy will help you identify the key themes, and in discovering the themes, you can more fully appreciate the context. Let this type of strategy simply be a guide for your human communication with the patient, and just notice what's revealed. The information obtained here can help you devise the best possible treatment plan, help you select strategies and approaches, and when the time comes for deeper work, help you identify the key issues for processing. The art of treatment planning and goal setting is discussed further in Chapter 8.

It bears mentioning here that as part of a trauma-informed assessment, we must learn about the client's sense of future orientation. One of the worst assumptions that we can make as professionals is that every client wants a better future. First, the patient may not be coming into treatment for himself or herself. It may be because a friend, a family member, the legal system, or an employer wants the client to come. External motivation does not necessarily mean that treatment won't work; it just means we have to take that variable into consideration in the treatment planning. Secondly, and perhaps most significantly, trauma can leave a person with a disintegrated sense of a future. This idea makes complete sense if you think about some of the messages people receive as the result of their trauma; for instance, "I'm never gonna amount to anything anyway," "I'm never getting out of here" (e.g., a war-torn country, an inner-city ghetto, a toxic work environment, an abusive family), "I'm damaged goods/I can't be fixed," or "I could die any day, so why bother?" If a person is operating with these beliefs, they will likely need to be addressed before that client can even consider future goals. Minimal or no future orientation does not mean that treatment won't work, but it does mean that these beliefs will need to be addressed as part of the treatment before a person can conceptualize future planning.

The addition of "negative beliefs about oneself, others, or the world" as a sub-criterion of the PTSD diagnosis in *DSM-5®* is one of the best updates to the manual. I smiled when I first saw it, because I've assessed using negative beliefs for years. Moreover, if you come from a traditional, CBT orientation, assessing for the impacts of trauma through a client's negative cognitions uses a concept that you already know, the negative schema. Trauma-informed assessment goes a step further by determining the origins of these negative beliefs.

Another viable way to assess for the impacts of trauma is through the body. A guiding principle of my work is that your body will tell you what's going on 10 steps before your head will. As was established in Chapter 4, unresolved traumatic memories are stuck in the parts of the brain most likely to play out in the theater of the body. Hence, simple questions such as, "As you're talking about this experience, what's going on in your body right now?" or "Of everything that you've tried in your quest to survive, what helps you to feel safe in your body?" can give you valuable information to guide treatment.

Certain body discomforts or distresses usually have powerful meanings. Having a basic understanding of these simple connections can also be a powerful gateway for learning about the client and his or her patterns. Some of the biggest connections to look for, based on teachings from energy and somatic medicine, include:

- Problems with grounding or sitting still: issues involving sexuality, stability, sensuality, security; possible subtle cue for dissociative issues

- Problems with hip pain or pain in the reproductive organs: issues involving reproduction, blocked creativity, diminished joy, diminished enthusiasm

- Problems with gastrointestinal issues or stomach pain/discomfort: issues involving personal power, value, and self-esteem, digestion (a metaphor for blocked mental processing), power, and personal growth

- Problems with pain or discomfort in the chest: issues involving love and compassion (blocks in giving and/or receiving), circulation issues, diminished passion/zest for life

- Problems in the shoulders, throat (tension, blockages) or jaw: issues involving expression, communication, independence, and security; often a direct manifestation of not being able to speak one's voice or truth

- Problems with head tension, headaches, migraines: issues involving doubting intuition or inner-knowing, clarity; possible spiritual blockages

Identification of pain or tension in these domains is not meant to imply medical diagnosis, and of course, we must remain within our scopes of practice by not diagnosing physical disease. However, if physical disease is disclosed and areas of distress are reported in the body, we can use these as a channel for further conversation about the possible emotional connections.

One of the most powerful measures of progress in treatment and healing is the quality of shifts within the bodily expressions. For instance, a person may come into treatment with severe stomach cramps or even simple fluttering in the stomach at the mention of home of origin. If that response no longer happens or happens with diminished intensity after a session or after a course of treatment, that is a powerful sign that something in the lower brain has positively shifted into the cerebral cortex.

In my delivery of therapy, I see reports about shifts in somatic symptoms to be the truest measures of change and growth in healing. Of course, you have the option of asking a patient to put a Subjective Units of Distress Scale

(SUDS) rating on the sensation, whether you are asking about the body in an initial assessment or later in treatment to evaluate change. Thus, if the person's subjectively rated stomach distress lowers from a 10 to a 6 in the course of a session, that is a sign of movement. Such a strategy, if appropriate, is a way to put both a qualitative and a quantitative element on an assessment.

QUANTITATIVE ASSESSMENT STRATEGIES

I prefer to see the world through a qualitative lens, so I am more likely to use the assessment strategies highlighted in the previous section. However, I recognize that many of you are quantitative thinkers and like to have numbers in place to help you make diagnostic and treatment decisions. Some of you may be required to use these types of strategies in your agencies or settings, especially as a way of tracking outcomes or pre-post treatment measures. This section describes some available methods for assessing traumatic stress and its concerns through the quantitative lens.

The Primary Care PTSD (PC-PTSD; text box) screen is one of the most popular tools available. As a semi-standardized interview instrument, it has quantitative and qualitative components. This tool may seem overly simplistic for those of you who already assess for trauma and its impacts. However, I think that it is an excellent place to start for those who are not used to asking questions about trauma. You can use it as a way to guide your questioning, and if you get a "yes" response to any of the items, you can follow up by asking the client to explain. This is what makes a tool semi-standardized. At the time of this writing, the PC-PTSD is being updated for *DSM-5*®, and you can visit the National Center for PTSD's website (http://www.ptsd.va.gov/) to keep abreast of these updates. (See Further Reading at the end of this chapter.)

Another popular assessment tool is The PTSD Checklist, also under revision for *DSM-5*® at the time of this writing. Both military and civilian versions of this tool are available. The PTSD Checklist gives a Likert scale score (1–5) to the *DSM* symptoms to rate symptom intensity, and a guide is provided at the bottom of the checklist to interpret the scores. A copy of the checklist can be accessed on the National Center for PTSD's website. Moreover, the National Center for PTSD catalogues more than 60 screens and assessments for various populations and specific trauma situations. If you are looking for a good "one-stop site" to see all that's available, I highly recommend visiting this website. (See Further Reading at the end of this chapter.) Although not all of these tools are available on the website, most can be obtained through an Internet search.

THE PRIMARY CARE PTSD SCREEN (PC-PTSD)

In your life, have you ever had any experience that was so frightening, horrible, or upsetting, that in the past month you:

1.) Have had nightmares about it or thought about it when you didn't want to?

YES   NO

2.) Tried hard not to think about it or went out of your way to avoid situations that remind you of it?

YES   NO

3.) Were constantly on guard, watchful, or easily startled?

YES   NO

4.) Felt numb or detached from others, activities, or your surroundings?

YES   NO

Current research suggests that the results of the PC-PTSD should be considered positive if a patient answers "yes" to any three of the items.

Prins, A., Ouimette, P., Kimerling, R., Cameron, R. P., Hugelshofer, D. S., Shaw-Hegwer, J., Thrailkill, A., Gusman, F. D., Sheikh, J. I. (2003). The primary care PTSD screen (PC–PTSD): Development and operating characteristics. *Primary Care Psychiatry, 9*, 9–14.

Many people like to use the simple questionnaire taken from the ACE study (discussed earlier in this chapter) to assess for childhood trauma. My only caution about using this tool as an assessment is that the questions are pretty closed ended; for example, "Did a parent or other adult in the household often or very often . . . push, grab, slap, or throw something at you? ever hit you so hard that you had marks or were injured?" Moreover, a person may feel overwhelmed answering these questions in an early meeting. It may be productive to use the ACE test a few sessions in, after rapport has been established, if the whole clinical picture is still unclear. You can get the ACE test and related resources measures, in addition to interpretations of the ACE data, online. (See Further Reading at the end of this chapter.)

You may also find the Dissociative Experiences Scale (DES), which can be found online through an Internet search, useful. Many training programs in trauma-specific therapies, such as EMDR, recommend that the DES be administered before any trauma counseling so that potential dissociation triggers can be identified and planned for accordingly. The DES (Bernstein & Putnam, 1986) is a 28-item screening inventory that asks questions such as, "Some people have the experience of looking in a mirror and not recognizing themselves. Select a number to show what percentage of the time this happens to you (0–100%)." Interpretations of DES data and cut-offs vary in different studies. However, a mean DES score of 45% is generally considered to be positive for a dissociative disorder. A client interview must be used to confirm the diagnosis, as the DES is considered a screening device, not an assessment tool. A DES ought to be treated as a semi-standardized interview instrument. If a patient indicates a score higher than 40% on any items endorsed, he or she ought to be more thoroughly interviewed to determine the impact of dissociative experiences. When I give the DES, I find that asking further about these items yields some pretty fascinating conversations that help me better get to know the client and his or her defensive responses, both adaptive and maladaptive.

Is That a Trauma?

There is a running joke among my team members at Mindful Ohio, my practice and training organization. At random times, either in the office or at trainings, one of them will ask me, "Jamie, is (insert such-and-such) a trauma?" This joke comes from the guarantee that at every training that I give publically, a trainee will come up to me over a break and ask me if something on his or her mind qualifies as a trauma.

"Jamie, what about losing a job? Is that a trauma?"

"What if you are working with a mean boss who's out to get you—is that a trauma?"

"What if you can't find work, or you're forced to do something you don't want to do to make ends meet—can we consider that a trauma?"

"What about going to prison? Going to jail? Are those traumas?"

"What if a parent went to prison?"

"What if you were cyberbullied?"

"What if you lost your family home to bankruptcy?"

"What if you were diagnosed with something like cancer?"

"What if someone you love is diagnosed with cancer?"

"What about things like long-term disability?"

"What about growing up with a disabled parent?"

"A mentally ill parent?"

"What if you had an abortion?"

"What if your partner had an abortion and didn't tell you about it?"

"What if you lived a very privileged life and then suddenly lost it all?"

"What about happy things, like having a baby. Can childbirth be considered traumatic? What about adjusting to having a child? Going back to work after having a child?"

In short, yes, all of these examples could be considered traumatic. Some may be traumatic in a general sense (e.g., as a wound that needs healing through validation, care, time, and support), whereas others may require clinical attention. It all depends on the context. Often, the value that a person places on what is lost determines whether something is traumatic. This is why major league executives have been known to commit suicide after losing everything (recall the 1929 stock market crash). Yet for millennia, history has shown us scores of people living in poverty who consider themselves fortunate because they feel enriched by values like family, community, and spirituality. Singing of her own childhood poverty and the blessings she managed to find within it, Dolly Parton declared, "One is only poor, only if they choose to be." In assessments, we get the information we need to best serve the client by trying to enter into his or her world and evaluate life from that person's perspective.

A guiding principle of my clinical life is that if a situation is traumatic to a person, then it's traumatic. I have been in situations with people whose issues may not seem traumatic to me, but that doesn't matter. My job is to validate and to educate. So many people coming into treatment don't even believe that they've been traumatized because they "haven't had it that bad." These are messages given to them by their abusers or in their family of origin. It may be helpful later in treatment to help the client put his or her trauma into a different perspective. However, assessment is not a time for pushing clients into seeing the silver lining.

Another way to look at this principle is that if it's true to the client, it is true. This idea is not without controversy, since much press has been generated around "false memories" coming up in treatment. Of course, I think it is completely unethical for a helper to push clients into places they're not ready to go, let alone plant ideas or memories that may not be there, but that is an entirely different issue. Often, clients may share memories with me that may not be literally "true," but they certainly are emotionally real, and I generally find it's best to validate what is real for the client. So many clients I've worked with over the years have been incredibly damaged by therapists who don't seem to believe them. Err on the side of believing and validating, especially at first. The truth will sort itself out.

In closing this chapter, I offer one more teaching tip on the importance of ending a session. One of the greatest errors I see in trauma treatment, be it in initial assessments, individual sessions, or groups, is saying "time's up," even if there's just been a big, tearful disclosure. Watch your clock, especially in a first session. Allow at least 10 minutes to close down, to come back to more general banter, teach a quick coping skill, or talk about positives. Although there's nothing wrong with leaving a client with something to think about, it's important not to leave a client viscerally activated. This may require that you allow the patient to sit in an empty office for a while, or encourage him or her to take a walk outside or get some air before leaving. Many of the simple coping strategies covered in Chapter 9, especially Clench and Release, are excellent, quick skills to teach at the end of a first assessment session. Another tip: If you set the tone of closure in your initial assessment, you set an effective message that the last 10 minutes of a session will be used to close down and come back to safety. The earlier you set the boundary, the better you'll be at avoiding problems that come up with clients who want to tell you everything in the last 10 minutes.

Also, think about what a patient may need to feel positively about returning for services. If he or she is in an inpatient setting or is incarcerated, what would he or she need to feel positively about really engaging in services? Sometimes it's a clear message from the therapist that hope is possible; other times it's something that the client needs to sense, a general feeling of acceptance and nonjudgment. Many clients want something concrete to work on right away, even if it's something simple like teaching Clench and Release (see Chapter 9) or asking the patient to experiment with journaling or making small changes in daily routine.

When I was in graduate school, one of my many part-time jobs was as a clinical actor at the local medical school. I had to learn a case and then act as the patient to help medical students and residents to hone their diagnostic skills. One afternoon, I acted as a young married woman showing all of the signs of Type II diabetes to eight different residents. The first seven residents interviewed me coldly and then left the room to talk to their supervisor. The eighth made an impression. He said, "Even if this ends up not being diabetes, I think getting you on a diabetic diet wouldn't hurt anything for starters. I'll have my nurse give you the information on that." I shared with the medical supervisor that this was something so simple, yet it allowed me, even as my character, to feel empowered right away. Thank you, dear medical resident, whoever you were, for teaching me that powerful lesson.

FURTHER READING

Centers for Disease Control and Prevention (2013). *Adverse childhood experiences (ACE) study.* Retrieved from http://www.cdc.gov/ace.

Curran, L. (2010). *Trauma competency: A clinician's guide.* Eau Claire, WI: PESI, LLC.

Dissociative Experiences Scale (DES) (n.d.). Retrieved from http://serene.me.uk/tests/des.pdf.

Hammerschlag, C.A. (1988). *The dancing healers: A doctor's journey of healing with Native Americans.* New York: HarperCollins.

Health Presentations (n.d.). *The adverse childhood experiences study.* Available at http://acestudy.org/home.

National Center for PTSD (2013). *DSM-5® validated measures.* In Professional Section. Updated 17 May 2013, Retrieved from http://www.ptsd.va.gov/professional/pages/assessments/DSM_5_Validated_Measures.asp.

National Center for PTSD (2013). List of all measures. In Professional Section. Created 14 July 2010, Retrieved from http://www.ptsd.va.gov/professional/pages/assessments/all_measures.asp.

CHAPTER 6

The Addiction Imperative

We're all addicts in a sense. We're all attached, if not addicted, to our possessions, careers, relationships, identities—to name a few. Everyone suffers from what Buddhists call the Three Poisons: attachment, aversion, and ignorance.

—Darren Littlejohn, from *The Power of Vow*

When my colleague Colleen McKernan took her EMDR basic training not too long ago, the trainer asked the hotel conference room, packed with people, how many work with addictions. Colleen was one of only two people to raise her hand. At the break, people came up to her and asked, "How can you work with *those* people?" Colleen, a dual addiction and trauma specialist who runs an innovative treatment center in Denver, Colorado, called Recovering Spirit, was floored, and wondered, "How can people who want to work with trauma think like that?"

In my years of mingling with trauma specialists in the EMDR community and in similar mental health systems, I have found myself just as miffed. The aversion to working with clients who identify as addicts is a major problem in our field, and it is no longer one that we can ignore. I've encountered the bias in many arenas, not just among colleagues who make the notorious "those addicts" comments. Even certain clients who book me to offer trainings on trauma suggest that I downplay the addiction component, or they have little interest in my "trauma and addiction" combined trainings. As one business figure said, "Addiction just doesn't sell amongst our target audience, but trauma is really hot."

His statement encapsulates the problem. Since the dawn of modern psychotherapy, a division has existed between mental health counseling and addiction counseling. Even Dr. Carl Jung, one of the fathers of our field, admitted defeat in treating the most hopeless of alcoholic cases with his methods and credited the spiritual experiences found in programs like Alcoholics Anonymous with helping such patients. AA was founded in 1935, and the social awareness raised by the success of this program in treating cases that psychiatry couldn't even touch ushered in addiction counseling as a separate field. Addiction counseling as a field was born in the 1950s with the advent of professional treatment centers. Although there have been some efforts at cooperative dialogue between the addiction field and mental health/psychiatry over the years, a great divide still exists. In this chapter, I argue that the divide is an impediment to quality client care, especially if we are serious about being trauma sensitive. Solutions for integrating our thinking and our approaches are also discussed.

THE GREAT DIVIDE

I learn a great deal from my husband David about how ordinary people think. By "ordinary," I mean people without formal training in this field who see the world with a common sense lost to many of us because of our education. David, a self-identified "simple redneck," grew up in a working class home, raised by his father in a tight-knit Pennsylvania community. He had little or no exposure to "my world" of recovery, professional counseling, yoga, or wellness, although he and those close to him were schooled in their share of hard knocks. When we got together, he asked why I had two professional designations after my name, one for mental health counseling and one for addiction counseling. I explained the divide to him.

"That doesn't even make sense!" he declared, "Isn't it all interrelated?"

If an *everyman* gets this, why can't professionals in our field? More specifically, why are people who want to work with trauma aversive to addiction, when, any way you slice the data, the comorbidity is so high? Comorbidity statistics on the trauma-addiction link are imprecise because operational definitions are imprecise. Consider that *addiction* is not a *DSM* term: It is more of a cultural construct that the medical community adopted decades ago. *Addiction* comes from the Latin *addicere*, meaning to be fixated on or favor something. The parallel to addiction in *DSM-IV-TR* is the diagnosis of Substance Dependence, a distinction no longer used in *DSM-5®* (text box). The most cited statistic in the literature on the comorbidity is now almost 20 years old: Through a national survey, Kessler and colleauges (1995) determined that approximately 34.5% of people with a PTSD diagnosis meet criteria for substance dependence, and an additional 28% meet criteria for substance abuse. Thus, if you are in a mental health setting diagnosing PTSD, you must be screening for substance use disorders and other addictions.

Other studies and surveys show equally high numbers, but it's safe to assume that they represent an underestimate. Generally, in the addiction field, what the statistics say are usually lower than what I've encountered in my clinical work. There's a great deal of underreporting in surveys due to fear or stigma. Moreover, there are inconsistencies in what treatment centers report, especially with mental health statistics, generally because they don't know what they're looking for.

If you use common sense, it's clear to see why there is such a high connection between unresolved traumatic stress and addictive or other pleasurable behaviors. As established in Chapter 4, the places of the brain where unprocessed traumatic memories are stored play out in the body. Because unresolved trauma kicks up body-level distress, it's only natural that a person would seek out ways to make the body feel better. Drinking, drug use, overeating, sexual compulsivity, gambling, and shopping, just to name a few, cause a profound dopamine release in the brain; in short, they can make a person feel better. However, all of these behaviors can be highly addictive and usher in their own set of problems.

DSM-5®: SUBSTANCE USE AND ADDICTIVE DISORDERS

A major update for *DSM-5®* is the elimination of the *abuse* and *dependence* distinction. In *DSM-IV-TR*, the abuse diagnosis was generally reserved for individuals whose substance use began reaching levels of clinical impairment; for instance, individuals getting a first driving under the influence charge or people starting to use substances in dangerous situations. The former diagnosis of dependence, parallel to the construct of addiction, required that three of seven possible criteria be met in a 12-month period, symptoms such as tolerance, withdrawal, use despite consequences, and inability to cut back or control. In *DSM-5®* (American Psychiatric Association, 2013), a singular diagnosis is used, Substance Use Disorder. There are 11 possible symptoms—basically the old dependence and abuse criteria combined, with the addition of craving. The diagnosis is rendered on a continuum. If no symptoms or only one criterion is met, there is no diagnosis. If 2-3 criteria are met, a *mild substance use disorder* is the diagnostic label; 4-5 criteria suggests a *moderate substance use disorder* diagnosis, and 6 or more criteria qualifies as *severe substance use disorder*.

Another major issue contributing to the divide, especially among trauma specialists, is the debate over whether addiction is a primary disease in and of itself or the symptom of a larger issue, like a traumatic experience. There are people like me who believe that both can be true. Let's examine this debate by exploring a little bit of history. Prior to the era of Alcoholics Anonymous, the predominant explanation for alcoholism and drug addiction was the moral model, which espoused that alcoholics lacked willpower and moral fiber, and that the solution was to toughen up and repent. The early physicians closest to Alcoholics Anonymous, such as William Silkworth, MD, were rebels in their day, contending that alcoholism was not the result of any moral failing. Rather, it was a disease in and of itself, better explained by a physical allergy.

Since 1952, the American Medical Association has classified addiction as a disease. The traditional conceptualization of a disease in the addiction field is that it's primary: It is not the result of any other emotional problem, although mental health problems and the disease of alcoholism and addiction can exist comorbidly. A main reason for this belief is that the best of the best in the psychiatric professions, even the likes of Freud and Jung, had long washed their hands of alcoholics and so-called *opiate inebriates* because conventional psychiatric methods were rarely effective. Other well-known addiction psychiatrists and professionals in the disease era, such as Dr. David Ohlms, have shared that when they first entered their profession, they sought out to treat the so-called "root cause" of addiction. As Ohlms recounted in one of his training videos, he treated one alcoholic with serious trauma for about five years with rigorous psychoanalysis, aimed to help him resolve those root causes. After much success in psychotherapy, the man ended up dying after relapsing and getting attacked in bar. At that point, it struck Ohlms that in rigorously exploring all of those root causes, he was giving the man more excuses for self-pity, when the time would have been better spent helping him to take responsibility for his disease and accept it, and working from there.

Those of us who identify as *recovering* addicts as opposed to *cured* addicts certainly see Ohlms' point. Speaking for myself personally, doing trauma work was only productive for me when I committed to not using what I found as an excuse for my addiction problems. I needed to commit to sobriety first before exploring the deeper issues. Now, there are scores of people who claim that by discovering why they drink and addressing it, they are able to get well. In my professional experience, I have not seen many successful cases of getting "cured" in the quest for discovering the *why*.

So, are people born with some addiction gene, or do they develop addiction problems as the result of trauma? Is addiction even a disease at all, or is that notion antiquated considering all that we've learned about trauma? Addictionologist Kevin McCauley (2009), himself a recovering addict and initially a skeptic of the *disease model* of addiction, offers a simple medical explanation to justify the disease model as still relevant. Consider this simple flow chart:

ORGAN → DEFECT (resulting from a cause or causes) → SIGNS &
                                                    SYMPTOMS

So let's look at a simple medical example:

PANCREAS → NO INSULIN → LOW BLOOD SUGAR, SORES,
                        FOOT & EYE PROBLEMS

Of course, this flow points to the disease of diabetes. As of the late 19th century, the medical community at large became savvy to the idea that it's not enough to treat the symptoms: You have to address the defects.

According to McCauley, here is how addiction, as a disease, fits into the flow:

LIMBIC BRAIN → DEFECT IN THE   → BIOPSYCHOSOCIAL
               BRAIN'S ABILITY   CONSEQUENCES
               TO PERCEIVE &   (E.G., LEGAL PROBLEMS,
               PROCESS   JOB PROBLEMS,HEALTH
               PLEASURABLE   PROBLEMS, FAMILY
               & PAINFUL   PROBLEMS,LOSS OF
               EXPERIENCES   MEANING/VALUES)

McCauley does a stellar job of encapsulating the defect in the brain of a person who's crossed the threshold into addiction. However, what caused this defect? And once again, we come back to the debate.

It's important to bear in mind that even some of the most common, purely medical diseases can have multiple causes. For instance, some people develop heart disease because of poor lifestyle choices in diet and exercise. Then there are people like my paternal grandfather who did everything right—lived on a diet of cottage cheese and wheat germ and worked out daily. He died at 67 while working out at his health club. The healthiest of all my grandparents was the first to go simply due to bad genetics. Even with diabetes, we have the distinctions of Type I and Type II: In one type, people are born with it; in the other, it is acquired over time due to lifestyle choices.

A similar phenomenon can occur with the disease of addiction. Some people are born with the genetic vulnerability to develop it, and if other variables fall into place, they will likely develop it. Of course, not everyone with the vulnerability develops it, just like not everyone who develops the disease of addiction has the vulnerability. The latter are more of a "Type II" phenomenon: Anyone can become addicted if they overwork the capacities of the limbic brain long enough and hard enough. This phenomenon often happens as the result of traumatic injury. Thus, it's not as simple as some people in the addiction field make it, that "Addicts are addicts, period." I do believe there is a place for us to examine how the disease develops so that we can more effectively treat it.

And here is where another layer of the debate ensues. I'm sure there are even some of you reading this book who like what you've read up until now but think I'm crazy for having all of this trauma knowledge and still accepting traditional concepts like the disease model of addiction. So many trauma and mental health professionals I work with think that the disease model is outdated. They prefer instead to see addictive responses as a symptom of unresolved trauma, largely using ACE data and other findings from neuroscience to support their positions. Several colleagues I respect have tried pleading with me: "But Jamie, I treated this woman with a long history of trauma with EMDR, and once the trauma cleared, her desire to drink went away." Although I've seen this happen, my experience suggests that treating *only* the trauma without addressing the damage the addiction has already done does more harm than good. With many cases of miraculous healing that I've read, and even seen clinically, there's been at least some foundational work in exploring the addiction and the problems it has caused.

Nikki Meyers, founder of Y12SR®, explains that addressing addiction and trauma issues concurrently is imperative. Nikki was clean and sober for 8 years, and like many people in recovery, she went back to school, got an advanced degree, and became very successful in her career field. As a result, her commitment to recovery slacked. Then, while on an overseas trip, Nikki ended up relapsing, causing her a great deal of devastation and consequence. When she came back to the States, she returned to her chosen 12-Step recovery fellowship and managed to get clean again. Shortly thereafter, she reconnected with yoga, a practice she had learned before her first exposure to recovery. She jumped into yoga with both feet, convinced that it was all she needed to help her with her overall wellness because it helped her work on the total self. However, after four years, Nikki relapsed once again. At that time, she made the connection, "I need both. I need yoga and a 12-Step program to address the whole package."

As a woman who identifies as a recovering instead of a recovered or cured addict, Nikki Meyers' experience resonates with me completely. The whole debate over whether the best alcoholics and addicts can hope for is to be in *remission* or whether they can be cured of their affliction plays out in the theaters of clinical treatment. For me, my identification as *recovering* parallels the concept of a cancer survivor referring to herself as *in remission*. This identification means that as long as I take care of myself and keep a watch over potential symptoms, I can stay well. This concept works beautifully for me, Nikki, and scores of others I've met in recovery.

I've also met other people who can get quite hostile when I call myself recovering, insisting that I am selling myself short by not seeking to be cured. My general view is that people have the right to pursue the path they feel will work best for them. However, because I have seen so many people get tripped up on finding the "cure" or going after the root cause of an addiction, I believe I am not the best professional to help those who are on that path. I am still a traditionalist and believe that many of the principles of 12-Step recovery, such as personal spirituality and interpersonal connection with others who have been through similar experiences, are vital to long-term wellness.

I addressed many of these issues on integrating traditional recovery approaches with trauma-informed material in my 2012 book, *Trauma and the Twelve Steps: A Complete Guide for Enhancing Recovery*. (See Further Reading at the end of this chapter.) If you are interested in learning practical ways of integrating trauma and addiction approaches in your professional work, I highly suggest that you check out this book. To me, we do more harm than good if we look at addiction only as a trauma issue. There is a lot about traditional recovery approaches that works wonders for people struggling with addiction. There has to be integration in our thinking, and part of that integration is not to throw the proverbial baby out with the bathwater. I agree that certain treatment centers and 12-Step groups have given traditional recovery a bad name by not wanting to look at trauma at all or by being excessively rigid. I am the first to admit that certain "recovery programs," if delivered without flexibility and absent the necessary emotional safety precautions, can be harmful.

I field this point of contention from many of my trauma colleagues: "But the 12 Steps are so outdated; they don't take trauma into account at all." True, certain groups, sponsors, centers, and counselors do not, and I agree that they do more harm than good. However, there are scores of us out there, recovering people like myself, Nikki Meyers, Dan Griffin (co-author of *Helping Men Recover*), Stephanie Covington (author of the landmark *A Woman's Way Through the Twelve Steps*), Kyczy Hawk (author of *Yoga and the Twelve-Step Path*), and Ingrid Mathieu (author of *Recovering Spirituality*) whose work can help you discover how integration of the traditional and the innovative is possible, and in our view, optimal.

Maybe I am biased as a person who identifies as recovering, but it continues to sadden me when I see addiction treatment centers ignoring the addiction and treating addicts and alcoholics through a mental health–only model. For instance, there is an established treatment center in my region that is moving away from doing anything traditional; it is even increasingly ostracizing long-term employees at the center who identify as being in 12-Step recovery. Those who run the center justify many of these changes as being state of the art or trauma informed, but in my community, I just don't see any improvement in the outcomes.

One of my highly respected colleagues, Susan Pease Banitt, author of *The Trauma Toolkit: Healing Trauma From the Inside Out*, speaks about the value in "claiming the connection." For instance, when Native Americans who are struggling with issues like depression and substance abuse can claim their connection to their heritage, Banitt notices improvement right away. I feel that the same thing happens for recovering addicts when we make that connection to who we are, to others like us, and to something outside of ourselves, be it something spiritual or some other external motivator. The centers that make addiction only a mental health issue lose this connection.

I am not saying that you have to be a recovering addict to help other recovering addicts and alcoholics, but what you do need is some ability to step into the recovering person's shoes. Another major cause of the great divide between trauma or mental health counseling and addiction counseling is misunderstanding of the alcoholic or addict. I am recovering and am the first to admit that it can be miserable to work with addicts. You can generally assume working with an alcoholic or addict that you're being lied to on some level, although I prefer to take the more humanistic view that you're not getting the whole story. An academic colleague recently disclosed to me, "I know you're not supposed to take them lying to you personally, but I do . . . I just can't work with them."

The other reality is that most alcoholics and addicts have done things that are morally reprehensible. People tend to hurt other people while in active addiction. I've met others in the mental health professions who've been seriously hurt by an alcoholic or addict and see all recovering patients that come their way through the lens of the original injury. I validate these injuries, yet if you are serious about working with trauma in the modern era, working through old wounds may prove to be imperative for your clinical success and overall wellness. Finally, I encounter people who say, "I just don't understand what an addict goes through, so I don't know if I'd be any good working with them. I don't want to do more harm."

As we segue into the section on solutions for bridging the gap and becoming more addiction informed in our delivery of trauma-informed services, consider the quote that opened this chapter from recovery writer Darren Littlejohn: We are all addicts, in one way or another, fixated on something or unhealthfully attached to something that doesn't serve us. Recognizing this idea as the great equalizer may help us to see the things you have in common with an addict, even if you don't identify as an alcoholic or addict. If you don't believe me, try giving up something that you like for two weeks and let me know how it goes.

SOLUTIONS FOR BRIDGING THE GAP

One of my colleagues, author and educator Linda Curran, calls trauma the proverbial *red-headed stepchild* of the mental health field, for some of the reasons explored in Chapter 2. I go a step further and contend that traumatized people with addiction concerns are even more stigmatized, more "red-headed" so to speak, than those with just unresolved PTSD or trauma-related issues. One of the worst things you can do if you are conducting a first meeting with a potential client who begins to talk about drugs, alcohol, or other addiction problems is to bluntly declare, "I don't deal with addictions." First of all, the client may not even identify as being an addict or alcoholic, so your getting nervous or jumpy may be more shaming. I am not saying that to be trauma competent you have to run out and train to be an addictions counselor, but you must maintain a calming presence when addictions come up. At very least, you must be trained to assess for problems related to substance abuse or addictive behaviors and then set the best plan of action, even if that means referring the client for specialized treatment or to a collaborative provider specializing in addiction who can work in concert with your care. So, how can you become more comfortable with addiction and related issues, especially if getting squeamish around the mention of addiction is an issue for you?

The first step is further educating yourself about what addicts experience in active alcoholism or addiction, in their attempts to get clean and sober, and in recovery. I believe you can engage in this education whether you hold firm to the disease model or prefer one of the alternative models, such as behavioral compulsivity or the allostatic (e.g., stress overload) model. I do not want to force the long-standing disease model on you if this goes against your view of mental health and wellness, but I do ask you to keep an open mind in what you may learn.

There are a couple of ways to expand your education. The first would be to take a continuing education course in addiction, especially if you didn't take an addiction course in your graduate training. (It is optional in most programs.) Second, reading autobiographies is another interesting avenue for expanding your learning, and I recommended some at the end of this chapter. If reading a story or watching a movie isn't sufficient, talk to one of us, we'll gladly answer your questions. Many of my colleagues who identify as not being in recovery will routinely approach me with questions, and I am glad to enlighten, especially for the sake of education and awareness. Another outlet is to consider attending an open 12-Step or other recovery meeting in your community. If you do an Internet search for "open 12-Step meetings," you will probably find several. An "open" meeting is just that: a meeting that is open to the public for the sake of learning and education. You never have to introduce yourself: You can simply sit there and listen.

Learning more will hopefully make you feel more at ease in conducting assessments and devising a plan of action. There are several screening tools you can easily access online if you are uncertain on how to start, like the CAGE or the TACE. Most formal assessments in clinical settings have some component of assessment for alcohol and drug use; for instance, "Do you drink alcohol? How much do you drink? How often do you drink? What happens when you drink?" Such questions should allow you to arrive at a *DSM* diagnosis. However, I am generally not the biggest fan of only using screening tools and these interrogation questions. First of all, someone who is resistant, in "denial," or quite frankly, ashamed about his or her use or behaviors will likely not answer in a straightforward manner. Additionally, many are not able to put an exact quantity or precision on the volume of their drinking, using, or other behaviors, so such assessments, although maybe clinically necessary, are not the most effective.

I included another "Greatest Hits" List tool in the appendix of this book containing many of the key beliefs that someone struggling with addiction may hold as true. You can also use this as an assessment tool the same way that you would use the standard "'Greatest Hits' List" introduced in Chapter 5, either in a first session or later, after some rapport has been established. For instance, a person may present for care in a standard mental health setting and may not disclose any issues with addiction in the first few sessions, which often happens because of lack of awareness, shame, or denial. However, after the person gets more comfortable with you, more may be revealed, at which time using the "'Greatest Hits' List of Addiction-Specific Beliefs" can help your client identify issues and help you both trace their origins.

Quite often, a person with a well-established history of both trauma and mental health concerns presents for an assessment and not want to look at or talk about addiction at all. I've had several colleagues consult with me on such cases, buying into the line, "I'm not an addict, I'm bipolar" or "I don't have a drinking problem—it's because of my PTSD." My colleagues generally end up feeling hurt upon realizing the manipulation. Of course, navigating dual diagnosis situations can be tricky. If a person comes in with the willingness to acknowledge mental health but not addiction issues, I generally do not shove addiction recovery down his or her throat, unless there is an imminent life-threatening issue (e.g., child's life in danger; potentially fatal withdrawal or overdose risk). I sometimes need to disclose that I may not be the best fit for the patient if he or she does not want to explore the addiction dynamics. After all, I can't make them: For the most part, I strive to practice empathy, meet the client where he or she is at, and don't press the recovery issue. However, I let the client know that if looking at their concerns only as a mental health problem is not resulting in improvement, I reserve the right to revisit the addiction issue at any time. Additional navigational dynamics with dual diagnosis clients are discussed in Chapters 8 and 9.

Another major facet of the solution is the promotion of dialogue. If you are an addiction professional primarily, educate yourself about trauma and talk to those doing trauma work. If you are a mental health/trauma professional, educate yourself about addiction and don't be afraid to reach out in the community and form collaborative partnerships. Throughout my career, I've been happy, as the trauma specialist, to partner with many addiction recovery treatment centers looking for a provider for the patients, either as an aftercare or collaborative referral. With one of our local treatment centers, I've often served as the trauma counselor that patients come to see so that they can better tolerate sitting through group. I am even more excited when such centers invite me to train their staff about delivering trauma-sensitive addiction care. However, not a single mental health program has invited me to train their staff on addiction-sensitive trauma care. For the record, I'm available for such training and would be delighted to offer it. I'm still awaiting your invitation!

FURTHER READING

Brown, B. (2010). *The gifts of imperfection: Letting go of who you think you're supposed to be and embrace who you are.* Center City, MN: Hazelden.

Covington, S. S. (1994). *A woman's way through the twelve steps.* Center City, MN: Hazelden.

Covington, S. S., Griffin, D., & Dauer, R. (2011). *Helping men recover.* San Francisco, CA: Jossey-Bass.

Griffin, D. (2009). *A man's way through the twelve steps.* Center City, MN: Hazelden.

Hawk, K. (2012). *Yoga and the twelve-step path.* Las Vegas, NV: Central Recovery Press.

Lawford, C. K. (2009). *Moments of clarity: Voices from the front lines of addiction and recovery.* New York: Harper Collins.

Marich, J. (2012). *Trauma and the twelve steps: A complete guide for enhancing recovery.* Cornersburg Media: Warren, OH.

Mathieu, I. (2011). *Recovering spirituality: Achieving emotional sobriety in your spiritual practice.* Center City, MN: Hazelden.

McCauley, K. (2009). *Pleasure unwoven* [DVD]. Salt Lake City, UT: Institute for Addiction Study.

Palaian, S. (2009). *Spent: Break the buying obsession and discover your true worth.* Center City, MN: Hazelden.

Silverman, S.W. (2008). *Love sick: One woman's journey through sexual addiction.* New York: W. W. Norton.

Sojourner, M. (2011). *She bets her life: A true story of gambling addiction.* Berkeley, CA: Seal Press.

CHAPTER 7

Empathy and the Therapeutic Alliance

We're all just walking each other home.

—Ram Dass

For Dr. Wayne Eastlack, a North Carolina–based clinical psychologist, there are so many "stories within the stories" when it comes to sharing his experiences as a noncommissioned Marine officer during the Vietnam War. Today, as an educator and helping professional, his message to those he serves is that healing is possible. Taking the higher ground to move past the bitterness is the road to freedom. However, it was a long and painful road for him to get to this place.

Wayne was the self-described "preacher's kid," so the notion of going to war was out of character. Wayne's gentle nature was not one of a killer. He explains, "I wasn't cut out to be a Marine." One of his strongest memories from Vietnam was of the first kill he ever had to make, a 12-year-old girl. For many years after his own daughter was born, Wayne would sit at her bedside, just watching her breathe, praying that some cosmic revenge wouldn't take her away because of what he did to that little girl in Vietnam. Wayne was on what was called a "suicide squad," so the chances that he would die with every mission were tremendously high. He ended up being replaced on a mission that proved fatal for everyone under his command, and when he was the only man left standing, he knew that he could never kill again.

There were more sources of trauma for Wayne on his return to the States. He remembers having eggs thrown at him by ordinary Americans, and his own fiancée ended up leaving him shortly before their wedding. The words in her parting letter pierced like any bullet: ""I've given it a lot of thought, and I just don't think I can marry a twice-decorated baby killer."

A beautiful point of redemption is that the young woman slated to be the maid of honor showed compassion for Wayne. Forty years and two children later, they are still happily married! Wayne's wife was the prime advocate for him getting help for his trauma, many years after he returned to the States. Already a practicing psychologist, Wayne was still distant and not able to optimally connect with his family. The tipping point was his first trip to the Vietnam Memorial Wall in Washington. When he found the name of the young man who replaced him on the fatal mission, he broke down in a torrent of emotion. He sought help shortly thereafter.

Wayne felt a kinship with his therapist, a man somewhat older than him. His therapist walked with a limp. It didn't originally register with Wayne that this man might be a veteran too, but he decided to ask when he noticed some tears well up in the therapist's eyes during a session. The man helping Wayne was wounded in the Battle of Ka-san during the Korean War, and he walked with a limp because his leg was full of shrapnel. After acknowledging their connection as veterans, Wayne's therapist said to him, "I will bring you home. I will walk with you all the way." For Wayne, that line was a turning point. It impacted his own healing, and it inspired him to become the type of therapist who also walks people home.

When it all comes down to it, when we wade through policy and procedure, technique and theory, that's all trauma-informed counseling is about—walking the survivor home. Home may be a literal place, an emotional state, or a haven of safety that the survivor never imagined possible. Through a working therapeutic relationship, the therapist may bring the reality of such a haven into focus for the survivor. In this chapter, we further explore this idea of walking the client to the proverbial "home" he or she is seeking as the hallmark of the therapeutic relationship. We will first explain why a therapeutic alliance is so important. Then, we will explore ways to deepen our sense of empathy and therapeutic relationship building as the imperative foundation of trauma-informed counseling.

It's All About the Relationship

I am not just a touchy-feely humanitarian promoting the values of empathy and the therapeutic alliance because I believe in our collective humanity and the importance of human connection. Although all of those things are true, it's important to state that I am not a renegade in my beliefs. There is pretty convincing evidence, in examining the totality of psychotherapy literature, that points to the importance of empathy and the therapeutic alliance.

For decades, helping professionals and the scientific minds of our fields have been on a quest to find that perfect modality, or just the right set of things to say to usher in change. In findings published by an American Psychological Association (APA) Task Force in 2002, distinguished professor and researcher Dr. John Norcross challenged that technique is not the most important element of what works in psychotherapy. Using a collection of empirical research studies and chapters from various psychotherapeutic professions, Norcross (2002) demonstrated that the therapy relationship, together with discrete method, influences treatment outcomes. He further concluded that therapists can hone these relational elements and that it is their responsibility to tailor these skills to the needs of individual patients. Thus, the relationship should drive the theoretical approach and delivery of technical elements, not the other way around.

The task force's findings do not give us blanket permission to dismiss theory and technique. However, if we value technique and theory above the therapeutic relationship, problems will ensue. A metaphor I first introduced in *EMDR Made Simple* (Marich, 2011) offers this modern-day example: Think about navigating a journey by car. If we put theory in the driver's seat and shove the relationship all the way back in the trunk of the car, the therapy isn't going to go anywhere. The therapeutic relationship needs to take the front seat. Typically, the client will steer the course of the treatment and the therapist will be the trusted front-seat navigator. At times, the client may need a rest, and the therapist will need to take the wheel. The technique is like a navigating passenger in the backseat with a map or a GPS system. It can give you good directions, especially when you're lost, but ultimately, the technique should never be the entity driving. To carry the metaphor further, sometimes maps are hard to read and don't take into account the creative elements of a drive (e.g., point A to point B may look quicker, but if you've actually driven the route before, you know there's a better way to go). For those of you who use a GPS, you know its lack of artistry can be even worse than a map! Many times, trusting GPS directions over my intuitive sense of direction has taken me way off course, and I realized later that my sense of direction was right all along.

If you have any interest in psychotherapy research, the volume *The Heart and Soul of Change: Delivering What Works in Therapy* (Duncan et al., 2009) is a must read. This team is at the cutting edge of investigating what works in psychotherapy, using massive meta-analyses (studies that statistically analyze the results of several studies) and literature reviews to examine what the canon of research recommends. The team concluded that the collaborative, therapeutic alliance between client and clinician is a primary factor in determining successful therapy outcomes and is more important than the specific execution of therapeutic protocols. Obtaining continuous client feedback throughout the therapeutic process is a critical element of enhancing client care, a practice that even the Substance Abuse and Mental Health Services Administration (SAMHSA) now considers to be evidence based. Little difference exists among the specific factors (e.g., technical elements) of *bona fide*, researched therapies that are intended to be therapeutic. Rather, there are a series of four common factors among these therapies that seem to be what's really contributing to change.

These common factors are 1) the clients and their extra-therapeutic factors (e.g., what they bring to the table in therapy and situations out of the control of the clinician), 2) models and techniques that work to engage and inspire the client, 3) the therapeutic relationship/alliance, and 4) therapist factors. The interplay of the factors is discussed more fully in Chapter 10 as we consider the art of matching technique to client preference and strengths. In the context of this chapter on the relationship, it's interesting to note that these four common factors were first proposed and published by psychiatrist Dr. Saul Rosenzweig in 1936. Most people in the field today do not recognize Rosenzweig's name, but you will likely make a connection when you learn that he was Carl Rogers' first clinical supervisor.

Carl Rogers, considered the father of client-centered, or person-centered, therapy, is the name that professionals likely associate with the importance of empathy. I contend, even in my own peer-reviewed publications, that the classic Rogerian constructs of empathy, genuineness, and unconditional positive regard still have relevance in the contemporary era, in which the influence of the medical model has placed more emphasis on standardization, treatment protocols, and manual-driven therapy (Marich, 2012). Metaphor is a teaching device heavily used throughout this book, and Rogers himself provided a helpful metaphor to describe empathy (Raskin & Rogers, in Corsini, 2000; p. 135):

> Being empathetic reflects an attitude of profound interest in the client's world of meanings and feelings. The therapist receives these communications and conveys appreciation and understanding, assisting the client to go further or deeper. The notion that this involves nothing more than a repetition of the client's last words is erroneous. Instead, an interaction occurs in which one person is a warm, sensitive, respectful companion in the typically difficult

exploration of another's emotional world. The therapist's manner of responding should be individual, natural, and unaffected. When empathy is at its best, the two individuals are participating in a process comparable to that of a couple dancing, with the client leading and the therapist following.

I know that this dance metaphor makes many therapists nervous, especially if you have the mentality that a patient is sick and needs guidance. As a former ice dancer and ballroom dancer who happens to be female (and thus, the party who is traditionally led), I have some insights to offer. When you fight where your leading partner wants to take you, the dance will be atrocious from a performance perspective; at best, it just won't feel as right or as magical as if you let the natural flow unfold. There is nothing wrong with being led, even if everything in your personality structure resists it. In training and practice, there is nothing wrong, as the female partner, with stopping the dance from time to time if something doesn't feel right and having a discussion with your partner about what needs to change. A communicative, healthy dance partner will listen to your concerns and make adjustments. These training habits, combined with a certain natural chemistry, are why partners like Fred Astaire and Ginger Rogers, Jane Torvill and Christopher Dean, and Margot Fonteyn and Rudolf Nureyev made magic as artistic legends of dance. As therapists and helpers, may we be open to the same suggestion that being led is a necessity for the magic to happen! This is the very essence of Rogerian empathy.

The importance of a solid, empathic therapeutic relationship takes on special relevance when we are working with traumatic stress issues. The literature in general traumatic stress studies suggests that the therapeutic alliance between client and clinician is an important mechanism in facilitating meaningful change for clients with complex PTSD (Courtois & Ford, 2009; Courtois & Perlman, 2005; Fosha, 2000; Fosha & Slowiaczek, 1997; Korn, 2009; Wilson & Thomas, 2004). One of the most significant studies on the role of the therapeutic alliance in PTSD training concluded that in clients with a history of early childhood sexual abuse, an early therapeutic alliance and positive social support are imperative to successful outcome (Keller et al., 2010). The authors of this study recommend that clinicians learn to assess for the quality of the alliance early in treatment. If clinicians do not feel comfortable doing this in the context of conversation in clinical session, several measures are available for this assessment, including the Working Alliance Inventory and the Session Rating Scale 3.0. (See Further Reading at the end of the chapter.)

STRATEGIES FOR ENHANCING EMPATHY

In their 2004 book, *Empathy in the Treatment of Trauma and PTSD*, John Wilson and Rhiannon Thomas contended that effective post-traumatic therapy is more than the application of a clinical technique. Effectiveness is the capacity to facilitate self-healing by helping the patient mobilize and transform the negative energies, memories, and emotions of PTSD and associated conditions into a healthy self-synthesis that evolves into a positive integration of the trauma experience. If you embrace the themes of humanity and tenderness in the treatment of human wounding in *Trauma Made Simple*, than this contention ought to make total sense to you. Yet some of you may struggle with how to be more empathetic, especially if your approach to human healing has always been more scientific.

Part of enhancing our capacity for empathy is to first understand what it means. Coined by German philosopher Rudolf Lötze in 1858, the German word for empathy, *Einfühlung*, literally translates as "in" + "feeling." The German derives from the Greek *empatheia*, meaning "in" + "pathos" (feeling). *Pathos* is also the root of *passion* and *pain*. Thus, being empathetic is different from feeling sorry for our clients and is more than experiencing a genuine sense of compassion for them. Rather, for the time that our clients are with us, we must be willing to take on their pain as we walk with them.

Taking this walk is easier for some of us than others due to factors like personality or life experience. Yet, empathy can be built. Sometimes it requires that the helping professional seek help and support if he or she is routinely struggling with being empathetic or releasing the empathy after sessions. (More on this in Chapter 12.) This support may come in the form of the professional seeking therapy or consulting with and seeking collegial support from others in the field. Ask them, "What works for you to help you be more empathetic? What has helped you during periods of struggle in your own career?"

A suggestion I give to supervisees, consultees, and professional friends is to remember what it was like when they experienced a trauma. Even if you are not in personal recovery from an addiction or from a mental health issue, all of us have been traumatized on some level, especially if we consider the broad definition of trauma. During the period of greatest struggle in your own life, what did you most need from others to help you get through that struggle? If you have to take a few moments to reflect, try meditating or using imagery to float back to the worst time in your life and remember what it was like.

Many times in my career, especially when I am going through a stressful period and clients seem ungrateful, I've been tempted to throw in the towel. One time I called a pastor friend during such a period. Upset, I said something like, "I am having such a hard time feeling sorry for these people! I mean, I was able to get sober and work on myself—why can't they?" After validating my frustration, she sensed that on some level I was forgetting what it was like to be newly sober and struggling to find my sanity. Her suggestion was that I go to a couple of recovery meetings in our community populated with newly sober people. The suggestion ended up being golden. Listening to people share their struggles while not in any professional capacity was a personal wake-up call, and it helped me with both my own wellness and to be more effective with my clients.

If going to a recovery meeting in your community is not feasible for you, consider going on a retreat of some type. Places like the Kripalu Center for Yoga and Health in Massachusetts and the Esalen Institute in Big Sur, California, offer a wide variety of retreats. Smaller organizations like my practice and community initiative, Mindful Ohio, offer regionally accessible retreats. Do an Internet search, and you might be surprised at what is available near you. Going on retreats is not only a wonderful self-care exercise, it can also help you with your empathetic capacities by getting to know and encounter others on a deep level.

My favorite exercise for building empathy is a guided imagery exercise that I like to call "Step Into Their Shoes." You can download a free version of me leading this exercise on this book's website. (See Further Reading at the end of the chapter.) You can complete this exercise as a guided imagery or as a simple meditation. To begin, think of a client, perhaps one currently on your caseload, or one you've treated in the past. Get as detailed as you want in your visualization: Picture what this client looks like, noticing details like height, weight, race, gender, ethnicity, and any other identifiable physical features. Think about this client sitting in your waiting room, or if you don't work in a conventional office setting, think about where this client would be as he or she was waiting for your visit. Notice what that person's motivation is for coming in to services; is it internal, external, or a combination of both? Then, if you are willing, allow yourself to step into the shoes of that client, if only for a few minutes. Allow yourself, in the role of that client, to notice what you'd be noticing sitting in that waiting room. Notice what would be going through your head and what would be popping up in your body as you wait to be seen by a helping professional. Then, imagine that the therapist or other helper comes out to get you. Notice what it feels like for you for this helper to shake your hand, and notice the experience of being led back to a strange office. Or, if you, as the client, are in a hospital or an in-home setting, be mindful of what it would be like to have a helper come into your space to ask you a bunch of questions.

You are asked some variation of the question, "How are you?" In your gut, what do you really want to say? Reflect on that for a moment, and then notice what you would actually say. Notice, as you begin to talk to this helping professional, how you feel, especially in your body, as you are asked questions about your life. Do you feel safe? Do you feel threatened? What are your impressions of this person who is supposed to help you? Do you feel as though you can trust him or her? If not, what is it about the helper, or about the dynamic of this interaction, that seems to be lacking? If you have a good vibe about your helper, what is it that seems to be working?

Continuing the exercise, let's say you are in this office during a first assessment or an early session. What do you most need to feel positively about coming back and continuing with counseling? If you are in an inpatient situation, what would you need to feel okay about staying and listening to what the helper has to say? If you are in a correctional facility, what would you need to feel optimistic about engaging in services? No answer is stupid or irrelevant. Sometimes, it is a simple experience of hope, an inkling of optimism that hasn't been present for a great while. For other clients, having a clear plan of action may do the trick. We've discussed the massive role of validation in trauma treatment throughout the book, and in most cases, experiencing that validation within the context of rapport is imperative.

Allow yourself, if you've engaged in this meditation, to step back into the shoes of your professional self. Take a few moments to notice or jot down any specific insights that emerged from that process. Notice, especially, if what you would have needed to come back and engage in services is different than what you, in the role of this client, would have required.

More issues regarding what makes a good trauma therapist are explored in Chapter 12. In many ways, this chapter and Chapter 12 complement each other in terms of content. It is important to introduce and to begin considering the important role of empathy and the therapeutic alliance before we dive too far into the technical elements of trauma treatment and developing a framework for healing trauma. Regardless of what approach, theory, method, or framework you are going to use to help a client heal, if you are not engaging in empathy, the process is not going to flow smoothly—in fact, it may even be futile.

An ancient Korean folk tale called "The Tiger's Whisker" taught this lesson many centuries before the dawn of modern psychology (Courlander &

Arno, 1959). In the story, a young wife named Yun Ok was saddened and frustrated, powerless to help her despondent husband after his return from the wars. A stubborn woman, she was reticent to seek the council of the old hermit living in the hills outside of her village, but when she grew fearful of her own husband's presence, she knew she must seek his help. She went to him seeking a potion to cure her husband's ailment, and he told her that to create such a potion, he would need the whisker of a live tiger. She protested vehemently, crying that such a request was impossible, but the hermit offered no alternative. He must have the whisker of a live tiger to make the potion and restore her husband.

Determined, the next day she went to a cave near the mountains where a tiger was known to live. She took a bowl of rice and meat with her. Making a gentle sound, she set the bowl down and then quietly hid before the tiger could see her. The tiger, after hearing her sound, came to the place where she had set the bowl and ate the young wife's offering. She repeated this pattern every day for the next several months, replacing the old bowl with a fresh bowl of rice and meat, each time making her gentle, clicking sound a little louder to desensitize the mighty tiger. One day, the tiger was sitting there waiting at the spot where she normally placed the bowl. His face looked like that of a kitten instead of a savage beast, and she was surprised that he let her approach him. The next day, he even let her gently pet his fur. This engagement continued over the next several days, and she even began talking to her new friend, complimenting him on his lovely, reddish fur as she continued to feed him.

One day, she had an intuition that it was the day to pluck off the tiger's whisker. While petting the tiger and talking to him gently, she was able, with one gentle motion, to pluck off a whisker! She trembled in amazement, and then graced the tiger with her thanksgiving. From there, she went to the old hermit, proudly waving the tiger's whisker.

"I have it, I have it!!!," she proclaimed.

He asked her how she managed to get the whisker, a task she once viewed as impossible, and she proceeded to tell him the story. After taking in her tale, he took the whisker and flicked it into the fire that burned to keep his dwelling warm.

"What have you done!?," she yelped in surprise.

The hermit told her, "Yun Ok, you don't need it any more. You no longer need the whisker. Tell me, is a man more vicious than a tiger? If the tiger responded to your tender and patient care, what's to say that your husband will not do the same?"

She left the hermit's dwelling that day, and she knew what she needed to do.

FURTHER READING

Duncan, B. L., Miller, S. D., Wampold, B. E., & Hubble, M. A. (Eds.) (2009). *The heart and soul of change: Delivering what works in therapy.* 2nd ed. Washington, D. C.: American Psychological Association.

Marich, J. Step Into Their Shoes [guided meditation], retrieved from http://www.traumamadesimple.com/audio-extras.html

Norcross, J. (2002). *Psychotherapy relationships that work: Therapist contributions and responsiveness to patients.* New York: Oxford University Press.

Session Rating Scale 3.0 & The Outcome Rating Scale (ORS), retrieved from http://www.centerforclinicalexcellence.com/site.php?page=measures.php (Instructions for administration & support also included).

Working Alliance Inventory, retrieved from https://www.niatx.net/PDF/PIPractice/FormsTemplates/Working_Alliance_Surveys.pdf(other variations available online).

CHAPTER 8

Creating a Framework for Healing Trauma

A whole is that which has beginning, middle, and end.

—Aristotle

KEEP IT SIMPLE

It seems as though not a month goes by in the psychotherapeutic professions without a new model being introduced to explain and treat trauma. Just about every number is covered in the naming of such models (e.g., the Four Activity Model, the 5-Stage Model, the 7-Stage Model). Some models implore very sophisticated, scientific-sounding names (e.g., the Adaptive Information Processing Model), whereas others carry the names of the scholars who devised them. Others still utilize a "healing sounding" word or series of words, punctuated by a °, ©, or ™ symbol. Interestingly, *model* comes from the Latin root *modus*, or something meant to be imitated. The French saying *à la mode*, which we generally associate with ice cream accompanying pie, actually means *according to the fashion*. And let's face it, psychotherapeutic models, especially when it comes to trauma, are very trendy.

The models that exist in the helping professions aim to accomplish the same thing: to offer a plan of action for healing to take place. Models often develop independently of each other and are largely influenced by the works and beliefs of their creators. I am not necessarily anti-model. If a certain model works for a professional and the setting in which he or she works (and ultimately provides a safe structure for helping a client heal), that's outstanding. However, in keeping with the theme of this book, I do get concerned when our field overcomplicates matters. As I stated in *Trauma and the Twelve Steps*, I don't think our field necessarily needs any new models when it comes to

121

understanding and treating trauma. We need a true integration of ideas in our thinking. The best way to do this is to keep it simple and return to the most basic roots of healing.

The simplest *framework* (a term that I prefer to *model*) for healing trauma is one of the earliest, Pierre Janet's Stage Model for the Treatment of Traumatic Stress. Tracing back to the late 19th century, it is still relevant because of its commonsensical potency. Even Janet's original model carries different names in the field today: The Three-Stage Model and the Triphasic Model are popular. I tend to prefer the title *Consensus Model* because, in the century plus since Janet published his ideas, just about every major scholar writing on post-traumatic stress can agree on the three-tiered structure. Anything on which we can collectively agree is worth studying!

Here are the three stages originally proposed by Janet (van der Hart, Brown, & van der Kolk, 1989):

- Stabilization, symptom-oriented treatment, and preparation for liquidation of traumatic memories.
- Identification, exploration, and modification of traumatic memories.
- Relapse prevention, relief of residual symptomatology, personality reintegration, and rehabilitation.

The Aristotelian simplicity is obvious: There needs to be a beginning, a middle, and an end (even if this "ending" is better conceptualized as *maintenance*) to the healing structure. Of course, there is room for scholars and practitioners to add their personal spin; hence, the reason we have so many named models today. However, when helping professionals who I train get tripped up on which model they should be using, I encourage them to keep it simple and come back to this most basic structure as a guideline.

One of the greatest misconceptions about trauma counseling is that it's all about catharsis, or the second component of Janet's structure (identification, exploration, and modification of traumatic memories). However, if a patient or clinician jumps into catharsis without having a foundation of stabilization, which includes a therapeutic alliance and a set of coping or affect regulation skills, further damage can result. As a former research subject of mine once put it, in stabilization, we make sure we aren't going to come *unglued* by what may come up in the identification and exploration of trauma (Marich, 2010).

Another great misconception about trauma counseling, especially with the savvy marketing around many of the newer approaches to trauma treatment, is that once something is *processed* or *cleared*, then it's gone—it's a non-issue.

This mindset, in my view, promotes an idea that trauma can be cured. A healthier approach is to look at trauma as something that can be healed. Even after a person has a major catharsis or breakthrough in counseling, there is still work to be done with his or her adjustment. Imagine if a person went into a hospital for major surgery, and the blockage or impediment was cleared but no postoperative follow-up or rehab was recommended.

Consider how the consensus model fits with the wound-healing theme of this book. Stabilization is commensurate to providing immediate attention to a wound. Using a simple scrape or cut as an example, stabilization might mean cleaning out the wound and disinfecting the area after it's had a chance to bleed for a while. Then, a dressing is generally applied to stop the bleeding and prevent infection or other impediments to healing. However, for a wound to truly heal, the dressing cannot stay on forever; the wound needs to be exposed to the light and air. Healing needs to occur from the inside out, a process that can take a great deal of time. This process is the middle stage. After a wound heals, it generally leaves a scar. In cases of relatively benign wounding, that scar may clear up altogether. With more significant injuries, a person may need to get used to living with a scar or whatever aftermath is left behind after the wound heals.

As "old" as the Janet stage model may seem, it is still cutting edge. In the autumn of 2012, an expert consensus panel of the International Society for Traumatic Stress Studies (ISTSS), comprising some of the biggest names in the field of trauma treatment, issued their recommendations for addressing complex post-traumatic stress. Even with all of the innovations since Janet, the panel still recommends his general sequence as the standard for trauma care (Cloitre et al, 2012).

Throughout the book, I contend that there is nothing neat and linear about trauma, grief, and how their wounds manifest. My biggest concern with models is that the more "steps," "numbers," or "components" they contain, the more likely clinicians and helpers are to get tripped up about how to deal with unpredictability. No model can capture the truly messy nature of unresolved trauma or grief, let alone offer the perfect solution for healing it. Thus, the fewer components of a model, the better, because simplicity allows for flexibility and the *ebb and flow* that characterizes human healing. This is why I refer to the consensus model as a framework, rather than a model: It's common sense to stabilize first—to make sure a person can deal with what may come up in the stage of deeper identification or exploration. However, if you enter the exploration stage and it's evident that the client is not adequately stabilized to do this work, you can always return to stabilization. Even if you are working with your client actively in that more cathartic phase, it's always wise to use skills acquired during stabilization to close sessions down or to remind the patient how to use these skills to stay safe between sessions.

Another major reason why the consensus model is not a perfect "stage" model is that if you are doing outpatient work, on some level, you are doing reintegration work throughout the entire process. Everything you do to help a client live more adaptively is reintegration work. Much of this can happen concurrently with the other two phases. Chapters 9 through 11 cover each of the stages in depth.

THE VICTIM-SURVIVOR-THRIVER CONTINUUM

I use the consensus model in this book to provide readers with a general framework, and because it stands the test of time in the psychotherapeutic professions. This framework, combined with the humanistic elements of empathy covered in Chapter 7, provide a beautiful context in which healing can take place. Another three-tiered structure to help frame the healing process from the perspective of the client is the victim-survivor-thriver continuum. The idea that identifying as a survivor or a thriver is more empowering than identifying as a victim is a notion that is not necessarily limited to our field—even popular culture has picked up on it. For instance, there's a great scene in the 2011 comedy hit *Bridesmaids* in which the clown of the film, played by Melissa McCarthy, told her story of falling off of a cruise ship and getting saved by a dolphin. In sharing her experience, she proudly declared, "I'm not going to say I survived; I'm gonna say I thrived."

Many clients with whom I've worked find the victim-survivor-thriver continuum to be a useful construct in gauging where they are at on any given day with their healing. There are powerful parallels to the consensus model. For instance, people working at the stabilization level are in the process of moving from victim traits into having survivor traits. Those in the reprocessing stages are working with a survivor's mindset with the goal of shifting toward thriving. Working in reintegration or maintenance is about keeping the thriver traits more constant, even while recognizing that ups and downs still happen and there will be days when feeling like a survivor is the best one can hope for.

One of my clients introduced me to the work of therapist, thanatologist, and healer Barbara Whitfield. She assembled the general traits of people in victim mode, survivor mode, and thriver mode into a table, which appears below. My client indicated that he likes to use Barbara's table as an inventory to assess his thinking and feeling on any given day. For my client, who is somewhere between survivor and thriver, evaluating where he is at and what blocks may be impeding him from more strongly identifying as a thriver is an important part of his continual healing process, informing our work together.

From Victim to Survivor to Thriver

Victim	Survivor	Thriver
Doesn't deserve nice things or trying for the "good life"	Struggling for reasons & chance to heal	Gratitude for everything in life
Low self-esteem/shame/ unworthy	Sees self as wounded & healing	Sees self as an overflowing miracle
Hypervigilant	Using tools to learn to relax	Gratitude for new life
Alone	Seeking help	Oneness
Feels selfish	Deserves to seek help	Proud of healthy self-caring
Damaged	Naming what happened	Was wounded & now healing
Confusion & numbness	Learning to grieve, grieving past ungrieved trauma	Grieving at current losses
Overwhelmed by past	Naming & grieving what happened	Living in the present
Hopeless	Hopeful	Faith in self & life
Uses outer world to hide from self	Stays with emotional pain	Understands that emotional pain will pass & brings new insights
Hides his or her story	Not afraid to tell his or her story to safe people	Beyond telling his or her story but always aware he or she has created own healing with Higher Power
Believes everyone else is better, stronger, less damaged	Comes out of hiding to hear others & have compassion for them & eventually self	Lives with an open heart for self & others

(Continued)

Victim	Survivor	Thriver
Often wounded by unsafe others	Learning how to protect self by share, check, share	Protects self from unsafe others
Places own needs last	Learning healthy needs	Places self first, realizing that is the only way to function & eventually help others
Creates one drama after another	Sees patterns	Creates peace
Believes suffering is the human condition	Feeling some relief, knows he or she needs to continue in recovery	Finds joy in peace
Serious all the time	Beginning to laugh	Seeing the humor in life
Uses inappropriate humor, including teasing	Feels associated painful feelings instead	Uses healthy humor
Uncomfortable, numb or angry around toxic people	Increasing awareness of pain & dynamics	Healthy boundaries around toxic people, including relatives
Lives in the past	Aware of patterns	Lives in the now
Angry at religion	Understanding the difference between religion & personal spirituality	Enjoys personal relationship with the god of his or her understanding
Suspicious of therapists/ projects	Sees therapist as guide during projections	Sees reality as his or her projection and owns it
Needs people and chemicals to believe he or she is all right	Glimpses of self-acceptance and fun without others	Feels authentic & connected, whole
Depression	Movement of feelings	Aliveness

Developed by Barbara Whitfield, RT (2003). Reprinted with permission.

For my client Jim,* who introduced me to this tool, unresolved trauma can strip you of your healing resources. That's the nature of trauma. As he shared in Chapter 1, "Trauma dries you out. It takes all of the natural oil and flexibility out of you and so you can't bend with life—that's why traumatized people are so defensive. They are so afraid someone can break them at any time." A survivor of early childhood trauma, including severe bullying, and spiritual trauma later in his life, Jim clearly identified that trauma causes shame, and shame causes you to push away the people who are trying to help you. He continued with this metaphor to explain his healing context of recovery: "So much of recovery is getting the oil rubbed in so you regain flexibility. Time doesn't heal all wounds; the oil does. For me, those oils are love, support, and caring people who want to listen."

Safety, Flexibility, and the Individual

As Jim so eloquently expressed, unresolved trauma can dry out your sense of flexibility and adaptation. People with unresolved trauma can be reactive instead of responsive to stressors, which is why, as professionals, it's imperative that we model what it means to be flexible. We also want to meet the client where he or she is *at*. There are so many different approaches, models, theories, and techniques for treating trauma. A major contention of the next three chapters is that no one approach, model, theory, or technique is best, because the hallmark of trauma-informed treatment is meeting the client where he or she is at on the journey. Thus, finding the right "fit" for that individual client is the imperative, and it is an art. Regardless of technique or approach, it is important that we create a crucible of safety for our clients and that we are flexible with them in the usually erratic process of wound healing.

One of the major problems with healing trauma in the professional service structure of modern America is that too many hospitals and agencies approach treatment as one size fits all. Sometimes they justify their unilateral focus under the guise of institutional mission (e.g., "We are a 12-Step facility," or "We maintain that the cognitive behavioral approach to treatment is the gold standard"). One-size-fits-all approaches may result from agencies feeling that meeting people at an individual level is too time consuming, emotionally exhausting, and cost prohibitive. Having neat models, manuals, and structures in place is a way to keep the ship sailing smoothly. If clients can't meet the treatment standards that an agency offers, they are generally written off as *resistant* or *not ready to change*. This practice is not acceptable if we are serious about creating trauma-informed systems of change in our clinical settings.

Maridee Costanzo has a great deal to say about the state of healing in contemporary America, having viewed the culture from a variety of perspectives. In the prime of her professional life, Maridee was an outspoken, no-nonsense criminal defense attorney known for her prowess in the courtroom. She built a successful practice defending criminals who most others did not want to come near. Maridee's addiction to opiates progressed along with the success of her career, and at a certain point, her life spiraled out of control before she realized what was happening. Maridee became one of the criminals she was used to defending, sentenced to eight years in a federal penitentiary on a murder-for-hire conviction, having ordered a hit on her estranged husband while she was in an opiate-induced rage.

For Maridee, whose entire life as an attorney was about control, having any semblance of control removed upon entering prison completely rocked her world. As she explained, being a criminal lowers your self-esteem, and then the dehumanizing treatment incurred in the prison system automatically compounds your traumatic responses. She calls trauma a chronic state, something that is with you always, and it comes out in one of two ways. Either you completely rage, because the anger at least feels good, or you have the complete opposite reaction and isolate into that curled up fetal position. Maridee noted, "I, at least had family support, intelligence, and a sense of humor to help keep me afloat. Even with that, being in prison was traumatizing; it overwhelmed me. I can't even image what it's like for people who don't have those resources."

Maridee managed to get clean while she was in prison, but when she was released after eight years, she experienced a total culture shock. In the eight years that she was incarcerated, society's technological explosion changed the landscape. Everyone had cell phones, and the digital age seemed to leave her in the dusk. "I felt like I was on the planet Zoltar when I got out!" she remarked. After her release, she was sentenced to spend time in a halfway house connected to a treatment center, and she directly experienced being treated by professionally trained staff who were not trauma informed.

Maridee explained, "People don't realize how it's the little stuff that makes all of the difference—getting assistance with being able to get clean clothes, a new pair of panties or a bra. Especially with the rapid changes in society, it's the little things we need help with. I remember when I was staying at the halfway house, and I was expected to use the bus to get to someplace like a job interview. We weren't allowed to carry cell phones, and they would insensitively say things like, 'If you get stuck, carry some change and use a pay phone.' But they didn't seem to realize just how few and far between pay phones were in our city. Then I had the situation of having to find a job. I had a law degree. Any place I applied, even Mickey D's wouldn't hire me because I was over qualified. And the staff at the halfway house told me I should just lie about my education. Isn't recovery about honesty? What kind of example were they setting?"

Maridee stated that after she completed her time at the halfway house, coming back to her hometown and working with a caring probation officer and a solid trauma-informed therapist made a huge difference in being able to heal. Maridee insists that professionals working with traumatized people must grasp that it's the little measures of humanity and attitude that make all of the difference. When I asked Maridee what message she wants professionals to hear on what constitutes a healing culture, she said, "If you're in this just for a job—do no harm, at the very least. If you want to make a difference, you have to truly believe there is some hope and that recovery is possible."

Maridee's words speak volumes about the culture we must create for the healing of trauma. If the consensus model is the guiding framework, the safety and flexibility that we create as professionals are what hold it together. Heather Bowser uses the metaphor of the basin: "I want to be that basin for my clients . . . to catch their emotion so that they can marinate on it. Then I want to give back their reflection with a hope that we can work through it." As Heather pointed out, basins tend to have drains, and the therapist catches a great deal of this energetic excess, which is why self-care for the helper becomes imperative (an issue covered further in Chapter 12). As I stated earlier in the chapter, doing trauma-informed work with a commitment to meet people individually does take more time and emotional energy; that is often the cost of being an effective helper for the people we are entrusted to treat. However, taking care of ourselves becomes a quality of care issue. If we are not dealing with what we catch in the drain, we run the risk of harming the client and providing him or her with a treatment culture that is antithetical to healing.

FURTHER READING

Cloitre, M., Courtois, C. A., Ford, J. D., Green, B. L., Alexander, P., Briere, J., Herman, J. L., Lanius, R., Stolbach, B. C., Spinazzola, J., Van der Kolk, B. A., Van der Hart, O. (2012). *The ISTSS expert consensus treatment guidelines for complex PTSD in adults*. Retrieved from http://www.istss. org/AM/Template.cfm?Section=ISTSS_Complex_PTSD_Treatment_ Guidelines&Template=/CM/ContentDisplay.cfm&ContentID=5185.

CHAPTER 9

Trauma Treatment: Stabilization

In a neighborhood, as in life, a clean bandage is much, much better than a raw and festering wound.

—Ed Koch

STABILIZATION IS TRAUMA WORK

"But if we talk to them about trauma, we run the risk of regressing them . . . what if we can't get them back?"

"It's just took risky to go into all of that trauma stuff when we have them for such a short time. We don't want them to leave and then relapse."

"I am afraid of making her worse."

These are the three most common objections I hear from fellow professionals when I introduce the idea of being more trauma sensitive in our delivery of clinical services. We tend to assume that trauma counseling automatically means that we are going to dive into the heavy emotional material, or that the risk is high of it coming up on its own. There tends to be such fear surrounding trauma within our professions, some of it legitimate, and much of it a reflection of fear-based ignorance of what trauma really means. (More on this in Chapter 12.)

Properly stabilizing a client is the ounce of prevention that's worth a pound of cure when it comes to delivering trauma services. Stabilization is just as important as the cathartic elements, if not more important. If a client isn't sufficiently stabilized, then yes, there is a high risk that working with the deeper, more subconscious levels of the story can trigger an abreaction that he or she is not prepared to handle. Janet indicated that stabilization must include initial building of rapport between therapist and client, delivery of moral guidance from the therapist, and what he called, "rest, isolation, and simplification of lifestyle." This recommendation could be the equivalent of an inpatient stay at a psychiatric or other treatment facility, or even an extended retreat. Janet also indicated that "stimulation and re-education" (what we might now call coaching or motivational enhancement) and the use of hypnotic relaxation strategies are also appropriate in this stage. (For reviews, see van der Hart, Brown, & van der Kolk, 1989.) Don't fret if you are not an officially trained hypnotherapist. Consider how some of the field's most popular strategies for relaxation, like guided imagery, implore hypnotic suggestion.

In this chapter, we explore the key elements for trauma-sensitive stabilization in contemporary times. Stabilization work involves coping skills training. Skills that are body based, action oriented, and holistic must be highlighted if we are serious about delivering them in a trauma-informed way. Such skills allow a client to more effectively regulate the intense affect that may be triggered in day-to-day life or in the therapeutic process.

Other activities that make for successful stabilization are also discussed in this chapter, such as assisting a client with identifying strengths and resources (both external and external). Introducing key ideas and attitudes, such as acceptance and empowerment, can get a client ready for deeper exploration of the trauma. If a client requires psychotropic medication following psychiatric consult, allowing the client time to get used to the medication is also critical before deeper trauma work begins. To reiterate my position, I am not anti-medication; I just get concerned when medication is over-prescribed, especially as a replacement for psychotherapy and psychosocial support. There are also clients who have legitimate, organic conditions, such as bipolar disorder or schizophrenia, along with PTSD or other trauma concerns. Ensuring that such clients are reasonably stable on their medication is required before going further.

It is imperative to realize that clinicians can begin doing stabilization-level trauma work from the moment they do a screening interview on the phone. Many of the best practices I described in Chapter 5 for assessment are stabilization-level functions. It is not necessary to explore relational elements in stabilization as a separate component in this chapter, because much of this is covered in Chapters 5, 7, and 12. Just know that building the relationship is an important part of this early sequence.

Whenever I hear hospital-based clinicians say things like, "We don't have enough time to do the trauma stuff," I cringe. Yes, you do. You can always assist a client in stabilizing and regulating in a more trauma-informed way. Hopefully, this idea will be even clearer by the end of the chapter.

COPING SKILLS TRAINING

Coping skills, affect regulation techniques, self-soothing mechanisms, distress tolerance activities. . . . Whatever term you use, the idea, especially within the context of stabilization, is to equip a client with a series of tools he or she can use to calm down when distressed and to keep from coming unglued when it is time for deeper work. In the human services profession, we talk a great game about coping skills and how we need to teach them to clients, yet many neglect to embrace the art of trauma-informed coping skills training. One of the fundamentals is to first assess the client's existing coping skills and discuss which of these skills are healthy or adaptive (especially in the context of the patient's goals for treatment) and which are unhealthy or maladaptive. Sometimes, it's not black and white. For instance, a coping skill like exercise may work very well in one context, yet be maladaptive in another (e.g., if it's being used primarily to avoid emotions). Spiritual practices are another type of coping skill that I've seen used both adaptively and maladaptively by the same person.

Thus, a conversation about what works, what doesn't work, and some of the contextual nuances surrounding both is the imperative first step in developing a solid, trauma-informed coping plan. Many clients will already have a set of adaptive coping skills in place, especially if they've had prior exposure to recovery, counseling, or healing. However, I've had to work with the vast majority of clients I've treated to build coping skills from the ground up. This is often a tedious process that involves trial and error. I adamantly believe that what works for one client in terms of coping may not work for another, and two variations of the same skills may work differently in different contexts for the same client. Developing a trauma-informed coping plan requires education and trial and error, with the client testing out the skills outside of the office. For clients who are inpatient or incarcerated, this testing may involve using the skills in the therapeutic milieu or when they are alone in the evening. For any client, nighttime is a prime time to test out newly learned coping skills, especially for those with problems falling asleep.

Trauma-informed coping skills are more than simple cognitive exercises like the classic thought-stopping. Trauma-informed coping skills are action oriented, which by their nature incorporate the body, or promote a holistic convergence of somatic, cognitive, and emotional/spiritual elements. There are literally thousands of books and training resources containing ideas about how to teach such coping skills to clients, and I've included some of my favorite recommendations at the end of this chapter. Covering all of the skills I use would exceed the scope of this book, so I have chosen to present this chapter in a summary format. I cover the major areas I believe need to be addressed in teaching coping—muscle relaxation, breathing, and multisensory grounding. I offer some thoughts on what makes each area vital and present summaries of my most popular skills in the chapter itself and in text boxes. If you are looking to expand your knowledge base and toolkit, check out the Further Reading section at the end of the chapter. I have used all of the books that I recommend, both personally and professionally, and believe they are valuable resources for any trauma-informed clinician's library.

Muscle Relaxation

One of my favorite "instant" coping strategies to teach clients is something I call Clench and Release. To optimally learn this exercise, I suggest that you try it yourself:

- Make fists.
- As you focus on your clenched fists, bring to mind something that stresses you out.
- As you reflect on the stressor, really notice the contraction of your muscles. Feel your fingernails dig into your skin if possible.
- Whenever it feels too uncomfortable for you to keep holding on, know that you can slowly, mindfully let go at any time.
- Notice your fingers uncurling, and feel the trickle of letting go all through your arms, up to your shoulders.
- Notice how good it feels to let go!

You can repeat this as many times as you need until you feel tension begin to release. This simple technique can be done with any muscle group (e.g., the abdominal muscles, muscles in the legs or feet) if fists are not an option. This simple technique is a modified, express version of a more involved technique, progressive muscle relaxation. In a full progressive muscle relaxation exercise, a person clenches and releases one muscle group at a time, slowly and deliberately. You could start with the left fist, clenching it for 20 to 30 seconds and then slowly gently letting it go. After taking a breath, you might move to the left forearm, clenching for another 20 to 30 seconds and then slowly, gently let it go. You repeat this process through the whole body, adding a bilateral variation if desired (e.g., begin with the left fist, then go to the right fist; proceed to the left forearm, then move to the right forearm).

Progressive muscle relaxation is one of the best techniques for promoting natural, restful sleep. For clients who struggle with falling asleep, I often devote a solid 20 minutes of a session to walking them through this exercise. I send other clients home with instructions on how to do it or provide them with a recording. Many clients have elected to record my voice on their phone as I walk them through the exercise. Hopefully, by the end of a progressive muscle relaxation experience, a person is well on his or her way to feeling more restful, or even ready to sleep. Adding another sensory component, such as soothing meditative music, white noise, or an essential oil/aromatherapy, can enhance the intended effect of the exercise.

I usually teach the modified Clench and Release to my clients at the end of an assessment session. Compared with some of the other skills I cover later in therapy, it is relatively easy to teach and learn. You can demonstrate it within the last few minutes of a session, and it is generally not as tricky to explain as breath work, nor is the potential for complications as high. So many clients come to me because they struggle with letting go of something. This exercise is a way to practice letting go with the whole body.

One of the benefits of the Clench and Release exercise is that it can be accessed virtually anywhere. You can be sitting at a 12-Step meeting or at your desk at work feeling agitated, and you can clench and release your fists a few times under the table to help release some of the muscle tension. If you are afraid that fists will draw too much attention, clench and release your feet. Obviously, doing a full-on 20-minute progressive muscle relaxation exercise is not feasible in most domains of life, so this simplified exercise helps you to access some of the benefits instantly. As someone who notoriously loses her patience with traffic and construction, I often use this exercise when I'm driving, clenching the steering wheel and then lightly (but not totally) releasing the grip. It's one of my favorite coping devices.

Breathing

Many people share with me that learning how to breath deeply and fully has been the key to healing from the aftereffects of trauma. Traumatic experiences quite literally take our breath away, and living in that state of chronic fight, flight, and freeze is like living with your breath held. Although we are generating enough air to stay alive, the fullness of its potential as a healing, enriching element of life gets stymied. Breath work is the ultimate bottom-up intervention when we look at the triune brain. Our ability to breathe is a reptilian function, a task of our most primitive brain. Thus, breathing fully, as we were created to breathe, offers the perfect gateway for whole brain healing.

The great Indian yogi B. K. S. Iyengar advised that the mind controls the body, but the breath controls the mind. This advice is perfect for both yoga teachers and helping professionals, as it emphasizes the vital importance of working with the breath. One of the axioms of cognitive-behavioral intervention is that to change the behavior, you must first change the thinking. As we explored in Chapter 4 on the brain, this is much easier said than done if the brain is riddled with the sequelae of trauma and thus is not working at its full potential. Iyengar's wisdom advises us that to change the thinking, we must first change the breath. Breath is an action-oriented intervention, and one of the principles of trauma-informed coping is that actions speak louder than words.

I rarely, if ever, let a client off the hook when it comes to using breath as a coping skill: That's how important it is for brain healing. Yes, some clients struggle with breathing, many for legitimate reasons. However, I find that these barriers, either real or perceived, can be worked with as part of stabilization. Please see the following text box for some time-tested strategies I've acquired and used with success over the years.

Tips for Dealing with Breathing Barriers: A Clinician's Guide

Client Comment/Resistance	Possible Clinical Response(s)
I just can't stay focused on my breath.	• "It's okay, a lot of people report they can't focus on the breath at first. Are you willing to give it a try again? Whenever you notice your mind start to wander, just notice that it's wandering and bring your attention back to your breath. Even if you have to do this 10 times a minute, just practice bringing the attention back to your breath. Breathing takes practice; it's normal not to get it right away." • Starting with an exhale or adding a count to the breath often helps people improve their focus. For others, music actually helps with staying focused on the breath.

(Continued)

Client Comment/Resistance	Possible Clinical Response(s)
Breathing just doesn't work for me.	• Engage the client in dialogue about how he or she has tried breathing in the past. From there, discuss how your approach to breathing may be different and see if the client is willing to try again. • There is likely a chance that, if a client has tried breathing before, he or she has given it less than a minute and given up if results didn't come quickly. Issue a three-minute challenge. Let the client know that you will breathe with him or her as encouragement (and modeling). • Encourage the client to pucker the mouth slightly on the exhale; this works with any breath to help enhance relaxation. Puckering the mouth directly stimulates the vagus nerve, and it's the same physiological mechanism accessed when babies nurse, people kiss, and yes, even when people smoke a cigarette. • Make sure that the exhales are longer than the inhales. People who report discomfort with breath are generally taking a longer inhale, which can make someone lightheaded or uncomfortable. • If a client has been exposed to clinical breath work in the past, it was most likely diaphragmatic breath. Consider teaching some of the other types of breathing, especially Ocean Breathing.

(Continued)

Client Comment/Resistance	Possible Clinical Response(s)
	• If a client still has a mental barrier to breathing, try a more direct body intervention like Clench and Release/ Progressive Muscle Relaxation. Suggesting this an alternative to breathing can make it more appealing, and as you're guiding a client through these exercises, you can insert gentle reminders about noticing the breath as the client moves or works the muscles.
I just can't relax when I breathe . . . it makes me more tense because I worry about whether I'm doing it right.	• Suggest that a client starts with an exhale. Starting with an exhale can create negative pressure on the lungs, so in contrast, taking the inhale automatically feels very relaxing. • One of Dr. Jon Kabat-Zinn's most famous teachings is that *if you are breathing, there is more right with you than wrong with you.* This wisdom serves as an excellent coaching statement for people with hang-ups about technique.
Getting that relaxed makes me nervous. I don't feel comfortable letting my guard down . . . what if someone sneaks up on me?	• Make sure the client knows that he or she does not have to close the eyes to do breath work. Closed eyes during breath work can increase trauma-related claustrophobic responses. • Take the breath work slowly and gradually. Start with just 1 or 2 breaths, and then have the client look around the room, perhaps repeating an affirmation, such as, "I'm here now, I'm safe." When the client feels ready, he or she can resume with deeper breathing. Remind the client that he or she can be aware of his or her surroundings while breathing and stop at any time.

(Continued)

Client Comment/Resistance	Possible Clinical Response(s)
I am prone to fainting spells. (Other medical reasons may also be given as reasons or concerns.)	• Get a release to correspond with the client's medical provider. This may help with the client's peace of mind and yours as well. • Take shorter sets (2 or 3 inhale-exhale repetitions) instead of more standard 5- or 6-breath sets and have the client check in with his or her body after each attempt. Learning to listen to the body is an important skill. • Begin with diaphragmatic (belly) breathing to see if the client tolerates the breath work before moving on to some of the exercises using fuller breathing.
Dissociating and *zoning out* is a problem for me. Breathing seems to make that worse.	• Take shorter sets, even if you are only taking one set of inhale-exhale at a time, then check back in. • Add another sensory element to the breath, even if it's holding on to a stone or using an aroma that keeps you present.

I have used breath work as a strategy with my clients since I first became a professional clinician; it's a critical part of being a trauma-informed counselor. However, since developing *Dancing Mindfulness* over the last few years and thus intensifying my own personal mindfulness practice, a critical insight emerged that I've translated into my work with clients: So many people struggle with breath work because we, as clinicians, jump right into the technique of breathing. People are much less likely to be harsh on themselves if we take a few minutes to have them simply notice the natural rise and fall of their breath as it is. Then, I introduce the simple encouragement that even if the mind wanders, it's alright—it's part of the process of learning how to do breath work! Sometimes, I even share with clients that I've been practicing breathing, yoga, and meditation for years and my mind still wanders! This diffuses people's tendencies to beat themselves up for "doing it wrong" and thus not being good enough.

There are hundreds of breathing techniques and variations a person can experiment with in learning how to use breath for stabilization. You can access these through the recommendations and resources listed at the end of this chapter. The three foundational breaths I am likely to teach all of my clients are diaphragmatic (i.e., belly) breathing, complete breathing, and *ujjayi* (ocean) breathing. The rationale for teaching the first two is simple: Fuller, healthier breaths originate in the gut, and shallower breaths originate in the chest. Diaphragmatic breathing teaches people how to use their abdominal region, controlled by the diaphragm, to help them achieve deeper breath. Complete breathing teaches that breathing with the chest isn't a bad thing; however, chest breathing becomes more beneficial when it originates with a diaphragmatic breath. For an explanation of both types of breathing, please see the following text box.

DIAPHRAGMATIC AND COMPLETE BREATHING

Diaphragmatic (i.e., Belly) Breathing

- Put one or both hands on the upper area of your stomach so that you can really pay attention to the motions of your diaphragm.
- As you inhale with your nose, allow your belly to expand as far as it will go.
- Exhale with your mouth, allowing the belly to pull back in.
- Continue this inhale-exhale pattern at your own pace for at least six or seven sets to find a rhythm and style that work for you.
- After finding your rhythm, consider puckering your mouth and really exaggerating your exhale, striving to make it somewhat longer than your inhale. This ought to help you relax even more.

Complete Breathing

- Begin with a diaphragmatic breath. Continue inhaling into the ribs and then the chest. You can put a hand on the chest to help with your awareness.
- At the top of inhale, bring your awareness to holding, or "cradling," the breath for a moment; this is a more meditative way to conceptualize holding your breath.
- Gradually release the breath with your exhale, allowing the chest, ribs, and belly to pull back in.
- Continue this inhale-exhale pattern at your own pace for at least six or seven sets to find a rhythm and style that work for you.
- As a variation, you can exhale quickly and suddenly, generating a "sigh of relief" experience.

Ujjayi (ocean) breathing is one of the best breath techniques to teach people who are stuck. *Ujjayi* is the Sanskrit yogic term for "ocean-sounding victory breath." For you movie buffs, think of Darth Vader's breathing— breathing in a vigorous way that may sound like the cinematic icon. There are two major reasons I like this technique in clinical work. First, yoga philosophy teaches that this breath is optimal for getting you out of a flight, flight, or freeze response. *Ujjayi* is naturally a very vigorous breath helps move some of that negative energy out of your body. I often advise my clients to step outside when they are able and take a couple of these breaths when they are feeling viscerally activated, It can feel like the body is somehow "resetting," like you've cleared out some negativity. Another reason I like to teach *ujjayi* is that the technique is different than the standard in-through-the-nose-out-through-the-mouth diaphragmatic or complete breathing, so it might be optimal for some clients who are reticent to try breathing because it didn't seem to work in the past.

Ujjayi (Ocean) Breathing

- This technique is different than the popular diaphragmatic and complete breathing techniques: You will be inhaling *and* exhaling through your nose.

- Inhale through your nose. Your belly ought to expand.

- Exhale through your nose. Although air may flow out of your mouth, think about doing the work with your nose.

- If you allow your throat to contract, you ought to hear a sound like the ocean.

- Attempt to keep the inhales and exhales even, especially while you're first learning this technique; eventually, work toward a longer exhale.

- Do not attempt more than five full sets during if you are new to this. It is more vigorous than other breathing techniques, and you may feel slightly lightheaded.

- It is completely normal to get lightheaded, but it should be a "good" lightheaded. If it does not feel good, chances are you tried too much too soon, or the inhales were longer than the exhales.

- For enhanced effect, pucker your mouth like you're sucking through a straw or about to kiss someone. Attempt to contract the back of your throat so it's slightly closed. Although there may be airflow through the mouth, remember that you are still doing the work with your nose.

Multisensory Grounding

Guided imagery exercises are one of the "greatest hits" of coping used by helping professionals. Although there is certainly a place for the use of guided imagery in trauma stabilization, with luminaries like Belleruth Naparstek using this modality as a primary approach, I want my clients and professionals that I train to start thinking in multisensory terms. Guided imagery and visualization exercises can be wonderful, but not everyone responds optimally to visual techniques. There are four other senses besides visualizing or sight, and I like to get clients thinking about how they can use all five senses to self-soothe in a healthful way and stay present.

Not all helping professionals are fans of guided imagery exercises, because they seem to promote dissociation as opposed to being present in the here and now. Some would argue that guided imagery can help with distress tolerance so a person can be in the here and now, and I have witnessed this with many clients. However, I do have concerns about the careless use of guided imagery out of context. For clients who are prone to dissociating in an unhealthy way or getting triggered unexpectedly (which describes the vast majority of trauma clients when they first start treatment), I try to use grounding strategies using the other senses first; for example, taking an object like a rock or a marble into the hand, rubbing it in the hands, and feeling the tactile sensation as an anchor to the present. This can work wonders to get a person back to the present if a guided imagery exercise results in dissociation or feels overwhelming. I use grounding objects in ways that are similar to how the totem was used in the hit movie *Inception*. Certain aromas and tastes can also serve a similar purpose. For instance, the smell or taste of peppermint alerts me and wakes me up to the present in a comforting way.

I highly advise creating a safe sensory anchor like the ones described before doing guided imagery work, especially for stabilization. I am also a fan of using simple guided imageries at first that don't necessarily "take a client to a place." Exercises such as Safe Place, Calm Place, and Happy Place are popular, but I rarely use these with clients in early stabilization. I think that they are usually more appropriate for reprocessing. Places can be emotionally charged: Many helpers go in with the good intention of helping a patient find his or her "happy place," but this can backfire. I have seen this happen many times with clients, such as with Claire.* In preparation for EMDR, Claire visualized going to the beach in her Safe Place exercise. For the first five minutes of the exercise, things seemed to be going well. I felt very optimistic because Claire chose the place and seemed excited about doing the exercise. Then, Claire visualized her young daughter showing up at the beach, and she started crying violently. Claire had lost custody of her daughter as a result of her own addiction and mental illness, and the last time she was actually at a beach, her daughter was with her.

At a later point in treatment, if Claire was more effectively stabilized, having such a reaction may have been productive. We could have used it for reprocessing. However, it was clear to me that she was not ready to go there, and she affirmed my suspicion when I asked her. Thus, I had to be creative and improvise in redirecting the exercise, bringing her Higher Power into the imagery to help calm her down. We also used breathing and grounding (e.g., pressing her feet against the ground, similar to Clench and Release) to make sure she was safe to leave the session.

After this experience with Claire and some others I witnessed or heard about going bad, I began using Light Stream (also called Color Stream) with clients when introducing guided imagery. I first learned this exercise during my EMDR training as a way to close sessions down, and I've picked up variations on it through my own mindfulness practice and yoga study. Because it is not connected to a place, this exercise tends to be less emotionally charged. You can read the full instructions on facilitating a Light Stream exercise in the following text box, and you can hear a recording of it on this book's website. Of course, use common sense. If a person's trauma was attached to a light, or if color was used in something like ritual mind control, proceed with caution. Having other grounding exercises using the other sensory modalities as a safety net is still advisable with this technique.

LIGHT STREAM GUIDED IMAGERY

- Imagine that a bright and healing light has begun to form overhead. This light can be whatever color you want it to be—whatever you associate with healing, happiness, goodness, or other positive qualities. If you don't like the idea of a light, you can think of it simply as a color or an essence.
- Now, think about this light beginning to move through your body or over your body (your choice), from the top of your head, moving inch by inch, until it reaches the bottom of your feet.
- If you want, you can think about this light grounding you safely into the earth.

(Continued)

- Spend a few moments just hanging out with the presence of this light or essence in your body. Notice if it has any other qualities besides color, such as a texture, a sound, or a smell.
- Draw your attention back to where you usually hold stress, tension, or craving in your body . . . what's happened to it?
- If the distress is still there on some level in your body, think about deepening your breathing so it makes the light or essence more brilliant and intense—so brilliant and intense that the distress can't even dream of existing within it.
- Keep practicing the exercise, keeping an attitude of patience if you don't notice much of a shift the first time.

There are several benefits to the Light Stream exercise. If a person develops a stream that works for him or her in stabilization, it can serve as a solid session closer. Helen,* the client introduced in Chapter 2, always used to alert me when it was time to go back to her "green light, " her chosen calming color, at the end of sessions. Another strength of the Light Stream exercise is that it can be nicely combined with other sensory modalities. For instance, a person can pair an empowering or calming piece of music with the light or color stream, or essential oils, such as soothing lavender or stimulating and balancing lemongrass, can be used to enhance the exercise.

Every sensory channel offers a modality through which relaxation, mindfulness, and empowerment can be accessed. All of the senses ought to be experimented with at the stabilization level so a client will discover what works best for him or her and in which contexts. With the sense of sound, using music is an obvious choice, whether it is making music or listening to music. I often assign my clients to make playlists for various needs: Calming, empowering, grounding, and spiritual connection are some of my favorite themes to suggest. Young people are nicely engaged by this exercise. However, other sound modalities like drumming, chanting, or even vibrational healing can be used. Amy Weintraub's *Yoga Skills for Therapists* and Susan Pease Banitt's *The Trauma Toolkit* are excellent resources for gathering more ideas. (See Further Reading at the end of this chapter.) Banitt's work is also a fantastic sourcebook for how aromatherapy can be beneficial in the treatment of trauma. She provides a detailed listing of how certain essential oils, herbs, and teas can help with various mood states. She extensively discusses ritualistic uses of smell for spiritual purposes, such as the practice of smudging in Native American traditions. When I attend drum circles and other ceremonies, I find the practice of smudging to be incredibly healing.

In my own clinical practice, I make extensive use of this sensory channel. I keep a drawer or basket full of scented candles, lotions, oils, and bags of herbs for the sake of experimentation. I have clients decide which smells are appealing to them and then make a note of whether the scent produces a calming or energizing response. In some cases, it's both. For instance, lavender is my go-to scent. Whenever I smell it, I immediately feel calmed and energized at the same time. For this reason, I carry a lavender essential oil roll-on in my bag at all times. When I'm feeling unfocused, overwhelmed, or just in need of something positive, I dig into my purse for my olfactory oasis. I've encouraged clients to find a portable scent to keep around the house, in the car, or on their person to access when they are feeling activated.

Tactile modalities, or those that use the sense of touch, can also be wonderfully portable. Exercises like Energetic Massage (see text box) or pressure point strategies derived from Eastern energetic healing can be remarkably helpful. I describe the major relaxation pressure points in *Trauma and the Twelve Steps*, and Linda Curran also covers these in both of her books. (See Further Reading at the end of the chapter.) Additionally, pairing a tactile object with a feeling state can be beneficial. During one of my own rounds of therapy, my counselor had one of those fuzzy stress balls in her office, and I routinely found that playing with it during our talk therapy kept me grounded and safe. One of my clients brought a blanket that her late grandmother knitted for her into session, and this was a resource she was able to access at home any time.

I advocate having a series of objects around your office of various textures so that clients can experiment with what works for them. Several years back, I found great success with having a tray of marbles on one of my tables. Marbles are fascinating objects for mindfulness and coping because they are intricately colorful, and they can feel good when you roll them around in your hands. Doing such an activity also promotes a natural, soothing bilateral stimulation with the hands. Many tapping techniques offer similar ways of accessing bilateral healing outside the context of EMDR. (See my book *Creative Mindfulness* and Laurel Parnell's *Tapping In* for more ideas.)

ENERGETIC MASSAGE

- Rub your hands together for at least thirty seconds (you can go longer if you want). Really work up some heat!
- Pull your hands apart and bring them to your forehead . . . there are many variations. You can close your eyes, and place the base of your palms over your eyes; let the rest of your hands curl over your forehead to the top of the forehead. Or you can rest the base of your palms on your cheeks and go around your eyes.
- Settle in, feel the energy you generated in your hands move into your brain. Let the energy work in you.
- Hold as long as you like.
- You can bring the energy from your hands to any part of your body that is feeling tense or anxious. Think about bringing the heat energy from your hands to your chest or stomach if you are noticing any tension or pain.
- The cranial hold position is an option after generating the energy. To achieve this, horizontally bring one hand to your forehead and the other hand to the back of your head.

Even the sense of taste can be used for soothing and grounding. I don't recommend mindlessly shoving 15 pounds of chocolate down your throat to self-soothe, although it's important to note that many trauma survivors do choose to cope in this not necessarily adaptive way. Sweets and carbohydrates offer the similar pleasure blast that drugs and alcohol afford to the limbic brain, one reason we tend to see overeating as a response to unresolved trauma. However, simple, mindful eating strategies are not only useful for coping or shutting down a session, but they can also help a survivor renegotiate his or her relationship with food. Consider how slowly unwrapping a peppermint or a piece of butterscotch, placing it on the tongue, and feeling a trickle move down the throat and into the rest of the body can create a sensation similar to that of the Light Stream exercise. Mindful eating is becoming an increasingly popular and useful approach for promoting weight loss and treating compulsive eating and other eating disorders. Several mindful eating resources are offered at the end of the chapter.

Mindfulness, as defined by Jon Kabat-Zinn, PhD (2004, 2011), is simply paying attention in the presence of the moment, nonjudgmentally, as if paying attention were your only job. Kabat-Zinn, founder of the wildly popular mindfulness-based stress reduction (MBSR) program for managing stress and illness, is the seminal figure in bringing the ancient practice of mindfulness into contemporary health care. A major inspiration I've drawn from his work is that any human activity can be engaged in mindfully—eating, walking, singing, dancing, jogging, stretching, lovemaking. Even something as simple as sipping water can be done mindfully, enhancing its impact in grounding and stabilizing a person. One of my favorite conceptualizations of mindfulness is the idea of slowing down activities that we normally do on autopilot. Even something as simple as getting up from a chair can seem hypnotically relaxing if we slow it down. Try it with anything!

In stabilization, I make sure to orient my clients to the meaning of mindfulness. Mindfulness is something that I think is necessary for a person to be able to understand and internalize. When a client is taught to be mindful during stabilization, he or she can use it when it's time to go further with trauma reprocessing, especially when it comes to ideas like "just noticing" something without judgment, a vital activity in reprocessing. Moreover, mindfulness promotes awareness of the self and the self's response, so a client used to practicing mindfulness is more likely to notice when he or she has gone too far with a reprocessing session and needs to come back to safety (e.g., a stabilization exercise, general conversation). Kabat-Zinn's work (see Further Reading at the end of this chapter) offers a wealth of ideas for practicing mindfulness in daily life.

IDENTIFYING STRENGTHS AND RESOURCES

There are many names in the literature for the art of using what is *good* in the treatment process. Some people like the term *strengths-based approach* or *Positive Psychology*. Others refer to *recovery capital* or *resources* in trauma work (e.g., anything organic or obtained in therapy that promotes recovery). Whatever term or approach you use, it is clear that highlighting a person's strengths constitutes a major part of trauma-informed counseling, especially at the stabilization level. The more wellness assets a person obtains at this level, the better equipped he or she will be for handling intense affect or emotional surprises during deeper work (i.e., reprocessing).

There is an art to identifying strengths and resources that can naturally flow from the therapeutic alliance. I've noticed that early in counseling, I've had to engage in many conversations with my clients about what constitutes healthy and unhealthy coping. The stronger the rapport we're able to build together, the more effective the conversation. One of the trickiest nuances of this art is getting a client to consider how something he or she has always identified as healthy or adaptive may, on some level, be unhealthy or maladaptive. Discussing the importance of family support often elicits such discussions. On one hand, many patients view their family as supportive. However, you as the helper may see patterns like enabling or codependency in those dynamics that are not optimal for the patient's health and wellness. Another fine-line distinction comes when evaluating the usefulness of hobbies or activities as resources. For instance, physical exercise is generally viewed as a productive, healthy pursuit, yet for some people, it can get taken to an unhealthy extreme or used in unhealthy ways. There is such as thing as exercise anorexia, or exercising to an unhealthy extreme for the purpose of weight loss or deprivation. Adam Lamparello's *Ten Mile Morning* is a touching memoir that explains this phenomenon in the context of his eating disorder.

Performer and drama therapist Liz Rubino, introduced in Chapter 5, explained that when she was in high school, the arts were an escape. A survivor of multilayered childhood trauma, she also dealt with numerous struggles surrounding her sexuality. As she explained to me, the arts became a passion rather than an escape after some much needed emotional work allowed her to realize how she used them in the past. Even though they helped her to cope during a very difficult time in her life, being in escape mode kept her from truly looking at herself and healing.

Any activity, physical or spiritual, that promotes getting up and *doing* instead of just dwelling on the problems of life should be considered a strength, as long as it serves the person and does no harm to others in the person's pursuit of wellness. Liz's story demonstrates just how powerful any of the creative arts can be in this process. When a person chooses to sing, dance, write, draw, paint, sculpt, make movies, play an instrument, or craft, the lower levels of the brain are engaged, and the potential exists for him or her to make powerful connections between self and the world. Some people in trauma recovery find these outlets for the first time. Others reconnect with creative channels in new ways through recovery. For instance, I grew up as a musician and a dancer, generally resenting these art forms because my techniques were "never good enough." Thus, I internalized that I wasn't good enough to call myself a musician or a dancer. Encountering these arts once again through the lens of recovery and wellness served as a reorientation to activities that I really love—activities that are clearly wellness resources.

Many forms of physical activity and exercise can be healing. I encourage my clients to find a form of physical activity and exercise they can passionately enjoy, not something that they feel required to do to lose weight or look a certain way. This is why I am a major fan of yoga and other Eastern practices, such as Tai Chi, Qi Gong, and other martial arts; their emphasis is on the process, not the outcome. I feel that these practices are wonderful ways for a trauma survivor to reorient himself or herself to exercise and body awareness. As helpers, it is our job to know what resources are available in our community in these wellness domains. For instance, I maintain relationships with several yoga studios in my area that offer come-as-you-are, affordable classes for people at all levels of fitness; thus, I have a good sense of where to refer people. Having awareness about the wellness resources in your community and fostering those connections promotes quality of care.

Silver Linings Playbook, one of the cinema hits of 2012, offers many powerful lessons about mental illness. The protagonist, Pat Solitano, Jr., recently released from a long-term hospitalization for bipolar illness, was befriended by recovering sex addict Tiffany Maxwell. She wanted to win a ballroom dancing competition and needed a partner. Every day, Tiffany and Pat practiced diligently. This became a positive development for the previously aimless, obsessed-with-his-ex-wife Pat. When Pat had a relapse in his symptoms and swore off dancing, his mother Dolores was distraught. She delivered a line about recovery that was right on: "The dancing gave him something constructive to do." I adored Dolores' use of the word *constructive*, because ultimately, we as clinicians are helping clients identify constructive uses of their time and resources during stabilization.

Hobbies support recovery. As with exercise, we must have careful conversations with our clients about whether their hobbies are helping or hindering recovery. For instance, I have seen working in advocacy function as a constructive, healthy outlet for many, such as Heather Bowser with her causes connected to Agent Orange survivors and children of Vietnam veterans. However, I have also seen people become so consumed with advocacy work, it ends up becoming more of a stress than a benefit. Think of how many people you may have encountered who are gung ho in their service commitments to 12-Step or other recovery groups, only to relapse because they fail to take care of themselves.

There is a balance to utilizing hobbies and other resources that we can help clients recognize as part of stabilization. Journaling is one activity for which I am careful to promote balance. I am a big fan of journaling. I've benefitted from it myself at various times in my recovery, and I've seen clients derive tremendous benefits from it. However, I find it necessary to caution clients that if journaling takes them to a dark place they are not ready to handle, they should step back and try another skill. Like one of my yoga teachers says, although yoga is designed to challenge you, it shouldn't hurt. I feel the same way about journaling and many other activities that have the potential to be intense.

When it comes to physical activities and hobbies, some clients may need help finding resources. Living in a rather economically depressed area, I routinely hear from clients, "There's nothing to do in this town." Therefore, I engage in a little of what I call *Metro Monthly* therapy. The *Metro Monthly* is a free publication in my hometown that can easily be picked up at places like gas stations and grocery stores. Many cities have such a publication. I encourage clients to take a *Metro Monthly* and highlight everything they see that is affordable and interesting to them. People are generally surprised at how much there is to do.

Having a pet is helpful to many people. Caring for the needs of an animal that will love you unconditionally is phenomenally healing. I experienced this when I was a graduate student. On returning to the United States from Bosnia, I lived with my ailing grandfather for a year, and after he died, one of my graduate school mentors was concerned that I would do something crazy in my loneliness, such as relapse or get into an unhealthy relationship. This mentor, an avid cat rescuer, suggested that I take one of her cats. Having grown up in a household without pets, I didn't think I was capable of caring for this little creature. My mentor encouraged me to take the kitty, whom I named Joy, home for a week to see if we were a good fit. Needless to say, I fell in love. Not only has Joy become part of my heart and my family, she was therapeutic for me during that difficult time and continues to serve a healing role. She gets me out of my own head every day. I've seen our dog, Scrappy, do the same thing for my husband, David. I was reticent to get a dog because of my husband's physical issues. Happily, I have been proven wrong. Scrappy is the best nurse we could ever ask for, and he provides David with a sense of purpose that is so magical, I don't think I can describe it in words. If you're an animal person, you know what I'm talking about!

Religion, spirituality, and spiritual practices are another resource that can be extremely beneficial to those recovering from trauma. For a variety of reasons, these are also areas that can be taken to unhealthy extremes and may serve as triggers. Many trauma survivors experienced a great deal of hurt at the hands of God or religion, which is why spiritual interventions ought never be forced on them. However, if a patient wants to renegotiate his or her idea of spirituality, it is certainly the clinician's place to support this and to help the patient do it in a healthy way. For instance, I get concerned when a person flips from having no faith to being a religious extremist overnight. I grow more concerned when this newly discovered zeal causes the client to start putting others down, so addressing these phenomena, when they happen, provides grist for the clinical mill.

As a very spiritual person, my feelings in this area are perhaps biased. Of course, I do not force exploration of spirituality on a client because this can be traumatic. However, I am all about promoting spiritual connection, especially when trauma can result from spiritual injury or religious systems. As Danyell,* a survivor of spiritual and emotional abuse whose case I presented in *EMDR Made Simple*, expressed during her treatment, "Everything about me wants to be spiritual; I just associate it with religion, and I shut down." Thus, my job became helping her to find a sense of spirituality that served her in her own time.

My approach is likely to garner criticism from both the staunch atheists and those who are devoted to a certain faith tradition. Feel free to tailor your approach based on where you work and your style—just never let your own agenda tarnish a client's goals for healing. (More on this in Chapter 12.) Even if deistic spirituality is something that doesn't work for you as a clinician or for your clients, I encourage you to at least consider the power of connection as a healing resource.

Many individuals in 12-Step groups who can't subscribe to the idea of God or a supreme being end up viewing the fellowship itself as their Higher Power or guide. A non–12-Step way to look at this concept is to consider the power of a support system. Without hesitation, I share that the most successful addiction and mental health recovery cases I've seen are those in which the clients had or learned to develop a solid support system. This doesn't mean that scores of people in a client's corner are required, and it certainly doesn't mean that the client needs to solicit the opinions of all of the people in his or her life. Quality is more important than quantity: I've seen patients who have the illusion of a support system—superficial friends and family members who only give lip service to their well being—and this is generally insufficient.

In general, people who enter services having and using a solid support system (e.g., actually calling or visiting support figures when distressed) tend to fare better with deeper levels of trauma work. The absence of a strong support system doesn't necessarily rule out your doing second-stage reprocessing work with a client. It does, however, mean that you will need to spend more time helping that client evaluate his or her existing support system and possibly rebuilding it. I know this is easier said than done, especially with clients whose only sources of support seem to be unhealthy people. However, I have seen patients start with just having a case manager and me as a support system and being able to identify healthier people in their community or check out a 12-Step group, a church group, or another community setting to build better connections.

A question of debate today is whether web-based connectedness via social media platforms is genuine and healthy. My essential conclusion is that it depends on how this technology is used; this is where we, as helpers, can help a client make critical evaluations. My former client Helen* readily admitted that she preferred Facebook for her social interactions because she could take on a different persona and interact with people without opening herself up to getting hurt. Clearly, this was an issue we had to evaluate in treatment. Our essential conclusion was that while certain uses of the computer served as a coping life raft of sorts (e.g., playing a game to get her through emotional outbursts), she needed to constantly evaluate her use of online connections for whether they were healthy.

In other cases, I have seen tremendous social connections made via technology. David and I met online, and many people whom I now consider to be close friends and colleagues, originally connected with me through social media groups. The distinguishing factor is that the technology was used as a vehicle to, not a replacement for, genuine human interaction. Engaging clients in discussions about the difference can be vital during the stabilization phase of counseling.

KEY ATTITUDES AND IDEAS

There are several important conversations during the stabilization phase that help collectively identify both subtle resources and any impediments to healing. For instance, motivation is a resource. It doesn't matter whether that motivation is largely internal (e.g., determination, willingness, the hope for a better future) or external (e.g., "I'm doing this for my kids," "I'm doing this so that I can keep a job"). As long as the motivation can be used in the treatment process, especially to keep it moving forward, it is a resource. From my experience, many clients present for counseling with a combination of internal and external motivations. One of the great misconceptions is that external motivation is somehow inferior to internal motivation, but my experience is that both are valuable (and a body of research in the addiction field concurs). Whatever gets a client in the door and keeps him or her engaged is useful.

A conversation about motivation must include a discussion of secondary gains, especially if the client's goal is to engage in deeper work at the reprocessing level. In sum, secondary gains are what a client gets out of staying "sick" or otherwise stuck in their trauma. Secondary gains can be tangible (e.g., a disability check) or intangible (e.g., an excuse for bad behavior, attention). Many clinicians, including myself, find it difficult to work with clients who continue to identify with the victim role and use their PTSD or trauma as an excuse when it's convenient. This problem is not unique to PTSD; it happens with other mental health and addiction issues as well. If secondary gains issues are manifesting, it is important to address them within the context of the therapeutic relationship early in treatment.

I have seen matters get worse if a person engages in reprocessing-level work unaware of secondary gains. Like Dr. David Ohlms experienced in his early work with addicts (see Chapter 6), delving into emotional issues with someone lacking a recovery or wellness focus can be disastrous. Such work can give a patient more excuses! One of television's most iconic therapy "patients," mob boss Tony Soprano of *The Sopranos*, epitomized such a dynamic. Although Tony experienced legitimate trauma as a child growing up in a culture of violence, it took his psychiatrist, Dr. Melfi, six years to realize that because he had no intention of changing his criminal lifestyle, dredging up and analyzing his past trauma was arguably making him worse. She even made a connection, prompted by a colleague, that Tony might have been using the emotional container of therapy as a venue for practicing his manipulation skills, a phenomenon that is now known as an empathy trap.

Another issue that could negatively affect a patient is if he or she goes into therapy without considering the consequences of making a positive change. Even progress can come with consequences, especially if a patient is living in an unhealthy system. The most common scenario in which I see this play out is when women come to me to work on issues of childhood sexual abuse. If a female client is in an unhealthy or abusive relationship, I must alert her that working on her early issues may cause a shift in the dynamic with her current partner. It is unfair, I believe, to take a patient by surprise. Many women state that they want the relationship dynamic to change, perhaps even becoming empowered to leave, whereas others need a longer period in stabilization to evaluate all of their options.

Whereas conversations about secondary gains and possible consequences of engaging in therapy can be difficult, they typically prove beneficial to the overall counseling process. Another difficult issue to address is the client's feelings toward acceptance. Acceptance has generated major buzz in the helping professions in recent years, especially with the popularity of dialectical behavioral therapy (DBT) and one of its skills, radical acceptance. Moreover, one of the new-wave cognitive approaches bears the word *acceptance* in the title: Acceptance and Commitment Therapy (ACT). The book *Alcoholics Anonymous*, first published in 1939, contains a line that is still highly regarded in 12-Step recovery: "And acceptance is the answer to *all* my problems today." One of the attitudes of regular mindfulness practice is acceptance.

Although the benefits of acceptance, both therapeutically and spiritually, are well documented, we must consider how difficult practicing acceptance can be for someone with unaddressed trauma. Many survivors believe that accepting something means that they are endorsing what happened to them. Very early in treatment, I introduce the idea that accepting something does not mean you have to like it. It simply means that you acknowledge something "is what it is." You can accept that your mother is a certain way and will likely not change, and as a result, all you can change is your own behaviors and reactions. You can accept that you lived through a hurricane. Of course, that doesn't mean you have to like it. You are simply claiming the truth that it happened to you, which could create a gateway for moving on. Acknowledging that you grew up in an unhealthy system where a great deal of trauma bonding took place with your family of origin does not mean that you automatically dismiss or forgive the dynamic. However, for many, the acknowledgment and owning of the reality is a vital step forward.

Many trauma survivors ask me if they need to forgive in order to move on. To me, forgiveness is more of a spiritual construct than a clinical one, so my feelings are mixed. I think that forgiveness can be a powerful pathway to healing for many, but I don't believe that giving lip service to forgiveness is very effective. To truly forgive, you need to work through the buried pain and emotion. Many clients are relieved to hear that they don't need to forgive to get better. I've seen many clients carry great shame around their inability to forgive. I maintain that acceptance is more critical than forgiveness. You may never forgive a person for what he or she did to you, but to move forward, it is vital to accept the reality of what happened as part of your story. Acceptance yields empowerment— empowerment to do something about changing your present and future.

Empowerment is another concept to which we give lip service in the helping professions without really stopping to consider what it means. In my previous books, I wrote about the importance of imparting hope and believing in the client's potential to change, as well as using the word *survivor* instead of *victim* in working with clients. Although I still believe these ideas to be true, my insights about empowerment and what it means continue to grow and to evolve. To me, empowerment means giving people a choice. One way to look at this is coaching a person to see that he or she has a choice about what to do with his or her present life, even though the past was horrible. As we've discussed throughout the book, this can be easier said than done, especially when we consider how unresolved trauma responses can shut down the part of the brain that has to do with rational thinking.

Thus, it's our job to offer choices so that clients can practice making them. Honoring a client's preferences and goals for treatment—giving him or her choices in the matter—is the most significant way that we can put this practice into action. I never tell a patient who comes in for services that we have to do things a certain way with a certain therapy. Of course, I give him or her my recommendations, but I always give the patient a choice in how we approach treatment. In the following chapter on trauma processing modalities and the hundreds of choices available for doing this work, I emphasize the significance of this idea of offering choice. Consider, however, that offering choice begins in stabilization, even if it's something as simple as promoting a trial-and-error approach to coping skill development instead of imposing your plans for wellness on the client. Fostering choice at every juncture is imperative to trauma-informed treatment.

Most of the trauma survivors interviewed for this book indicate that keeping or developing a sense of humor is imperative to survival and ultimately to healing. For some people, this comes naturally; for others, it is a process. For many of the clients I've treated, arriving at the balance of using humor in a healthy way, instead of to deflect emotional response, is a vital part of stabilization.

During the height of the Bosnian war, a group of journalists based in Sarajevo used their collective senses of humor to ride out the siege by authoring what they called *Sarajevo Survival Guide* (Prstojevic, et al, 1993). Written like a Lonely Planet tourist guide, the book's tongue-and-cheek tone offers tips on surviving day-to-day life during the siege. In the concluding pages of this classic, they offer insight on surviving the siege, emphasizing the importance of humor, practicality, and keeping emotions in check:

> When you come to Sarajevo, be prepared and be mature. It might prove to be the most important decision you ever made in your life. . . . You should know when to skip a meal, how to turn trouble into a joke and be relaxed in impossible moments . . . Give up your former habits. Use the telephone when it works, laugh when it doesn't. You'll laugh a lot. Despise, don't hate.

Issues to Consider Before Going Further

There is no perfect science in determining when to segue from stabilization (Phase I) into reprocessing (Phase II). Some people are well stabilized when they present for treatment, so you may be able to move into the trauma reprocessing rather quickly. Others may need to learn the basics of stabilization and coping from scratch. This list is not meant to be a hard and fast checklist because, like many aspects of trauma counseling, stabilization must be assessed through qualitative rather than quantitative means. Think quality of stabilization over quantity. Consider asking yourself the following to help determine whether you and the client can collectively move into reprocessing work:

- Does the client have a reasonable number of coping skills to access?
- Is there a sufficient amount of *positive* material in the client's life?
- Is the client willing (and ready) to look at past issues?
- Does the client have a healthy understanding about the role of psychotropic medications in recovery (e.g., medications are not going to "fix" them, but can support the process)? If the client is on psychotropic medications, are they stable?
- Have you assessed for secondary gains?
- Have you evaluated the number of sessions or time frame in which to work with the client?
- Is the client living in a reasonably safe environment that supports recovery?
- Have you checked your own issues or biases surrounding the client and his or her trauma to optimally support him or her going further?

Further Reading

Baranowsky, A.B., Gentry, J.E., & Schultz, D.F. (2010). *Trauma practice: Tools for stabilization and recovery.* Boston, MA: Hogrefe Publishing.

Curran, L. (2010). *Trauma competency: A clinician's guide.* Eau Claire, WI: PESI, LLC.

Curran, J. (2013). *101 trauma-informed interventions: Activities, exercises, and assignments to move the client and therapy forward.* Eau Claire, WI: Premiere Education & Media.

Hanh, T. K. & Cheung, L. (2011). *Savor: mindful eating, mindful life.* New York: Harper One.

Hawk, K. (2012). *Yoga and the twelve-step path.* Las Vegas, NV: Central Recovery Press.

Light Stream Guided Meditation led by Dr. Jamie Marich, available: http://www.traumamadesimple.com/audio-extras.html.

Marich, J. (2013). *Creative mindfulness: 20+ strategies for recovery and wellness.* Warren, OH: Mindful Ohio.

Naparstek, B. (2004). *Invisible heroes: Survivors of trauma and how they heal.* New York: Bantam Books.

Parnell, L. (2008). *Tapping in: A step-by-step guide to activating your healing resources through bilateral stimulation.* Louisville, CO: Sounds True Books.

Pease Bannit, S. (2012). *The trauma toolkit: Healing PTSD from the inside out.* Wheaton, IL: Quest Books.

Progressive Muscle Relaxation Guided Meditation led by Dr. Jamie Marich, available: http://www.traumamadesimple.com/audio-extras.html.

Prstojevic, M., Razovic, M., & Wagner, A. (1993). *Sarajevo survival guide.* Sarajevo, Bosnia-Hercegovina: FAMA.

Three Breathing Exercises by Dr. Andrew Weil, available: http://www.drweil.com/drw/u/ART00521/three-breathing-exercises.html.

Weintraub, A. (2012). *Yoga skills for therapists: Effective practices for mood management.* New York: W.W. Norton.

CHAPTER 10

Trauma Treatment: Reprocessing

Everybody has won and all must have prizes.

—The Dodo Bird's verdict, *Alice in Wonderland*

FUNDAMENTALISM AND OUR FIELD

Not too long ago, I presented a conference keynote on EMDR therapy. EMDR is the approach to psychotherapy with which I am most identified, because it is my primary clinical specialty, and I've written extensively on it. A gentleman many years my senior approached me after the presentation to tell me about the great success he's experienced using Somatic Experiencing®, a therapy whose premise makes sense to me, although I've never been formally trained in it. He declared that while EMDR sounds like "good stuff," it is very simple to learn, compared with the intricacies and nuances of being a Somatic Experiencing® practitioner. He surmised that he could pick up a book on EMDR and learn to do it in a night, whereas training in Somatic Experiencing® takes three years of intense study to really get it right. While I meant no disrespect to him, I laughed at his comments and shared that I've heard EMDR colleagues make similar claims about EMDR—to do it right, it takes years and years of study and practice within a regimented model. In contrast, these same colleagues have dismissed Somatic Experiencing® as a simple technique that is really just EMDR without the bilateral stimulation and with more direct movement.

Herein lies the problem with our approaches to treating trauma— everyone believes his or her school of thought has it *right*. I most dreaded writing this chapter because of that reality. Inevitably, there will be camps that think I've done this chapter on trauma processing a disservice because I left out their approach or didn't give it adequate attention. I hear these protests at trainings all the time. After I talk about trauma processing and other material you will be reading in this chapter, arguing that there is no clear-cut "best" modality, people come up to me in a fury. Yes, I tend to focus on the therapies I know best—EMDR, Gestalt, Trauma-Focused CBT, mindfulness-informed interventions, Narrative Therapy, and the expressive arts. People say things to me like, "I just got trained in Hakomi. And it is far and away better than anything you talked about," "Why didn't you give Life Span Integration therapy more attention?" or "What about Internal Family Systems (IFS)? This is great stuff that finally makes sense." A colleague from graduate school even posted something on Facebook that made me chuckle. She commented, "Nothing else besides (insert her model of choice here) works for trauma, and if you're not doing it, you're missing the boat."

I've heard talk like this before, growing up in two highly dogmatic churches. For those of you who haven't read *EMDR Made Simple*, let me give you some backstory. I was born to two Catholic parents, and when I was five years old, a late-night televangelist converted my father. Soon thereafter, he joined an extremely fundamentalist, charismatic church where the message at each service was how "right" this specific church's interpretation of the Bible was and how "wrong" all others were. My father made no qualms about publically declaring that my mother and all of her Catholic relatives were going to hell unless they repented, got saved, and joined the true church—his church. All the while, my mother remained a devout Roman Catholic.

My brother and I went to both churches for many years to keep both parents happy. Although this experience came with some spiritual trauma, it also made me incredibly diplomatic and open minded. Even as a child, it struck me as odd that any church's primary message would be fear based, with so much energy focused on what made the other party "wrong" instead of focusing on what it had to offer. My brother ended up committing to Catholicism at age 14, and as I was seeking paths of recovery in my early twenties, I also decided to focus on Catholicism. While spending a great deal of time in very conservative facets of the Catholic Church (such as working for a Catholic parish while in Bosnia-Hercegovina), I saw how there was war within the Catholic church over which faction was "right:" the more liberally minded parishes and thinkers or those that could best be described as old-school traditionalists.

When I entered graduate school and ultimately began working in the field, I was amused by how much this dynamic plays out in the helping professions. Theoretical School A believes that it has the market cornered on the truth of what works in helping others. Meanwhile, a flood of people who left Theoretical School A because they did not feel sufficiently helped formed

Theoretical School B and now shout from the rooftops why their approach is the new answer. Theoretical School C has a totally different approach and a loyal group of followers, and so on. There are literally thousands of approaches, theories, models, and modalities to explain human distress and provide a structure for how to treat it, just as there are tens of thousands of religious denominations in Christianity alone! I am not saying that having variety and choice is a bad thing, either in religion or in psychotherapy. What concerns me now is what concerned me as a child sitting in my father's fundamentalist church: putting down other approaches to promote the superiority of your own, when all of them are really paths to the same destination.

Dr. Saul Rosenzweig (1936), whose work I introduced in Chapter 7, voiced concerns about the "religious" nature of psychotherapy as far back as the 1930s! The variety of therapeutic approaches available in the thirties was more limited than in the present, but Rosenzweig held even firmer with his original contention, even as the field spawned new theories, models, techniques, and approaches. In a 2000 interview with Dr. Barry Duncan, Rosenzweig, shortly before his death, surmised, "Psychotherapy models and their followers are more like cults: charismatic leaders with legions of worshippers" (Duncan et al., 2009, p. 16). I completely agree with Rosenzweig, and this is a major reason why I had difficulty immersing myself in the EMDR community even though I got trained in it at the highest levels. The "Francine Shapiro worship" concerned me. To be clear, I don't mean this as a slam against her specifically. I've seen the "putting the founder on the pedestal" phenomenon with all other schools of therapy I studied. I don't even think that the problem is having a charismatic leader who can inspire those who believe in the work; the problem is the elitism that certain approaches proclaim and the degradation of other approaches. This is when our field looks like a dogmatic religion.

As far back as the 1930s, Rosenzweig proposed what we now call the dodo bird verdict, deriving from the classic quote in Lewis Carroll's *Alice and Wonderland* that opens this chapter. Rosenzweig asserted that all approaches or models that are intended to be therapeutic have merit; they all have the potential to work as long as a series of implicit or common factors are present:

- The client and his or her extra-therapeutic factors (e.g., what a client brings to the table in therapy and situations out of the control of the clinician)
- Models and techniques that work to engage and to inspire the participants
- The therapeutic relationship/alliance

- Therapist factors (e.g., training/competence, belief that a therapy will work, ability to work through countertransference)

One of the most comprehensive reviews of psychotherapy literature is the American Psychological Association (APA)–published volume *The Heart and Soul of Change: Delivering What Works in Therapy.* If you have any interest in psychotherapy research, this book is compulsory reading. The editors, Drs. Barry Duncan, Scott Miller, Bruce Wampold, and Mark Hubbell, prove that the common factors are the most "evidenced-based" idea ever proposed, as literature reviews and meta-analyses continue to demonstrate that these four factors, especially when working in concert, are the most likely agents of change. The editors explain the interplay as such:

> We conclude that what happens (when a client is confronting negative schema, addressing family boundaries, or interpreting transference) is less important than the degree to which any particular activity is consistent with the therapist's beliefs and values (allegiances) while concurrently fostering the client's hope (expectations). Allegiance and expectancy are two sides of the same coin: the faith of both the therapist and the client in the restorative power and credibility of the therapy's rationale and related rituals. Though rarely viewed this way, models and techniques work best when they engage and inspire the participants (p. 37).

I believe that the phrase "models and techniques that work to engage and to inspire the participants" is the most brilliant line in all of psychotherapy literature. Those of us who believe in the merit of the common factors are not opposed to model or technique, but we believe that if the client isn't buying what you as the therapist is selling, you'd better switch things up! Staying true to your specific approach out of stubborn, even dogmatic loyalty will not work with traumatized clients; you need flexibility to meet people where they are (Charman, 2005). This may entail trying several different techniques or approaches or blending some of your existing competencies. In short, if the client isn't inspired by the therapy, if the client doesn't have hope that what you're doing will help him or her to get better, it will likely not be a success.

I am a fan of growth in the field; I support the development of new models and techniques that may help a person who has been previously frustrated with therapy to become engaged. However, I think that we as a field, especially as trauma-informed counselors, are wasting our time in the search to find the ideal therapy for treating trauma. The recovering fundamentalist in me simultaneously laughs and cringes every time I see a workshop on a specific technique billed as the latest, greatest, most researched-based approach that will be the panacea to cure the pandemic of trauma worldwide. I get even more amused when such approaches proclaim to do this healing work rapidly, instantly, or painlessly. The reality of wounding, both physical and mental, is that wounds take time, effort, and usually a little discomfort to heal. I fully acknowledge that certain newer approaches have found ways to help people reprocess trauma with less affective intensity and distress, but the idea of completely painless trauma resolution does not resonate. Moreover, what I know from being human is that no two people heal in exactly the same way. While certain approaches may be very effective for most, no one therapy will serve as the cure-all. Thus, our efforts at the preprocessing level must be focused on finding a model and approach that are the best fit for the client in question.

Many of you may be asking, "What does the research say?" This is a valid question, especially when policymakers, insurance companies, and professional organizations have been shoving that phrase "evidence-based practice" down our throats. The way I've seen advocates of a certain approach use research in the modern era is similar to the way religious fanatics use the Bible or other sacred texts—they cherry-pick the verses (or, in this case, studies) they want and don't look at the big picture. Leaders in our field are notorious for finding five or six studies that support their position and another few studies that negate the other's position without looking at the totality of research. Additionally, many ordinary clinicians who have research presented by teachers and leaders as gospel truth don't realize the politically charged climate of research and how peer-reviewed journals are run.

After many years of experience submitting to peer-reviewed journals, my general impression is that the peers doing the reviewing are largely academic in their orientations. Although there is a place for academic study of psychotherapy, the intense academic focus of research makes it less likely for ordinary clinicians on the front line to engage in research. My experience also reveals that a bias against qualitative research exists amongst peer-reviewed journals in our continued efforts to "scientifically" legitimize what we are doing. Yet, so much of what we are asked to do clinically is qualitative in nature, and nonacademic clinicians are much more likely to follow and comprehend the flow and findings of a qualitative study (Reisetter et al., 2004).

Many problems exist when it comes to taking published research at face value. There are many methodologically solid *quantitative* studies that don't get published each year because they don't demonstrate statistically significant findings. Essentially, they affirm a status quo or fail to demonstrate that some radical, new twist is any better (Duncan et al., 2009). One can only wonder how many pieces of good research or research ideas have never seen the light of day. Consider that there are many solid clinicians around the country who have phenomenal ideas for research, but because they can't procure funding, the research goes undone. Speaking strictly for myself (and I know I'm not alone), I have tons of great research ideas, but I'd rather spend my time actually working with clients or doing community outreach instead of doing research that may or may not get published. To be honest, since I'm not affiliated with a university, doing research takes away from time spent on projects that will pay the mortgage and feed my family.

I recommend reading meta-analytic studies. A meta-analysis is a statistical research design that looks at several studies, combining and contrasting methodologies in an attempt to observe patterns and effect sizes to make broader conclusions. Of course, meta-analyses can be flawed, especially because researchers set criteria for what gets included and what doesn't in the studies, and researchers are fallible. However, overall, they are the best studies available when attempting to arrive at conclusions about what "the literature" really says.

There are several major research teams conducting meta-analyses on PTSD, two of which continue to go back and forth about which researchers are conducting them correctly. An often-cited meta-analysis comes from Bisson and Andrew (2007) of the Cochrane Collaboration in the United Kingdom. In examining 30 studies over an eight-year period (1996–2004), they found that *trauma-oriented* PTSD treatments were far superior to *coping skill–only* PTSD treatments. Essentially, those treatments that helped the patient go back to the past and reprocess unresolved hurts were more effective than those that kept him or her in stabilization. Past-oriented or trauma-oriented treatments can include Trauma-Focused CBT, exposure therapy, hypnosis, or EMDR; however, there were no major effect sizes among these different modalities. No clear-cut leader emerged.

Another major PTSD meta-analysis (Benish, Imel, & Wampold, 2008) revealed similar findings, in that no modality emerged as clearly being best. This meta-analysis examined all studies on *bona fide* treatments for PTSD that compared two or more treatment interventions (e.g., desensitization, hypnotherapy, psychological debriefing, trauma treatment protocol, EMDR, stress inoculation, exposure, cognitive, present centered, prolonged exposure, Thought Field Therapy, imaginal exposure) conducted between 1989 and 2007. The authors found no statistical significance in effect size among the treatments. They ultimately concluded that although there is strong evidence that the treatments studied work for PTSD compared with no treatment, *no one therapy should be considered the only option for PTSD clients*. Thus, according to Benish and colleagues, "Having several psychotherapies to choose from may enable a better match of patients to type of psychotherapy that fits the patient's worldview and is more tolerable to that particular patient" (pp. 755–756). Of note, one of the therapies examined in this meta-analysis, present-centered therapy, represented the control group condition in a major research study conducted by Dr. Edna Foa and her team. Present-centered therapy is essentially void of specific techniques: It means creating a supportive container for change and focusing on current life concerns. As demonstrated in the meta-analysis, present-centered therapy can work just as well as other, more sophisticated approaches.

Although the meta-analysis by Benish and associates (2008) is not without its critics, specifically over what constitutes a *bona fide* treatment (Ehlers et al., 2010), their conclusion resonates with clinicians who do not believe in a one-size-fits-all approach to therapy. Benish and colleagues and other meta-analytic scholars (Ehlers and others related to the 2010 response) go back and forth in their findings, which, to me, reflects the larger, impassioned discussion about what works in the treatment of PTSD. For me, as a qualitatively minded clinician and researcher, this back and forth shows that quantitative science doesn't hold all of the answers, since imperfect human beings with their biases and proclivities are the ones designing the research. Dr. Scott Miller, who I see as one of the major voices of reason in the field of psychotherapy today, publically shares that he and his research associates have received hateful letters about the findings of their meta-analytic research. Considering the connections that I readily make between religion and psychotherapy, Miller's having this experience doesn't surprise me.

Although I see errors and subtle biases in the meta-analyses of both Benish and colleagues (2008) and Bisson and Andrew (2007), both demonstrate that we, as clinicians, have choices in how we treat PTSD. **The key is not finding the perfect treatment; it is finding the right fit for each client.** To parallel, in my own spiritual journey, I abandoned organized religion several years ago and currently practice a very integrated spirituality. Although I still identify as a Christian, many Buddhist practices sustain me, and I connect with the god of my understanding through many other channels, such as nature and in my work with people. Of course, the people with whom I grew up in both the fundamentalist church and the Catholic church might now label me as aimless and wishy-washy, but that is of little concern to me. I've found an integrative spiritual path that works for me.

Naturally, clinical colleagues accuse me of similar "spinelessness" because I am so integrative. I once got a critique from a peer-reviewed journal in which the editor, well known for her rigidity, chided my "piecemeal, qualitative" approach to constructing the case study article. I giggled when I read it, because her words, *piecemeal* and *qualitative* define my integrated approach to psychotherapy and working with human beings. From my experience in working with PTSD, *piecemeal* can better be described as *fusion*: an integration of techniques, approaches, and strategies that form a tapestry or a collage. In the reasoning of Rosenzweig, if this integration works to engage and inspire the participant, and it yields positive outcomes, who are we to question its worth?

In Their Own Words

Dr. Baute

Dr. Paschal Baute is one of my personal mentors and heroes. A retired clinical pastoral psychologist, former Catholic priest, veteran, and storyteller, Paschal carries a great deal of folk wisdom, which he shares with others through the art of parable and storytelling. Paschal and I first met when he attended a workshop I gave on spiritual abuse. One of his stories not only explains the trauma of spiritual abuse and how it affects people, but also personifies the challenges in our field that Rosenzweig identified in the 1930's.

Satan and His Apprentice: A Teaching Tour

Satan went for a walk with an apprentice devil, a teaching tour. Soon they saw a human over on the right reach down and pick something up. He looked at it, was delighted, and tucked it under his hat.

"What does that mean?" asked the young devil.

"Wait. We need a contrast," said Satan.

Soon, they saw another human over on their left find something, reach down, pick it up, and he also was delighted with the finding. He put it in his vest.

(Continued)

"See the difference," said Satan.

"What does it mean?" asked the devil.

"The man on the right put what he found under his hat, in his mind," said Satan. Even though we can turn the piece of truth he found into belief, he will use his belief to judge others. When those persons gather to compliment themselves as having the Right Teaching, they are in our pocket. 'Right Teaching' is our great secret weapon. We have used it to create much mischief, violence, and hidden idolatry for ages."

"How about the other, the one who put it in his vest?" asked the young devil.

"That's a horse of a different color. He put it next to his heart. Even though we turn it into a belief, that human received it as a gift. He knows it is undeserved and he can only use it for himself, with wonder and awe. These types we have no leverage with," said Satan.

"Wow!" said the devil, "Aren't we shrewd. We can so easily use belief to promote our own kingdom."

"Yep, anytime Christians, Jews, or Muslims remind themselves that they alone have the 'Right Teaching,' they belong to us already. They are in our bag and don't even know it," said Satan.

"I think I got it, teacher. They think they are safe with Right Teaching, but it is really an idol in disguise, working on the dark side for us," said the devil.

"Yep, you got it," said Satan.

"Wait a minute," said the apprentice devil. "I do not yet understand how we trick them so easily to the Dark Side?"

"Well," said Satan, "Actually, humans trick themselves. As soon as they find a concept or a text about our Enemy, they think it represents the mystery of the Enemy. Soon, humans assume the authority of the Enemy is contained in that text or concept. They invest the human word with the authority of the Divine. This way, humans turn the concept or text into an idol. They judge others by their precious text. When this happens, humans belong to us; they belong to the Dark Side. They have needed little help from us to do this down through the ages, which is why we have been able to accomplish so much violence through humans' belief," Satan cackled. **"They do it even in the name of our Enemy."**

Satan laughed uproariously.

"Now, I really get it," said the devil. They both laughed at the easy way they used belief. And they continue to laugh, down through many centuries and across the world in our own times. They find it easy to shape human belief for their dark and mean purposes.

REPROCESSING MADE SIMPLE

We've established that there are multiple techniques and modalities that can work for treating trauma. Selecting a modality that is right for each patient is often the most challenging task in this phase of treatment. Trial and error is often required, although forging a solid therapeutic relationship in stabilization can give you, as the provider, enhanced insight on where to begin. Inquiring about what has or has not worked in past attempts at therapy is a good place to start. For example, when I work with people who have gone through every type of talk or cognitive therapy imaginable, I am likely to suggest one of the more body-centered or holistic psychotherapies that they haven't tried before. However, if a person reports that cognitive modalities seemed to help in the past, I might start there and then make suggestions for bringing in other modalities if the client stays stuck.

I strongly advocate for body-centered, holistic therapies in the treatment of trauma. However, there is a simple idea from cognitive work to simply conceptualize reprocessing that applies across the modalities. Let's say that the trauma leaves a survivor with a message that crystallizes into cognition. As discussed in Chapter 5, some common messages include, "I'm not good enough," "I'm to blame," and "I'm defective." (See Appendix for a full list.) In more complicated presentations, there are often multiple negative cognitions tangled together, like in the metaphor I introduced in Chapter 4. For the sake of teaching, let's use "I'm not good enough" as our example.

If the traumatic experience(s) leaves a cognitive imprint of "I'm not good enough," this is likely to manifest in other areas of human experience. Think of how "I'm not good enough" might play out emotionally, somatically, or even spiritually in the lives of our clients. A solid course of reprocessing allows the ingrained "I'm not good enough" to shift to a more positive, natural opposite, such as "I am good enough." It is not enough for the belief to be confronted. Many patients who've had therapy before know what their negative beliefs are and may even know what they *should* believe, but the shift hasn't internalized. For some people, cognitive behavioral approaches do it (although I am of the belief that the *behavioral* components of these interventions are the most healing elements, concomitant with the "actions speak louder than words" operation of the limbic brain).

However, for people who continue to manifest distress at an emotional, somatic, and/or spiritual level, the processing work must incorporate those other channels. As Shapiro (2001) explained in her adaptive information processing model, unprocessed components or manifestations of memory can be stored in a variety of states. These can be visual, cognitive, sonic, emotional, somatic, existential, or a combination. These states can transform during processing to an adaptive resolution. Information processing transmutes information though all accessed channels of memory. For Shapiro, the modality of choice is EMDR, but there are many other ways to process stuck information. The key is finding out where a person is still "stuck" and accessing that channel. For many of our clients, the cognitive work has been done, but the emotional, somatic, or existential work still needs to be completed.

There is no shortage of therapies, models, and approaches available for reprocessing trauma. Because I believe in the dodo bird verdict logic of Rosenzweig, I have elected not to go into each of the popular therapies in detail. I believe that readers allegiant to certain modalities would feel left out that I didn't give their approach ample coverage. Moreover, there is no way I can cover every modality in the scope of this book. My suggestion is that if you are interested in a modality with which you have little familiarity, do some further research. The Internet makes information access easy, and every major school of thought has one or more books or manuals describing the approach, with information on how to pursue further training in that modality if you are interested.

To understand reprocessing work, let's take a look at Pierre Janet's original thoughts on what needs to happen during this stage of trauma treatment. In finding the best fit for a client to engage in the healing process, it is useful to ask whether a potential modality or therapy will help him or her to achieve these tasks. Janet wrote that traumatic memories must first be uncovered and then neutralized (van der Hart, Brown, & van der Kolk, 1989). Although Janet largely used hypnosis to achieve this task, just about any contemporary modality can be used. One of the great misconceptions of trauma reprocessing is that a person needs to "relive" it all to feel the emotions or somatic states that have been long repressed. However, a patient does not have to regress to first claim the connection to the memory and then neutralize it. As Dr. Wayne Eastlack, introduced in Chapter 7, explained, reprocessing allows a person to transform hot, charged memories into just bad memories.

Janet also made use of what he termed the substitution method for patients who might be too traumatized or destabilized by identification and neutralization. Examples, as used by Janet, include pairing pleasant imagery or stimuli with traumatic responses or introducing cognitive reframes or restructures. Janet considered simple morale building and encouragement to be part of substitution, techniques we associate with the solid therapeutic relationship serving as a therapeutic container. I have tended to use a combination of these substitution activities employed by Janet with clients I've treated who were not adequately stabilized for deep levels of processing.

You may be asking, "What does the evidence say about what works best?" I relayed some of my opinions about research and evidence in the previous section, but I know I must address the issue again, since most contemporary clinicians are trained to ask, "But is what you're doing an evidence-based practice?" *Evidence-based* is a phrase that generally makes me squirm, because there is no uniform definition of what constitutes evidence. From my experience, the standards set by a particular company, organization, or governing body for what they define as evidence are agenda driven, and the research used to justify these standards is generally cherry-picked to justify the agenda.

I know that many of you reading this book are expected to use "evidence-based practices," but if anyone ever questions your methods, I challenge you to ask, "Evidence-based according to whom?" Get some specific information about whose standards you're expected to uphold before proceeding. If you're dealing with third-party payers, for instance, it usually involves knowing how they expect services to be documented in your notes. Think in broad categories (e.g., insight-oriented therapy, mindfulness-based interventions) instead of obsessing over whether a specific modality is covered.

In my clinical opinion, the most humanistically sound definition of what constitutes an evidence-based practice that I've read over the years comes from the American Psychological Association. A 2006 task force issued the following definition (p. 280): "An evidence-based practice in psychology is the best available research with clinical expertise in the context of patient characteristics, culture, and preferences." Thus, it does not come down to research alone.

So What Are My Options?

Following is a short list of options available at the time of this writing for reprocessing traumatic memories. I present a blend of some traditional modalities and others that are more innovative. All have some type of research base supporting them, although some would be seen as more credible by the mainstream because the supporting research is quantitative. As you glance through the list, consider how many of these approaches you use. On this list, I've excluded name brand models and approaches that carry a trademark or a copyright, even though many of these trademarked approaches are wildly popular. Some of

---

(Continued)

the approaches on this list started out as trademarked approaches (e.g., EMDR), but the founders' release of the trademark has allowed for broader interpretation, variation, and dissemination on their original discovery in clinical settings. As an adjunctive exercise to reading the book, you might consider doing an Internet search on the therapies with which you are not familiar to read more about them.

- Accelerated Experiential Dynamic Psychotherapy (AEDP)
- Acceptance and Commitment Therapy (ACT)
- Cognitive behavioral therapy (CBT)
- Cognitive processing therapy (CPT)
- Dialectical behavioral therapy (DBT)
- Developmental Needs Meeting Strategy (DNMS)
- Emotional Freedom Technique (EFT)
- Eye Movement Desensitization and Reprocessing (EMDR)
- Energy psychology
- Equine-assisted therapy
- Exposure therapy
- Expressive therapies (art, music, dance, drama)
- Focusing
- Gestalt therapy
- Hakomi
- Hypnosis and hypnotherapy
- Internal Family Systems (IFS)
- Interpersonal neurobiology
- Mindfulness-based cognitive therapy (MBCT)
- Narrative therapy
- Neurofeedback
- Neuro-Linguistic Programming (NLP)
- Pet therapy
- Progressive counting
- Psychoanalysis
- Psychodrama
- Stress inoculation
- Trauma-focused cognitive behavioral therapy (TF-CBT)
- Yoga therapy

SAMHSA now lists The Partners for Change Outcome Management System (PCOMS): The Heart and Soul of Change Project as an evidence-based practice. Thus, if you are an integrationist or innovator but aren't really sure what to label your approach or how to justify it with research, consider learning this simple outcome tracking system to support your approach and help obtain valuable client feedback. Learning to track outcomes is the heart of gathering practice-based evidence.

Fusion, Combination, Integration

We must use a modality or series of modalities that are the best fit for each client. It is not trauma sensitive to impose our way of doing things on a patient and then, when he or she does not respond, to write it off as resistance. Thus, being an eclectic or integrative therapist is optimal if you are serious about being trauma competent.

In the spirit of integration and developing an approach for working with a client, consider what you've learned through the assessment. Is his or her culture important to the patient? If so, what are some ways that culture frames the healing process? For Paula Bossert, a Native American therapist working with Indian Health Services in Sisseton, South Dakota, incorporating Native American folklore, stories, and healing rituals into her work with children is imperative. Paula is trained in EMDR and several other modalities for healing, and she believes that cultural folkways can be incorporated into just about any approach to enhance healing. The Native American healing arts excite me, even as a person without Native American blood. The Wellbriety recovery movement is an example of such a program. Wellbriety can serve as a complement to traditional 12-Step recovery approaches, and what I like about it is that the 12 steps of recovery are seen as a circle that can be continually experienced, not as a linear series of steps. Susan Pease Banitt's *The Trauma Toolkit* offers powerful suggestions for how to integrate Native American healing arts into Western therapy.

I once had the privilege of hosting a survivor of the Rwandan genocide at one of my trainings. This man presented as the very picture of joy, and he certainly struck me as someone who lives in the thriving state. When I asked him about his culture's perspective on healing trauma, he shared a very simple strategy with me: "When people in our villages experience a great trauma, we send them to the elders, and the elders share their stories. A person is nourished by the sharing of those who have lived so much life." This is such a simple, beautiful healing art. Cultures around the globe are filled with such humanistic rituals for healing trauma. We must wonder, as our professions push to systematize and legitimize psychotherapy as a science, have we lost touch with healing folkways that have stood the test of time?

Heather Bowser's journey with reprocessing her trauma fascinates me. We've looked at Heather's case throughout the book. I was surprised to hear that she has never been through her own course of professional therapy, especially when one considers her level of thriving. I was eager to hear how Heather did it—what worked in helping her heal from the multilayered trauma of being born with a disability into a family system riddled by war and illness. Heather recalled that she actively participated in the band in middle and high school, which was a healthy, positive outlet for her. She also acknowledged that leaving the small town after high school where she had experienced the early trauma was a freeing experience.

Studying art as an undergraduate afforded Heather multiple outlets for processing buried emotion. In her senior project, she painted a three-panel mural that told her father's story and her story. She admitted that this experience helped her to get out many emotions that she had been holding in. As an adult, working as an advocate for victims of Agent Orange exposure continues to play a vital role in her healing and grief work. Heather has even made three trips to Vietnam as a guest educator, forming very powerful bonds with other survivors in this work. Heather has said that even outside of the Agent Orange causes, working with children and families of veterans is a major part of her healing. She encourages veterans to talk to their kids and sees family systems work as vital to the healing process.

With Heather's case, we literally strip away all the hype about what therapeutic modality "works best" to heal trauma, because she was never exposed to any of them as a client. There are many lessons we can draw from Heather's story about what works to help a person heal—creativity, expression, connectedness, feeling and freeing repressed emotion, creating therapeutic distance, and advocating for others. In helping a client to reprocess trauma, it may be useful to consider the healing power of these constructs in evaluating what strategies to use and how to approach the reprocessing component of therapy.

In trainings, I have no qualms about publically sharing my experiences with healing from the aftereffects of unresolved trauma. I am the first to admit that no one "thing" did it for me, which is why I get concerned when I see clients and therapists in search of "the instant cure." I share some of my odyssey in *Trauma and the Twelve Steps*:

> For me, a combination of having my traumatic experiences validated, having a trauma-sensitive provider care for me, and going to meetings early on are what helped me get sober. Really digging in and doing a lot of self-discovery with journal writing, songwriting, and "stepwork" are what helped me stay sober. Doing EMDR therapy at around two to three years of sobriety is what helped free me from many of my mental burdens, helping me transition from victim to survivor. Engaging in bodywork (like

cranial-sacral massage, aromatherapy, and hydrotherapy) helped me to enhance my self-care potential as an addicted survivor of trauma working as a professional. In recent years, continuing to write, perform music, dance, practice yoga, and engage in a few other therapeutic techniques like NET™ and coherence therapy have helped me move from survivor to thriver, all while staying in touch with the relationship I've fostered with my Higher Power. Because of my history of trauma and emotional vulnerabilities, I have had to seek a variety of outlets for stabilization, reprocessing, and reintegration—that has worked for me and I'm grateful. One time, early on in my recovery, I was sharing my healing ventures with my brother Paul: going to meetings, going to therapy, going to church, going for massage, writing music, and performing it with my partner. He jokingly said, "It takes a village to help my sister." Although he and I laugh about this comment today, it is a true observation—one that I feel has helped me to thrive (p. 135).

Generally, healing does not occur in a vacuum. My own research on EMDR with women in addiction continuing care addressed this idea: A context of support is needed for overall healing. The actual EMDR therapy was one component of this larger network of care, and it likely would have been ineffective on its own, according to the lived experiences of the participants (Marich, 2010).

No two trauma clients are created equally, nor are any two trauma clients in the same place on their journey. My story describes how what worked at one point in my recovery was not optimal at other times. Healing is an evolution. Being well attuned to relational dynamics is half of the battle in determining how you can best work with a patient, wherever he or she may be on the journey.

In Their Own Words

Dave

Many of us working with trauma believe that whereas discovery can happen in an office-based setting, clinical locations are often insufficient for healing the deep wounds of trauma. So many exciting things are happening in retreat and community settings across the world that help

(Continued)

survivors of trauma reprocess, either as an adjunct to traditional therapy or as a healing modality in their own right. Dave Ferruolo, MSW, a former Navy SEAL, is on a team in his home state of New Hampshire offering retreats with a focus on equine-assisted therapy for returning veterans. Consider some of Dave's key insights about the experience and what he's learned about creating a safe space for healing:

> My first insight revolves around how gracious and thankful the veterans were to have us provide them with the equine retreat. At first I dismissed their behavior as courtesy and tact; however, the meekness of manner hinted at something deeper. I hypothesized that this behavior (while they were genuinely grateful) came from a place of low self-esteem, insecurity, and feelings of worthlessness. Low self-worth often is a byproduct of post-traumatic stress disorder. My instinct suggested that these veterans were experiencing dissonance about why so many resources were being spent on them; this dissonance birthed from a place of deep-seeded worthlessness. When working with veterans, practitioners must investigate whether low self-worth stems from traumatic events, from worth and esteem issues or, a combination of both. One monumental insight I had when working with combat veterans, an insight that seems to elude current PTSD literature, is that combat-related PTSD may be very closely related to what a veteran personally did as a combat soldier. As one veteran put it, "God did not make me a killer." A lot of the veterans I work with question their morality and their worth as a human being. This seems to be a result of the actions they took as combatants. "I did things," an army veteran stated, "Things I want to forget. Things I am not proud of. Things I have to live with." Practitioners must understand the dual relationship of these constructs and how it relates to the etiology and treatment of PTSD in combat veterans.
>
> The loss of purpose and identity is something many veterans struggle with. As a veteran myself, I can relate to this. I empathized with one of the veteran participants of the equine program when he stated that his name was "Sargent" and he felt like he was still living in Iraq. For many years, I continually identified myself with my former military life. This caused

(Continued)

many problems and unnecessary strains in my life. Veterans typically have trouble shedding their military mentality. The military does a fantastic job of creating a military mindset, but lacks significantly when it comes to re-civilianization, or humanization.

As I worked with the aforementioned veteran on redefining himself and his life, three things were asked of him after we had worked on connecting his passions with his strengths: 1) what vision did he have for his life, his future, and himself as he moved forward from this point; 2) what aspects of himself did he need to let go of and leave behind to be able to move forward and create this vision; and 3) what did he need to let go of for all of this to happen. After the equine program finished, this veteran revealed that for the first time in many years he no longer felt like "Sargent," but instead he felt like "Patrick."

Further Reading

Duncan, B. L., Miller, S. D., Wampold, B. E., & Hubble, M. A. (Eds.) (2009). *The heart and soul of change: Delivering what works in therapy* (2nd ed.). Washington, D. C.: American Psychological Association.

CHAPTER 11

Trauma Treatment: Reintegration

Your joy is your sorrow unmasked.
And the selfsame well from which your laughter rises
Was oftentimes filled with your tears.
And how else can it be?
The deeper that sorrow carves into your being, the more joy you can
contain.

—Khalil Gibran, *The Prophet*

Healed Versus Cured

A Roman Catholic parish in the village of Medjugorje, Bosnia-Hercegovina hosted me during my time of service in the country. As a result, I had a chance to hear sermons by priests from around the globe. One sermon stands out, delivered by a young, Filipino priest. I don't even remember his name, but I remember his message. Medjugorje is a famous pilgrimage site in the Roman Catholic world; places of mystical events or Marian apparitions usually are. Pilgrims the world over have come to Medjugorje in droves since the early 1980s, even during the war. Many pilgrims are looking for a miracle, usually to cure a medical or emotional ailment, inspired by miraculous stories of what people have experienced in the village over the years. In a friendly, human style, this young priest challenged the craving for the instantaneous that was present in so many pilgrims. He simply stated, "Do you want to be cured, or do you want to be healed?"

His challenge remained with me over the years. Even when I heard him speak these words in 2000, at the height of my own addiction, the concept of healing sounded much healthier to me. To fully explore this idea, let's break down the definitions. In popular medical dictionaries, the words *cure* and *heal* are synonymous: to restore to health. So naturally, I turn to word origin. *Cure* (n.d.) comes from Latin, meaning "to take care of." *Curé*, a French term for an associate parish priest, comes from the same derivation. *Heal* (n.d.), however, comes from Old English, meaning "make whole, sound, and well."

I don't know about you, but I prefer to be healed! Today, being *cured* implies the quick fix, or at very least, the idea that once you are cured, the problem is no longer an issue. Everybody wants to be cured; wanting a cure is human nature. So many people approach mental health in this way. They want to take that pill or go through that guaranteed program that will make the trauma, addiction, or other mental condition simply go away. I saw this play out at a famous Catholic pilgrimage site. En masse, people came to say prayers, kiss a statue, and climb a mountain, with the hope that God would cure their problems.

Similar actions go on all the time in the secular world. I remember a conversation I had with a woman in my community who goes to the same chiropractic office that I do. We were talking about the stellar approach the chiropractors in our office use, called Neuro Emotional Technique^{TM} (NET^{TM}), a way of releasing blocked energy in the body connected to emotional trauma using chiropractic adjustment. I love NET^{TM} as a complement to other healing arts. I take the material that comes up during NET^{TM} sessions and spend some time with it, journaling, dancing, reflecting, or taking it back to dialogue with my sponsor or other support people.

The woman's view of NET^{TM} was much different. She declared, "I hate talk therapy. I hate journaling. I don't want to talk about it. I don't want to write about it—I just want it to be gone. NET^{TM} lets it all be gone." Interestingly, she talked with such contempt in her voice that it made me wonder if "it" was really gone. There's no doubt in my mind that the NET^{TM} helped her on some level, but she was clearly using it as a cure, not a mechanism of larger healing, and as a result, I perceived that she shortchanged herself.

The debate over whether something can be truly *cured* has raged in the mental health and addiction fields for decades. I have witnessed people get into sparring matches at conferences and on Facebook about whether addiction is a disease that requires ongoing effort and recovery to be kept in remission, or whether it is something that can truly be cured if you look deeply enough to resolve the root causes. For me, the concept of an ongoing recovery has always made the most sense, so I acknowledge that slant as I present this chapter. I want healing, not a cure; I want to be made whole through continued growth and effort.

In my estimation, we set ourselves up for greater failure if we think that something is cured, especially when it comes to the treatment of post-traumatic stress issues. I fully recognize that I may be stepping on many toes by saying that, since so many trauma clinicians and trainers readily promote the merits of trauma resolution. I've gotten into some heated debates with colleagues I respect about whether a traumatic memory can be totally resolved. Many of these colleagues see resolution or clearing as the ultimate goal, yet my experience teaches me that trauma can be so existentially wounding, you may never be the same after the experience. Of course you can heal, you can grow, you can thrive, but we must ask, is true resolution ever possible? For some people it may be. Speaking for myself, it's not. Trauma recovery is about adaptation, and this stage of treatment, reintegration, is about continuing the adaption process in as healthy a manner as possible.

The definition of what *resolution* means varies from person to person. As Dr. Wayne Eastlack described (see Chapter 10), it can mean experiencing a shift from hot, troubling memories to just having bad memories. Heather Bowser, whom we've read about throughout the book, readily acknowledges that she is still going through her grieving process with her dad, but this has not stopped her from living at the *thriver* level. As a workshop attendee once shared with me, "I hate that word *resolution*. I don't think it's ever going to be possible for me. But I can resonate with the ideas of *reconciliation* and *renewal.*"

People have a right to define what is possible with their trauma recovery. Expecting them to be totally "resolved" at the reprocessing level before moving into reintegration strategies is just not realistic. For Pastor Todd,* placing this expectation of resolution on his own trauma recovery set him up for failure. Todd, a Protestant minister, came to me for EMDR therapy many years ago, hearing rave reviews about the approach and its merits. A survivor of multilayered emotional abuse in his home of origin, Todd continued to see the world through the cognitive filters that his demanding parents instilled. Todd went through two years of EMDR treatment at intermittent levels, which helped with his most acute symptoms of depression. He continued to beat himself up because the emotional "charge" surrounding these negative memories and beliefs diminished, but they still surfaced from time to time during periods of high stress. Everything he read about EMDR told him he should be "cleared" and that these memories should no longer be an issue.

At one point, Todd made the stark realization that he was setting himself up for more self-degradation by not being gentle with himself. One day, he came into session and told me that approaching his emotional trauma recovery would be best handled by viewing it as an addict in long-term recovery might view his sobriety. He commented, "This trauma digs down to the core of who I am. It would be unrealistic to think that the impact can all just go away. I am so much better overall than I was when I started therapy, so I'm going to accept that, and when I identify that I'm having a bad patch with my issues, I am going to take care of myself like I need to." For Todd, this *care* meant using the skills he had learned as part of his treatment in the service of his healing.

THE ART OF REINTEGRATION

At its essence, reintegration is taking the skills one learns during stabilization and the insights one gains during reprocessing and using them for long-term wellness. If embraced as such, a person can live in the thriver stage on more days than not. Most of us helpers are familiar with the saying, "Give a man a fish and you've fed him for a day; teach a man to fish and he'll never go hungry again." In reintegration, the client internalizes the skills needed to fish for the rest of his or her life.

IN THEIR OWN WORDS

Bill*

If you've been to any of my live trainings, you're heard me talk about Bill as one of my great inspirations during my time as a counselor. I introduced the case of Bill in *EMDR Made Simple*. In that book, written two years after Bill's major motorcycle accident, he shared some of his reflections with EMDR therapy and the major coping skill he derived from his therapeutic experience, writing. He graciously agreed to offer some reflections at five years following his accident. Listen for the signs of post-traumatic growth and the maintenance process involved in his healing experience:

> My life after the motorcycle accident and being diagnosed in 2008 with PTSD following the accident has had its ups and downs. I went through almost two years of EMDR, which helped a great deal. At this same time I was taught several coping skills; some worked better than others. However, the coping skill that worked the best for me was writing.
>
> The writing started out as an exercise to bring out the events the day of the accident; from our (my wife and I) waking up the day of our ordeal, continuing through the entire day and into the evening following our motorcycle accident. This exercise has culminated in a complete book accompanied with photos pertaining to the accident and our ordeal. Definition of ordeal: medical recovery, motorcycle

(Continued)

repairs, and the obnoxious insurance representatives. All of these were contributing factors to my PTSD and the need for EMDR.

I worked hard at trying to overcome this; I did what I could by researching PTSD online and through books. My recovery is a long one and is not over, but I am tough and a survivor. It is still a group effort.

Back to the writing—I do write almost every day, whether it is in a journal or one of my books of fiction. At present, I have completed four books in all; the first one is about the motorcycle accident, and then there are three books of fiction, with a fourth one about half done. I am very optimistic about getting my work published. Writing for me seems to be the perfect outlet, or coping mechanism. These books (sequels), with their almost 60 characters at this point and the many complex scenarios, seem to be the perfect getaway.

I still on occasion use the coping skill of visiting my "happy place." Of course to us bikers, that would be the "garage" that houses our motorcycles. There has been many a time that I would pull out a lawn chair right in the garage and do my writing. On occasion, I still have the "red truck dreams/nightmares" and wake up in the middle of the night with night sweats wide awake, reliving the accident in my dream/nightmare. The dreams/nightmares always seem so real! I had one of the dreams/nightmares a few weeks ago just prior to the anniversary of our motorcycle accident. It was not a big deal; I was able to use a coping skill taught me, and I was able to return back to sleep. I do continue to ride my motorcycle every day. I've been on motorcycles for some 45 years, and now's not the time to call it quits.

There is something that my wife and I do each year on the anniversary of our accident. We ride the motorcycle the almost 70 miles to the scene of our accident and relive the events of that day, sort of like visiting the scene of the crime, except for the accident, of course. Riding through the crash site without incident is for us a form of closure, I suppose. Again I am a biker, and any old reason for a motorcycle ride [works], although sometimes having a destination is nice.

(Continued)

These visits to the scene of our accident and the small resort town have been named the, "Crashing Sucks Run." We even had shirts made up! We did this for a few years as a way of showing our overcoming the ordeal of the accident, I guess making a mockery of it. A lot of photos are always taken, even though we have many of the area from throughout the years. Obviously, [these are] more tools of closure.

All in all, my problem has been diminishing but more than likely will always be there. Such trauma just doesn't disappear. Here are a few quotes that were given to me that I utilize regularly:

"Focus on what I can control."
"Progress not perfection."
"*Acceptance* is the key to all my problems today."
"Coping is not about making the waves stop—it's about learning to surf."

Bill's case offers us a perfect example of how a client can take the skills acquired during treatment and put them to use in his life once therapy terminates. Bill hasn't been my client in almost three years, yet he continues to make use of the skills. Whenever he sends me the occasional follow-up email, he usually includes the line "P.S., Thank you for pointing me to the pen."

As Bill's case showed us, reprocessing is the art of taking the skills that we learn in stabilization and repurposing them for lifelong wellness. Whenever a person formally leaves therapy but continues to use the breath skills obtained in the helping process, that's an example of how healing comes full circle. As I said in Chapter 9, I often ask my clients to make music playlists with a certain quality, like relaxation. These playlists are intact as long as the person holds on to the technology. I continue to make playlists for myself whenever I need to listen to music with a certain theme, and several of my friends also use this strategy. Mandy Hinkle, my collaborator introduced in Chapter 2, commented, "For me, making playlists is spiritual."

A vital part of my own stage three, continued healing, has been developing the *Dancing Mindfulness* practice. Although techniques like EMDR helped me get through the most acute symptoms of my traumatic stress, I still found that more healing was available to me at a spiritual, existential level. As I referenced in Chapter 11, finding yoga was a vital part of my continued healing because it so dynamically fused somatic and spiritual elements. While on a retreat at the Kripalu Center for Yoga and Health in Massachusetts several years ago, I discovered the genre of conscious dance (sometimes called yoga dance). In conscious dance, the focus is not on mastering precise steps or measuring up to a certain technical standard. Rather, it is on being in the moment, in the process in the art form of guided free dance. The first time I took one of these classes at Kripalu, I knew instantly that I had to teach it. The healing potential of being in a space with other people who are moving with intention and joy struck me as tremendous. The emphasis of this practice is not on measuring up; it is on just being yourself!

I originally went to Kripalu to train in several conscious dance forms, but I ultimately developed *Dancing Mindfulness* as a way for people to safely, mindfully, and nonjudgmentally explore the healing potential of their moving body. *Dancing Mindfulness* is not dance therapy per se; it is a mindfulness practice that uses dance as the primary channel through which to cultivate mindful awareness. Although it can be used in clinical settings, I've envisioned it more as a community practice. *Dancing Mindfulness* is a class that can be taught at yoga schools, community centers, churches, or retreat centers. Other movement classes, such as yoga, Zumba®, Tai Chi, Qi Gong, Pilates, and other dance forms, are beautiful outlets for clients to continue accessing wellness and growth, even after formal therapy terminates. Many yoga schools, community centers, and places of worship also offer meditation courses or other spiritual practices that are ideal for stage-three healing. As stated in Chapter 9, clinicians have a responsibility to be aware of what is going on in our communities so we can inform clients of these resources as an adjunct to their treatment or as follow-ups for continued maintenance after treatment terminates. A little of this old-school social work, as I like to call it, goes a long way.

Janet identified three primary tasks to address in this phase of care: 1) relapse prevention, 2) reintegration of the personality, and 3) management of the residual symptoms of traumatic stress (van der Hart, Brown, & van der Kolk, 1989). These tasks are compatible with my understanding of the ongoing recovery effort I learned in addiction recovery. Janet acknowledged that a person could have a major shift take place while uncovering and addressing the traumatic memories (stage 2). However, such a shift does not usually yield instant healing. Continued maintenance is needed, and I strongly advocate working with clients in the wellness paradigm for learning maintenance strategies. For Janet, education in such strategies is a part of reintegration. He also used the term *excitation* as a stage-three function—the use of awareness exercises and coaching clients to master new tasks that they previously neglected. Bill's yearly "anniversary" bike run to commemorate surviving the accident is an example of an excitation strategy. According to Janet, if psychotropic medications are part of long-term maintenance, a plan for follow-up with an appropriate provider must also be arranged during this period.

THE FLEXIBILITY IMPERATIVE

One of history's most physically flexible men, martial arts legend Bruce Lee, is credited with the following advice: "Notice that the stiffest tree is most easily cracked, while the bamboo or willow survives by bending in the wind." What a great guiding principle for clinicians doing trauma work! The wind is unpredictable, as are the manifestations of human pain. The phases of the consensus model are not meant to be a perfect, rigid stage model. Janet recognized that a certain degree of flexibility is needed within the stages, depending on the client (van der Hart, Brown, & van der Kolk, 1989), an idea that I first introduced in Chapter 8. A major theme of this book is that safety and flexibility are the two primary elements of successful trauma therapy. The three-stage framework encourages us to be flexible if the clinical situation dictates. Van der Hart, Brown, & van der Kolk concluded, in their major review of Janet's work on trauma, that Janet was "a flexible clinician who viewed the different stages of posttraumatic syndromes as constantly shifting and returning, requiring different treatment approaches at different times" (p. 9).

Part of being a trauma-informed clinician is to recognize that a degree of reintegration goes on throughout the treatment, especially if you are working with patients on an outpatient level. Of course, they may need many stabilization skills and still have reprocessing work to do, but the real challenge is to help them "reintegrate" to an outside world from which they may feel estranged. This is often seen in working with veterans. As Dave Ferruolo, introduced in Chapter 10, explained:

> The Veterans Administration has very effective reintegration programs, yet only a fraction of military personnel will have the opportunity to go through one when they separate from service. Mental health workers assisting veterans must recognize this attachment to the military identity and help the veteran establish

his or her new civilian identity. I have found that this can be accomplished by helping the veteran redefine his or her life and purpose. Many veterans went in to the military when they were in their late teens or early twenties, before they had the opportunity to discover certain things about themselves. Helping a veteran to discover what they like and what they are good at—linking their passions with their attributes—can greatly redirect a veteran's life and assist in creating a new civilian identity. Building on former skills taught in the military can assist this process. Using a strengths perspective and highlighting the veteran's already existing strong points but redirecting those strengths toward civilian pursuits, will help the veteran de-identify with the military and identify with his or her true, genuine self.

Ferrulo's describes just how much interplay exists between the stages. In my experience, clinicians and helpers who truly understand trauma and how its wounds manifest in the human experience are best positioned to comprehend this interplay. More on what makes an effective trauma therapist is explored in the next and final chapter.

A question that many of us ponder is what time is ideal to formally terminate therapy in clients with traumatic stress issues. Many theories exist regarding termination. My general view is that these dynamics must be evaluated on a case-by-case basis. To me, the imperative is that while long-term follow-ups may be appropriate, we should never enable a client to become dependent on us. The healing arts are about allowing a client to identify and to develop his or her own strengths and community resources so that he or she won't need us any more. Janet's insights on termination are noteworthy (van der Hart, Brown, & van der Kolk, 1989) and may serve as a useful guidepost for us today:

- Reduction of the therapeutic influence signaled the beginnings of termination.
- The patient developed a quieter attitude, was more open to positive influences, and relapses were less severe and of shorter duration.
- "Ingratitude" is the best sign of recovery: when the patient started to forget appointments, he was on the road to recovery.
- In severe and complicated cases, infrequent appointments maintained the therapeutic influence over time.

IN THEIR OWN WORDS

Dee*

Just as I ask workshop participants and clients to give me their working definition of trauma as a starting off point, I also ask how they would define *trauma recovery*. Asking such a question of a client can give you a solid sense of what he or she wants to get out of treatment or help him or her to realize the extent of their post-traumatic growth. I asked this question of Dee, a trauma survivor I met through the yoga community in my city, and here is her "gut level" response:

> Recovery to me has been learning to live with and move on from the trauma. It's part of me, part of my story, part of who I am, but it is such a little part that it does not define me— realizing that there is so much more life to live and that I have the right to love it, enjoy it, and be happy.
>
> What's helped me is having an excellent foundation, and that's a therapy team I trust and feel safe with. I love my team! I think another thing you have to have when you're in recovery is to want it. Sure, plenty of people NEED recovery, as their trauma opened them to vices or harmful lifestyle choices, but until a tiny, itty-bitty part of them WANTS recovery, it isn't going to happen.
>
> Recovery has ups and downs. You go three steps forward and four steps back sometimes. It's scary, exhilarating, boring and mundane, exciting, and sometimes feels never ending (which can be a comfort at times while pissing you off at other times).
>
> When you want it so bad you can taste it, you go full force. Don't let others make you feel bad and/or selfish when they think you're good or healed enough. You'll know when you're finally there and until then, don't stop. Use your newly learned coping skills, set healthy boundaries for yourself, and never let someone make you feel bad because you said "no" and put yourself first. You aren't selfish.
>
> I've done many things to help in my recovery. Yoga; going to the gym; eating healthy; weekly therapy; taking my medications; standing up for my stability and saying "no" to others; seeking comfort in the arms of my boyfriend or parents;

(Continued)

asking my support system for help; making my sleep schedule a priority; self-help books, workbooks, and exercises; learning as much as I can about what I "have" and then learning even more about others who overcame it before me; and the list goes on.

FURTHER READING

Marich, J. (in press). *Dancing Mindfulness*. Los Angeles, CA: StartAgain.

Website: www.dancingmindfulness.com [Live video available].

van der Hart, O., Brown, P., & van der Kolk, B. (1989). Pierre Janet's treatment of post-traumatic stress. *Journal of Traumatic Stress, 2*(4), 1–11.

CHAPTER 12

What Makes a Good Trauma Therapist?

In my early professional years I was asking the question: How can I treat, or cure, or change this person? Now I would phrase the question in this way: How can I provide a relationship which this person may use for his own personal growth?

—Dr. Carl Rogers

SEYKHL

Between the movies and my Jewish ex-husband, I picked up my fair share of Yiddish over the years. This rich language contains a word that is so brilliant because of everything it's able to capture in two syllables: *seykhl*. Someone with *seykhl* is someone who has street smarts, common sense, and the wisdom of the ages. My ex first taught me this word as I prepared to enter a doctorate program in counseling. It was a rough time professionally, as I strived to reconcile the professional identity I really wanted with the professional identity that the counseling field was imposing on me. As I wrote in *EMDR Made Simple*, it was also a time when I deeply ensconced myself in technical EMDR training to become an "expert," at the expense of abandoning many core values I learned about helping in Bosnia. However, when my ex taught me this word and what it meant, I knew I wanted to have *seykhl* as a counselor. That quality would put me in the best position to help clients. In the years since, I've strived to make *seykhl* my professional identity.

When I began my doctoral program at a nationally acclaimed counseling institution, I heard many a discourse on *counselor identity*, yet I sensed no *seykhl* in the faculty. I started the program as a part-time student so I could maintain my full-time job as a counselor. The already joyless faculty frowned on my unwillingness to totally commit to their academically rigorous program. During the second meeting with my two faculty advisors,

I experienced an intensely negative visceral reaction to their condescension and lack of compassion. I literally ran from the building that night, vowing never to go back. That moment was a major turning point in my life, for not only did I honor my being's internal message, I claimed *seykhl* as my professional identity. I claimed that having *seykhl* is what made me good, and no academicians were going to make me feel otherwise. Fortunately for me, I soon found a doctoral program that embraced my identity and prompted me to grow in ways I never thought possible. So much of that program's secret was honoring my interests and beliefs while challenging me to the limits of my potential, just like a solid trauma-informed therapist would do with a client.

Although this chapter goes into some detail on what makes a good trauma therapist and why professional development issues matter, we can summarize this chapter with the word *seykhl*. A good trauma therapist has *seykhl*, or at the very least, strives to cultivate more of it in his or her practice. Let's look at the three components of the word: street smarts, common sense, and wisdom of the ages.

Having *streets smarts* does not literally mean that you had to live on the streets or come from an urban, impoverished culture. *Street smarts* generally connotes that everything to learn in life cannot be learned from a book. In general, clinicians who practice strictly from what they learned in classroom settings do not impress me. Sure, you may be able to recite your *DSM* inside and out, but have you been through the school of hard knocks yourself, or at very least, are you open to embracing the experiences of those who have?

Urban Dictionary, the go-to online source for looking up what words *really* mean to many of our clients, offers several solid definitions of *street smarts*. A particularly useful definition comes from a contributor who identified four primary traits of someone who is street smart (retrieved November 3, 2013 from http://www.urbandictionary.com):

1. Getting along with others: Knowing which questions to ask and not asking too many, being polite and friendly, but also being assertive.
2. Common sense: Knowing who you can trust, which areas in town are good and which are bad, etc.
3. Self-defense: Knowing how to fight and fend off an attacker, especially if you are small.
4. "BS detection": Knowing when people are trying to fuck you over, reading their intentions, and knowing that most corporate advertisements are complete bullshit.

This list is an excellent guide for clinicians! As a note, my interpretation of point three is more than self-defense in a physical sense; it also means the ability to set solid boundaries with people, an essential trait for a therapist if you are doing trauma work.

Another *Urban Dictionary* contributor expressed that while book smarts and streets smarts are seen as being mutually exclusive, they certainly don't have to be. Think of Dr. Sean Maguire, Robin Williams' character in the film *Good Will Hunting*, a classic example of someone who has both. We don't even have to look to fiction: Dr. Viktor Frankl, Holocaust survivor and author of the classic *Man's Search for Meaning* (1959), is a prime real-life example from our field. Any clinician seeking a role model for striking the balance between book smarts and street smarts needs to read this classic, or any work by Frankl.

Common sense, the second component of *seykhl*, comes up quite a bit in definitions of street smarts, but it deserves extra attention. One of my main teaching points is that a little humanistic common sense goes a long way in working with trauma. The common factors of Rosenzweig, (explored in Chapter 10) contain so much common sense they baffle people. "It can't be that easy!" people protest. Sometimes the answer is so simple, we miss it. As one of my colleagues said in her quintessentially sassy way, "Common sense just ain't common!"

I am reminded of a dear friend from high school, Ross,* a genius debater and all-around academic wizard. During our freshman year, the state of Ohio instituted statewide proficiency tests that we needed to pass by the end of senior year in order to graduate. For academically gifted kids, passing on the first try was typically a given. Not for Ross. It took him three times to pass the math portion of the exam. He explained to his friends, "I looked at the questions and they just seemed too easy—they had to be trick questions." As a result, he kept tricking himself out of passing.

The same thing happened to another close friend and former student, Becky. Becky is the smartest math student I've ever met; she eventually went on to get an advanced engineering degree from an Ivy League school. When I was in graduate school and learning how to give a Weschler Intelligence (WAIS) test, I recruited Becky as a test subject. I simply had to see what a math genius looked like taking this test! What happened to Becky was very similar to what happened to Ross—she kept tricking herself out of the right answers! She overthought things in the spirit of "It can't be that easy."

How often do clinicians think this same thing? We get so caught up in trying to find that right intervention based on the latest practice standards because, after all, we're dealing with very complicated people! Yet, often, the answers are so simple and right before our eyes. We get too caught up in the technical to really *see* them.

That brings us to the final component of *seykhl*: the wisdom of the ages, the things we can learn from those who've gone before us, the richness of tradition, legacy, and folk knowledge. The Korean folk tale in Chapter 7, *The Tiger's Whisker*, is one example of how ancient sources of knowledge are marvelously relevant today. As a field, we get worked up about the latest innovations in trauma treatment; yet, if we look into the annals of folklore, the answers for healing have been there all along. The folklore traditions of every culture are filled with tales and healing rituals that carry so much common sense. Two favorite tales I first read in childhood are O. Henry's "Gift of the Magi," and Charles Dickens' *A Christmas Carol*, filled with themes of love and healing. When I was a young adult, Victor Hugo's *Les Misérables* taught me lessons of redemption and grace, and I identified the protagonist Jean Valjean as an inspiration when I struggled to heal from my own trauma. Many people intone the poetry of Rumi, a 13th century Persian, as inspiration for healing and wellness. A Rumi quote opens Chapter 1 of this book, if you recall. We think that so much of our learning about trauma is new, but Rumi taught on emotional wound healing centuries before the dawn of modern psychology, and others predate Rumi with their own teachings on healing.

Wisdom implies more than just knowledge. Wisdom is being able to practice keen discernment and then use that knowledge. We can look to teachers, healers, and stories from the past for a greater appreciation on what worked in terms of healing and what may have been lacking. A teaching attributed to the ancient Chinese philosopher Confucius (551–479 BC) is that there are three ways to obtain wisdom: by reflection, which is noblest, by imitation, which is easiest, and by experience, which is bitterest. In my view, the most trauma-competent counselors are those who can learn through all three channels and let the interplay of what they've learned manifest in sessions.

FROM THE CLIENTS

Clients seem to know when a therapist has *seykhl*. In a major study I conducted, the element of common sense came up as a primary trait in what female trauma clients valued in their therapists (Marich, 2012). Other positive traits the women identified were caring, trustworthiness, intuitiveness, being natural, being connected, being comfortable with trauma work, skill, being accommodating, being wonderful, common sense, being validating, gentleness, being nurturing, being facilitating, being smart, being consoling, and being magical. One research participant even identified her counselor as "the bomb," a colloquial expression implying excellence.

I presented literature in Chapter 7 demonstrating the significance of the therapeutic relationship in trauma counseling, and of course, the relationship is one of the Rosenzweig common factors explored in Chapter 10. It's important to give these dynamics a bit more of a human face, from a client's perspective, so that we can learn what most resonates with clients about what worked. In essence, we know that the relationship is important, but we must explore what makes it important to people who come to us for help.

Fawn*, a survivor of multilayered trauma, explained that she had "a compassionate and patient therapist, who was willing to try many different types of approaches until she found the ones that 'fit.' For me, it was art therapy . . . drawing my way out until I could talk. She believed in me and 'my' perception of the trauma." Willa* stated that she had an excellent therapist who "didn't run from anything," a testament to the importance of being comfortable with trauma. For Donna, introduced in Chapter 2, having a psychotherapist as a "guide" to take her through the mindfulness treatments that ultimately worked for her, in concert with spiritual practice and massage, was a vital part of her healing.

The word *guide* is a powerful descriptor. Ultimately, we cannot *cure* anyone. Rather, we can guide people to do the work they must do to *heal* themselves. We can guide them in the direction of the physical, emotional, social, or spiritual resources they need for this healing work. Several contributors to this book identified the power in that therapist guidance, most notably, Dr. Wayne Eastlack (Chapter 7). Wayne's therapist clearly issued the invitation to bring him home (from Vietnam), to walk with him all the way. When Wayne tells the story of how he made the vital connection with this therapist in that healing moment of human exchange, his eyes still become filled with tears.

Holly Ann Rivera, introduced in Chapter 2, offered several keen insights on what constituted a good therapist for her, especially since she was shuffled in and out of the mental health system for many years before finding a good therapist. She identified the therapist she met at age 18, whom she later made her permanent therapist, as the first professional to truly validate the terms *abuse* and *trauma*, which was significant for Holly. She maintains that her therapist's eclectic nature works well for her, because someone with an eclectic orientation can better accommodate to changes in what Holly needs and changes in her own development as a therapist. Holly also believes that a good therapist lives what he or she teaches, and she picks up on this trait in her therapist.

To revisit Maridee Costanzo's words from Chapter 8, "If you're in this just for a job—do no harm, at the very least. If you want to make a difference, you have to truly believe there is some hope and that recovery is possible." I could fill volumes with clients' praise for their therapists as being critical forces in helping them heal from trauma. Yet, I could fill just as many pages with horror stories of what trauma survivors often *don't* get from therapists. Perhaps Maridee's comments shed light on one of the key differences between good trauma therapists and those who are harmful. Might it be fair to say that therapists successful at forging a connection with clients can communicate that sense of hope and possibility, whereas those who are unsuccessful have lost hope?

Jeff Zacharias, introduced in Chapter 5, speaks about his work as a clinician with such energy and optimism. In speaking to me for this book, he shared, "I love what I do. I love paying it forward. I love getting people to believe that life can be different for them." My wish is that one day, every client with unresolved trauma can have the good fortune to work with someone like Jeff. The reality is that so many trauma survivors in need of such a therapist with a healthy, optimistic attitude cannot find this connection. (Refer to Anna's story in the following text box.)

In Their Own Words

Anna

We first met Anna, a woman diagnosed with DID, in Chapter 4. Anna shared this list of traits in a therapist she feels she deserves, but has been unable to find. Anna's list is so powerful, I believe all helpers would benefit from reading it:

The thought I have is that a paid helping professional needs:

- To know and understand your diagnosis.
- To get to know *you*, where you're at (are you externally and internally safe???), where you've come from (historical context; triggers, traumas, what to be aware of), and where you want to go (short- and long-term goals).

(Continued)

- To be a person who believes in TEAMWORK. Both the professional and the client do work, lots of it. There is not an aggressor in the equation, ever. When/if it happens, stop.

- To have compassion and empathy—NOT PITY, ever. I have seen pathological psychiatrists who don't like humans. Pity is just destructive to what is supposed to be happening: growth and healing. Pity is never a foundation for that.

- To have a sense of connectedness. For people without a diagnosis, when they're going through a hard time, the baseline is to find someone you connect with.

- To never, never, never put their own moral thing (e.g., Christianity) above the code of treatment. Ever!!!!! No dogma at all should be in the way of the client finding her way.

- To have connectedness, the basis for going forward together. This ends up not being possible for me, because if I can't find someone who understands the diagnosis and they don't have a clue, they can't connect any information. They are only logical, they absolutely cannot connect emotionally—they can fake it, while we all know they're faking it.

- Bad therapy is worse than no therapy. I have learned this experientially.

Anna's comment, "Bad therapy is worse than no therapy" ought to grab our attention. We must ask ourselves why there is so much "bad therapy" going on, especially when this puts trauma survivors at an especially high risk of being retraumatized. Yes, there is evidence to show that, overall, therapy works; people who receive psychotherapy are less likely to be symptomatic than their untreated counterparts (Duncan et al., 2009). Yet, there is more to the picture.

Drop-out rates in therapy tend to average around 47%, and therapists consistently are unable to identify people who are regressing in their symptomology (Lambert et al., 2004). In a 2004 survey conducted by Penn and colleagues, one of the nation's most respected polling companies, about half of the sample felt they could benefit from therapy. For those who had not sought it, cost or lack of insurance was the greatest barrier (81%), and lack of confidence in the quality of service was the second-highest factor (78%) (Penn, Schoen, & Berland for the American Psychological Association, 2004).

In contrast, fewer than 20% reported stigma as a barrier. There is a major problem when so many people cannot access the care they need and/or have little confidence that it will work. We have to wonder what that says about the job we're doing and how this enters into the "word of mouth" marketing about therapy.

The perspectives of women from the study I cited earlier and contributors to the book may shed some light. In my study on the use of EMDR in addiction continuing care with women (Marich 2010, 2012), the respondents had a chance to reflect on their experiences with all of the trauma therapists at the facility, not just those who practice EMDR. Participants who initially had a bad experience with EMDR before switching to another therapist had negative qualities to report about their therapists. They described the ineffective therapists as rigid, scripted, unnatural, unclear, and uncomfortable with trauma work. As JoElle,* one woman in the sample, indicated, "I felt that I had to protect that therapist . . . it was like she couldn't handle the dark things I had done."

Inability to handle trauma and the dark side of human nature is a major problem if you are going to encounter human wounding. Holly Ann Rivera, in her search for the ideal helper, actually had two therapists say to her, "You are more than I can handle." I have mixed feelings when I hear that. On one hand, it is important for therapists to know their limits, but in this day and age, is trauma something that should be over our heads as therapists? As I wrote in *EMDR Made Simple*, when a therapist shies away from emotional trauma, it's like a physician who winces at the sight of blood. You wouldn't want a squeamish physician handling your medical care, so why are so many patients exposed to therapists who are squeamish emotionally?

Another insight that Holly shared regarding her unsuccessful therapy involved therapist ignorance. Holly was raped several times as a young adult; one perpetrator was a man, the other was a woman. One of Holly's therapists asked, "How is even being raped by a woman possible?" As Holly declared, looking back on that experience, if you have to ask that question, you should not be working with trauma, and, ". . . you shouldn't even be a therapist."

FOR THE HELPERS

Not only is there a trauma pandemic on our planet today, there are alarming numbers of clinicians and helpers who are not comfortable looking the realities of human wounding square in the face. As JoElle,* the woman in my research study (Marich, 2012), indicated, clients sometimes feel like they need to protect their therapists from the horrors of their trauma. For JoElle, holding back was not about her own resistance. In the first session after she switched therapists, she sensed something that told her she was safe to share with her new therapist. As JoElle indicated, "She just got it."

So, what is that mysterious "it" factor? Beutler and coworkers (2005), in their review of extant literature on connecting therapist traits to client outcomes, concluded that effective therapists are interested in people as individuals, have insight into their own personality characteristics, are sensitive to the complexities of human motivation, are tolerant, and have an ability to establish warm and effective relationships with others. An Australian review article (Charman, 2005) assembled a related list of traits: mindful, not having an agenda, having a concern for others, intelligent, flexible in personality, intuitive, self-aware, thoughtful, knows own issues, able to take care of self, open, patient, and creative.

All of the traits listed here are certainly trauma sensitive. The question remains, how do therapists acquire these skills? Are they traits that people are just born with—you either have them or you don't? Does it have to do with being a good human being and living life with your eyes open? Are these qualities that come with experience? Believe it or not, there is little evidence to show that therapists, as a whole, are any better at measuring performance outcomes later in their career than they were at the beginning (Hiatt & Hargrave, 1995; Duncan et al., 2009). Do therapists have to do their own therapeutic work to acquire these skills?

The jury is still out on whether a clinician needs to do his or her own therapy to make a good therapist. On one hand, there is little conclusive evidence linking clinician therapy history to client outcomes (Cooper, 2008; Duncan et al., 2009). On the other hand, many respected leaders in the helping professions boldly write about the importance of doing one's own therapeutic work (Corey, 2009; Norcross, 2005; Yalom, 2001). When I was a graduate student, I learned that it's impossible to take a client further than you yourself have gone in terms of health and wellness. I still firmly agree with this idea, which has been a guiding principle throughout my career. I believe that Holly Ann Rivera's statement on therapists needing to practice what they preach is something that most clients would echo agreement.

Whether handling your own emotional issues comes in the form of professional therapy or not, your issues must be addressed. As the principles of trauma and human wounding that we've discussed throughout this book dictate, if they weren't dealt with, they're going to come out somehow. For many therapists practicing with unresolved issues, they come out in the therapeutic context, to the detriment of the overall process. Remember that therapist factors are one of the four common factors.

I am pretty firm in my belief that all clinicians, especially those striving to be more trauma sensitive, should go through their own personal therapy. It's hard to promote the usefulness of an art that we've not experienced ourselves. I know that I couldn't do it, but I cannot speak for others. Whether our healing comes in the form of psychotherapy or involvement with a 12-Step support group or a church group, or working through self-help books and journals, it is something on which we must be committed to work to be more trauma competent.

When people ask me, "Jamie, what things should I get trained in if I want to specialize in trauma?" they are typically asking me for recommendations about techniques and models that they can learn, master, and use with their clients. As I've established throughout the book, the technique isn't nearly as important as the container that we establish for healing. Moreover, being able to handle the intense affect that can accompany abreaction (e.g., the discharge of tension and anxiety when material shifts from the unconsciousness into the consciousness) is vital to working with trauma, especially at the reprocessing level. No amount of technical training can prepare you for handling abreaction—it is about your comfort with trauma and ability to create a healing presence. In my view, creating that healing presence is more about you doing your own work and looking at yourself than it is about any specific intervention you can learn.

Of course, the process of clinical supervision is ideally set up for young therapists to examine some of these issues, especially when clients trigger certain issues within them. However, as someone who supervises and has been supervised, I fully contend that supervision is an imperfect process in most contexts. If you have a supervisor who has control issues, the supervision process can be traumatizing, and a perfectly competent new clinician may be left to wonder if he or she is really cut out for this field. In many instances, the supervisory process is imperfect because supervisors are asked to juggle both administrative and clinical duties, causing some blurred lines about what can be discussed. Even with the healthiest dynamic, supervisees can run the risk of feeling powerless if they confess a weakness or an insecurity that comes up for them in session to a supervisor who controls their future licensure and employment.

The bulk of doing our own work in the quest to become more effective, trauma-competent therapists is up to us. My colleague Susan Pease Banitt shared her opinion that clinicians must take active steps to desensitize themselves to the horrors of the human condition if they are serious about being therapists.

Susan suggests, "Watch horror movies, go to inner city soup kitchens, make yourself confront what may shock you." I am not saying that every clinician who struggles has to go to therapy, but he or she at least needs to be open to the idea. Therapy may be one of many self-care measures that a clinician chooses in his or her wellness plan. It's absolutely vital to have a wellness plan in this field, where we are asked to confront the dark side of human nature every day. Instances of vicarious traumatization and burnout are high, because too often, clinicians are ill equipped to deal with the emotional, energetic toll that helping others demands.

I recently experienced something disturbing that I fear is a microcosm of a larger problem within the helping professions. Along with clinical counselor and fellow *Dancing Mindfulness* facilitator Abbey Carter Logan, I presented an appeal to the education and training standards committee in my home state, connected to one of the licensing boards. This "standards board" consistently rejected continuing education presentations I offered at conferences, saying they were too "experiential" and "self-discovery" in nature. I pled my case not only for myself but also for other practitioners after hearing stories of alternative methodologies (e.g., Qi Gong, art therapy) being rejected for continuing education credits. One continuing education sponsor even shared with me that a workshop on compassion fatigue was rejected! When I met with the board and one of the academic members referred to alternative therapies as "expressive crap," I knew that I was in for a treat.

They decided that my *Dancing Mindfulness* trainings, which instruct professionals on how to teach the practice, were eligible for hours, but sections of the training that were purely experiential or meditative could not be counted. They contended, "That's self-discovery, not education." Of course, my response was, "What's the difference?" They were afraid of establishing a precedent that clinicians in our state would want to count every self-care activity as education. I said to myself, "Maybe if we gave people some educational credit for self-care, we wouldn't have such a problem with burnout?"

I don't mean to demonize all regulatory boards. Certainly, I've had several splendid experiences with other boards in my state and approval boards around the country that see the need for expressive healing modalities, experiential learning, and clinician self-discovery. For example, the Ohio Psychological Association hosts a continuing education retreat every year on the theme of integrating psychology with spirituality. I've made this retreat a yearly part of my own wellness program. It sustains me to teach and to receive at this wonderful event! When I deal with such organizations, I have a great sense of hope for our field.

WHAT MAKES A GOOD TRAUMA THERAPIST

Dr. Parnell

My favorite EMDR clinician, trainer, and writer is Dr. Laurel Parnell. Originally a trainer for the EMDR Institute (founder Francine Shapiro's organization), she broke away early on to teach her own style of EMDR. Her intuitive style is, in my view, the pinnacle of clinician- and client-friendly EMDR. In her 2007 book, *A Therapist's Guide to EMDR*, Parnell presented six qualities of a good trauma therapist. I used these in my own 2011 book, *EMDR Made Simple*, as a guideline for my own commentary, which I've modified for this book. You can use this list and the questions I've posed under each of the six Parnell items as a guide for your own self-evaluation:

1. *Good clinical skills*

   • What abilities or special skills do I have going for me as a clinician?

   • How comfortable am I with implementing the most basic clinical strategies for safety (e.g., risk assessment, contracting for safety, seeking outside help when necessary)?

   • If a client abreacted or experienced intense affect in a session, what clinical skills do I have to work with so that I would not harm the client?

2. *Ability to develop rapport with clients*

   • What strategies worked for me so far in establishing rapport in the first meeting with a client?

   • What are my struggles with forging a solid therapeutic relationship?

   • Are there certain populations of clients with whom I find it especially difficult to connect?

   • If it becomes clear that the client and I are not connecting after several sessions, am I willing to explore the potential problems and solutions? Would I be willing to make a referral?

3. *Comfort with trauma and intense affect*

   • How do I feel when a client enters a state of extreme emotional catharsis in my office (which can include, but is not limited to,

(Continued)

intense crying, screaming, abreaction, and lashing out at a figure from the past who is not in the office, such as a past abuser)?

- What issues of my own do clients seem to provoke the most?
- What aspects of trauma and its sequelae might I still find hard to grasp clinically or personally?

4. *Spacious*

- Have I ever forced a client to work on an area that he or she might not be ready to handle?
- What might my motives be for pushing a client to work on traumatic material he or she is not yet ready to address?

5. *Well grounded*

- Have I worked on my own issues when it comes to trauma, addiction, and mental health?
- What were my motives for wanting to become a therapist? For wanting to work with trauma?
- Do I let the client lead the session, or is it the other way around most times?

6. *Attuned to clients*

- What issues may keep me from staying present with my client during sessions?
- At what times might I find myself drifting off or distracted during sessions?
- Am I able to read nonverbal and paraverbal cues (e.g., inflection, tone, nuance)?

TYING IT ALL TOGETHER

Dr. Scott Miller and associates continually assert that clinicians who solicit feedback from their clients about their own clinical performance consistently display the best outcomes. Miller, founder of the International Center for Clinical Excellence, advocates the use of the Session Rating Scale 3.0 and the Outcome Rating Scale (see Chapter 7) to obtain this feedback. SAMHSA now lists this feedback-informed approach as an evidence-based practice. The Session Rating Scale 3.0 gives clinicians a simple, four-question metric to complete this assessment (Duncan et al., 2003). These tools are obtainable online and very easy to learn, especially if you benefit from quantitative feedback or are held to measurable outcomes standards in your practice.

There is compelling evidence to support the use of client feedback, especially regarding the therapeutic alliance, in services. Miller and associates (2006) compared the retention rates of 6,424 clinically, culturally, and economically diverse clients in a real-world setting. In cases where the therapists "opted out" of assessing the alliance at the end of a session, clients were twice as likely to drop out, and three to four times more likely to have a negative or null outcome.

Although I highly respect the work of Miller and others who are part of The Heart and Soul of Change project, the reliance they place on quantitative feedback has never fully resonated with me. Numbers give me very little useful data as a qualitatively minded person, even though they do wonders for proving the legitimacy of a concept to the scientific minds in the field. To accommodate my own learning and desire to improve as a therapist, I've taken Miller's approach with the Session Rating Scale and weave it into the closing conversation I have with clients at the end of a session. The Session Rating Scale asks clients to put hash tags along a continuum, rating the relationship (i.e., "I felt heard and respected today" on one end and "I did not feel heard or respected" on the other). Goals/Topics, Therapist's Approach and Method, and the Overall Quality of the Session are rated along a similar continuum. The hash tagging system is thought to take the numbers out of the equation for clients, but therapists are advised to place a ruler along the 10-inch line to get a traditional 0-to-10 scale. A computer algorithm and/or paper-and-pencil charts are available for purchase to track clients' overall satisfaction with sessions and the relationship over time. Early alliance continues to positively correlate with successful outcome.

As I've shared throughout the book, I don't believe that numbers paint the whole picture. Although many feedback-minded scholars and clinicians disagree with me, I use the same areas of feedback in a more conversational way. I let a client know that the feedback is important to help me do my job better and for us to more effectively work in collaboration. I encourage honest, open, sharing of preferences from the first session. Especially in those early sessions, I want to have conversations about whether the client perceives how we're working together as a good fit, and if we are accomplishing what he or she wants to accomplish in treatment.

We must strive to assess the quality of the alliance as a prime factor in being a good trauma therapist. Doing this requires us to leave our egos and "expert mindsets" at the door. We must see ourselves as mere collaborators in the client's journey towards his or her goals. The therapists qualities that Charman (2005) identified in her review are on point for enhanced trauma sensitivity: mindful, not having an agenda, having a concern for others, intelligent, flexible in personality, intuitive, self-aware, thoughtful, knows own issues, able to take care of self, open, patient, and creative.

So, what do we need to do to further cultivate these qualities? The first thing is to recognize that we have never "arrived," we are never the "expert," and we can always learn—from our clients, our colleagues, and the world around us. Dr. Paschal Baute, introduced in Chapter 10, exemplifies what it means to be a lifelong learner. He is a gem, one of the last living links that I have to my grandparent's generation. I hope that I will be so blessed to age as gracefully as he has, a thriver through and through. When he attended a *Dancing Mindfulness* class I led at a professional retreat and danced with vigor to Madonna's *Like a Prayer*, I decided that I must get to know him better. The helping professions need more people like Paschal. I consider him one of my most cherished mentors, because even in his eighties, long retired from regular clinical practice, he still thirsts for continued knowledge and development. Our email exchanges are evidence of his thirst, and his desire to learn from me, a relatively young professional by the field's standards, impresses me greatly. I hope that when I'm in my eighties, I will be open to learning from those who are new to the field.

Our journey of self-discovery must never stop. My friendship with Paschal reaffirms this cherished belief of mine every day. Whether that self-discovery comes in the form of doing our own healing work in therapy, committing to regular self-care practices, or engaging in endeavors where we continue to learn new things about ourselves, it will only benefit those we serve. Plus, it will help us to be more sane and grounded working in a professional field that is emotionally demanding. In sum, take care of yourself the way you want your clients to take care of themselves. You're worth it, and the people you help will thank you for it.

Continued growth and study in the field is important. Having an interactive community for consultation and general support is vital. Those who are masters in every field are well studied, well practiced, and comfortable with accessing support (Miller & Hubble, 2011). One of the most powerful ways to educate yourself in a person-centered manner is to examine your biases and address them through education and collaborative, collegial support. Dan Griffin, author of *A Man's Way Through The Twelve Steps*, a friend and colleague, regularly teaches that we must encounter and address our biases about gender. Jeff Zacharias, introduced in Chapter 5, believes we must encounter our biases about sexuality and strive to educate ourselves about experiences for which we have no personal frame of reference. Jeff has declared, "It's not enough to be tolerant; we have to be fully accepting of who people are if we are serious about helping them with recovery. You've got to dig in, do your own work, examine your biases, and learn."

When it comes to working with veterans and their families, Heather Bowser, introduced in Chapter 1, put it very bluntly: "Do your research. Don't retraumatize someone by being an idiot." Heather's guidance does not just apply to working with veterans. We should take this advice whenever we find ourselves working with a population about which we know little or if we find ourselves working based on stereotypes. Jeff Zacharias shared that his team at New Hope Recovery Center is happy to answer any questions that professionals might have about better understanding people who identify as LGBTQI. Speaking for myself, I love answering questions that colleagues have about addicts/alcoholics and our general experiences. It's a generally accepted practice to avoid making your client your cultural informant, so ask others; educate yourself. For instance, I enjoy asking Dan Griffin questions that I might have about a man's experience with the healing process. My collaboration with Dan gives me an enhanced understanding of my male clients. It has even helped me to work with my female clients on their relationship issues more effectively.

A phrase often attributed to Aristotle (384–322 BC) is that knowing yourself is the beginning of all wisdom. I couldn't agree more. His words are sage guidance that every helper ought to take seriously. Knowing your biases is part of this self-knowledge. Knowing the areas where you need more learning and training is another part of this, but knowing your emotional, spiritual and/or existential self is of prime importance. In your work with clients, if something gets viscerally activated in you and does not pass, that is likely your body's signal that it's time to address something emotionally. Doing that work does not make you any less of a therapist. Being attuned to that cue and recognizing that you need to do that work makes you a better therapist.

If you work in the field of healing human wounds, I thank you. The work that we do isn't easy. On most days, the stressful work is accompanied by heavy doses of under-appreciation. That does not make the work that you do any less important. As a client who benefitted from the healing arts of many helpers, I'm sure that I did not adequately express my thanks to these individuals for all that they gave me at the time I saw them. They provided the bandages I needed to stabilize my wounds, the patience I needed to let them heal, and the skills I needed to thrive in a spirit of post-traumatic growth. They saw resilience in me even when I couldn't see it in myself. So, I end this book with an open expression of thanks to them, and in thanking them, I thank all of you who make a difference in the lives of the wounded. The healing light in me bows, honors, and salutes the healing light in each and every one of you. Together, let us illuminate the paths of healing in this wounded world, and may these paths bring us home.

QUESTIONS FOR SELF-EVALUATION

Consider using the following questions for reflection. You might benefit from free-verse journaling on these or meditating on them. If you have a group of peers that you use for collegial support, discussing such questions together may prove fruitful. Notice what others have to share on these topics. You may find out that you're not alone, and the experience, strength, and hope you get from trusted colleagues may provide you with the needed guidance.

- How do I handle intense affect and abreaction?
- What are my personal barriers with trauma and grief?
- What factors may inhibit me from being effective with someone struggling with trauma and/or grief?
- What are my biases? For instance, do I struggle working with addicts, with clients from a gender or culture that is not my own? Am I working on stereotypes with clients from traditionally oppressed groups?
- What is my plan of action for addressing these biases?
- How knowledgeable am I about resources available in the community where I practice? Am I comfortable linking my clients with these resources? If not, what keeps me from doing so?
- When is the best time to use collaborative referrals?

FURTHER READING

Dr. Paschal Baute: http://www.paschalbaute.com.

Frankl, V. (1959). *Man's search for meaning: An introduction to logotherapy.* New York: Simon & Schuster.

Gentry, E. (n.d.). *Understanding compassion fatigue: Fitness for the frontline* [Recording]. Sarasota, FL: Compassion Unlimited.

Nepo, M. (2012). *Seven thousand ways to listen: Staying close to what is sacred.* New York: Atria Books.

Rothschild, B., & Rand, M. (2006). *Help for the helper: The psychophysiology of compassion fatigue and vicarious trauma.* New York: W. W. Norton.

Urban Dictionary: http://www.urbandictionary.com.

References

American Psychiatric Association. (2000). *Diagnostic and statistical manual of mental disorders* (4th ed., text revision). Washington, D. C.: Author.

American Psychiatric Association. (2013). *Diagnostic and statistical manual of mental disorders* (5th ed.). Washington, D. C.: Author.

American Psychological Association Presidential Task Force on Evidence-Based Practice. (2006). Evidence-based practice in psychology. *American Psychologist, 61,* 271–285.

Baranowsky, A. B., Gentry, J. E., & Schultz, D. F. (2010). *Trauma practice: Tools for stabilization and recovery.* Boston, MA: Hogrefe Publishing.

Benish, S., Imel, Z., & Wampold, B. (2008). The relative efficacy of bona fide psychotherapies for treating post-traumatic stress disorder: A meta-analysis of direct comparisons. *Clinical Psychology Review, 28*(5), 746–758.

Bernstein, E. M., & Putnam, F. W. W. (1986). Development, reliability, and validity of a dissociation scale. *Journal of Nervous and Mental Disease, 174*(12): 727–735.

Beutler, L., Malik, M., Alimohamed, S., Harwood, T., et al. (2005). Therapist variables. In M. Lambert (ed.). *Bergin and Garfield's Handbook of Psychotherapy and Behavior Change* (5th ed.,pp. 227–306). New York: Wiley.

Bisson, J., & Andrew, M. (2007). Psychological treatment of post-traumatic stress disorder (PTSD). *Cochrane Database Syst Rev, July 18*(**3**), CD003388.

Burana, L. (2009). *I love a man in uniform: A memoir of love, war, and other battles.* New York: Weinstein Books.

Cacciatore, J. (2008). Appropriate bereavement practice after the death of a Native American child. *Helping Families in Crisis.* Retrieved from http://www.nationalshare.org/Cacciatore_Native_American_Child_death_FIS.pdf.

Carlin, G. (Performer), & Urbisci, R. (Dirctor). (1990). "Euphemisms." *Doin' It Again* [TV Movie], United States: Home Box Office.

Centers for Disease Control. (2013). Major findings, In *Adverse Childhood Experiences (ACEs) Study.* Updated January 18, 2013, Retrieved from http://www.cdc.gov/ace/findings.htm.

Charman, D. (2005). What makes for a "good" therapist? A review. *Psychotherapy in Australia, 11*(3), 68–72.

Cloitre, M., Courtois, C. A., Ford, J. D., Green, B. L., Alexander, P., Briere, J., . . . van der Hart, O. (2012). *The ISTSS Expert Consensus Treatment Guidelines for Complex PTSD in Adults.* . Retrieved from http://www.istss.org/AM/Template.cfm?Section=ISTSS_Complex_PTSD_Treatment_Guidelines&Template=/CM/ContentDisplay.cfm&ContentID=5185.

Cooper, M. (2008). *Essential research findings in counselling and psychotherapy: The facts are friendly.* Thousand Oaks, CA: Sage Publications.

Corey, G. (2009). *Theory and practice of counseling & psychotherapy* (8th ed.). Belmont, CA: Thomson Brooks/Cole.

Courlander, H., & Arno, E. (1959). *The tiger's whisker and other tales from Asia and the Pacific.* New York: Henry Holth & Co.

Courtois, C. A., & Pearlman, L. A. (2005). Clinical applications of the attachment framework: Relational treatment of complex trauma. *Journal of Traumatic Stress, 18*(5), 449–459.

Courtois, C. A., & Ford, J. D. (2009). *Treating complex traumatic stress disorders: An evidence-based guide.* New York: The Guilford Press.

Cure. (n.d.). *Online Etymology Dictionary.* Retrieved September 20, 2013, from Dictionary.com website: http://dictionary.reference.com/browse/cure.

Curran, L. (2010). *Trauma competency: A clinician's guide.* Eau Claire, WI: PESI, LLC.

Curran, L. (Director). (2012). *Trauma treatment for the 21st century* [Educational Documentary]. United States: Premiere Education & Media.

Curran, J. (2013). *101 trauma-informed interventions: Activities, exercises, and assignments to move the client and therapy forward.* Eau Claire, WI: Premiere Education & Media.

Dickens, C. (1843). *A Christmas carol.* London: Chapman & Hall.

Dugard, J. (2011). *A stolen life: A memoir.* New York: Simon & Schuster.

Duncan, B. L., Miller, S. D., Wampold, B. E., & Hubble, M. A. (Eds.) (2009). *The heart and soul of change: Delivering what works in therapy.* 2nd ed. Washington, D. C.: American Psychological Association.

Dykema, R. (2006). How your nervous system sabotages your ability to relate: An interview with Stephen Porges about his polyvagal theory. *NexusPub,* March/April 2006. Retrieved from: http://www.nexuspub. com/articles_2006/interview_porges_06_ma.php.

Ehlers, A., Bisson, J., Clark, D. M., Creamer, M., Pilling, S., Richards, D., . . . & Yule, W. (2010). Do all psychological treatments really work the same for post-traumatic stress disorder? *Clinical Psychology Review, 30,* 269–276.

Engel, G. L. (1961). Is grief a disease?: A challenge for medical research. *Psychosomatic Medicine, 23,* 18–22.

Evans, K., & Sullivan, J. M. (1995). *Treating addicted survivors of trauma.* New York: The Guilford Press.

Fosha, D. (2000). *The transforming power of affect: A model for accelerated change.* New York: Basic Books.

Fosha, D., & Slowiaczek, M. I. (1997). Techniques to accelerate dynamic psychotherapy. *American Journal of Psychotherapy, 51*(2), 229–251.

Frances, A. (2013). *Saving normal: An insider's revolt against out-of-control psychiatric diagnosis, DSM-5, big pharma, and the medicalization of ordinary life.* New York: Harper Collins.

Frankl, V. (1959). *Man's search for meaning: An introduction to logotherapy.* New York: Simon & Schuster.

Gentry, E. (n.d.). *Understanding compassion fatigue: Fitness for the frontline* [Recording]. Sarasota, FL: Compassion Unlimited.

Grey, E. (2010). *Unify your mind: Connecting the feelers, thinkers, & doers of your brain.* Pittsburgh, PA: CMH&W, Inc.

Hammerschlag, C.A. (1988). *The dancing healers: A doctor's journey of healing with Native Americans.* New York: HarperCollins.

Hanh, T. K. & Cheung, L. (2011). *Savor: mindful eating, mindful life.* New York: Harper One.

Hawk, K. (2012). *Yoga and the twelve-step path.* Las Vegas, NV: Central Recovery Press.

Heal. (n.d.). *Online Etymology Dictionary.* Retrieved September 20, 2013, from Dictionary.com website: http://dictionary.reference.com/browse/heal.

Henry, O. (1913). The gift of the magi. In *The four million.* New York: Doubleday, Page & Co.

Herman, J. L. (1992). *Trauma and recovery.* New York: Basic Books.

Hiatt, D., & Hargrave G. (1995). The characteristics of highly effective therapists in managed behavioral providers networks. *Behavioral Healthcare Tomorrow, 4,* 19–22.

Howell, E. (2008). *The dissociative mind.* New York: Routledge.

Hugo, V. (1862). *Les Misérables.* Paris: A. Lacroix, Verboeckhoven & Cie.

Keller, S. M., Zoellner, M. A., & Feeny, N. C. (2010). Understanding factors associated with early therapeutic alliance in PTSD treatment: Adherence, childhood sexual abuse history, and social support. *Journal of Consulting and Clinical Psychology, 78*(6), 974–979.

Kessler, R. C., Sonnega, A., Bromet, E., Hughes, M., & Nelson, C. B. (1995). Posttraumatic stress disorder in the national comorbidity survey. *Archives of General Psychiatry, 52,* 1048–1060.

Korn, D. (2009). EMDR and the treatment of complex PTSD: A review. *Journal of EMDR Practice and Research, 3*(4), 264–278.

Kübler-Ross, E. (1969). *On death and dying.* New York: Simon & Schuster.

Lambert, M. J., Whipple, J., Hawkins, E., Vermeersch, D., Nielsen, S., & Smart, D. (2004). Is it time for clinicians routinely to track client outcome? A meta-analysis. *Clinical Psychology, 10,* 288–301.

MacLean, P. D. (1990). *The triune brain in evolution: Role in paleocerebral functions.* New York: Plenum Press.

Males, Trauma, and Addiction Summit. (2013). *Eight agreements on males, trauma, and addiction treatment.* Retrieved from http://dangriffin.com/wp-content/uploads/2013/06/The-Eight-Agreements.pdf.

Marich, J. (2010). EMDR in addiction continuing care: A phenomenological study of women in early recovery. *Psychology of Addictive Behaviors, 24*(3), 498–507.

Marich, J. (2011). *EMDR made simple: Four approaches to using EMDR with every client.* Eau Claire, WI: Premiere Education & Media.

Marich, J. (2012). What makes a good EMDR therapist?: Exploratory clients from client-centered inquiry. *Journal of Humanistic Psychology, 52*(4), 401–422.

Marich, J. (2013). *Creative mindfulness: 20+ strategies for recovery and wellness.* Warren, OH: Mindful Ohio.

Marich, J. (in press). *Understanding and treating spiritual abuse* (Continuing Education Full-Length Article) Sacramento, CA: CME Resource.

Miller, A. (2006). *The body never lies: The lingering effects of cruel parenting.* New York: W. W. Norton & Company.

Miller, S. D., Duncan, B.L., Brown, J., Sorrell, R., & Chalk, M. B. (2006). Using formal client feedback to improve retention and outcome: Making on-going, real-time assessment feasible. *Journal of Brief Therapy, 5*(1), 5–22.

Miller, S. D., Duncan, B. L., Sparks, J. A., Cloud, D. A., Reynolds, L. R., Brown, J., & Johnson, L. D. (2003). The session rating scale: Preliminary psychometric properties of a "working" alliance measure. *Journal of Brief Therapy, 3*(1), 3–12.

Miller, S. D. & Hubble, M. (2011). The road to mastery: What it takes to be an exceptional therapist. *Psychotherapy Networker, 35*(3), 22–31.

Mitchell, E. C., & Hoover, J. E. (2010). *The elders speak: Two psychologists share their lifetimes of experiences.* Knoxville, TN: Authors.

My Chemical Romance. "Sing." *Danger Days: The True Lives of the Fabulous Killjoys,* Warner Music and Reprise Records, 2010, CD.

Naparstek, B. (2004). *Invisible heroes: Survivors of trauma and how they heal.* New York: Bantam Books.

Nepo, M. (2012). *Seven thousand ways to listen: Staying close to what is sacred.* New York: Atria Books.

Norcross, J. (2002). *Psychotherapy relationships that work: Therapist contributions and responsiveness to patients.* New York: Oxford University Press.

Norcross, J. (2005). The psychotherapist's own psychotherapy: educating and developing psychologists. *American Psychologist, 60*(8), 840–850.

Nouwen, H. (1974). *Out of solitude: Three meditations on the Christian life.* Notre Dame, IN: Ave Maria Press.

Nouwen, H. (1990). *The road to daybreak: A spiritual journey.* New York: Bantam.

Olfman, S., & Robbins, B. D. (Eds.) (2012). *Drugging our children: How profiteers are pushing anti-psychotics on our children and what we can do to stop it.* Westport, CT: Praeger.

Paris, J. (2013). *An intelligent clinician's guide to DSM-5®.* New York: Oxford University Press.

Parnell, L. (2007). *A therapist's guide to EMDR: Tools and techniques for successful treatment.* New York: W. W. Norton & Company.

Parnell, L. (2008). *Tapping in: A step-by-step guide to activating your healing resources through bilateral stimulation.* Louisville, CO: Sounds True Books.

Pease Bannit, S. (2012). *The trauma toolkit: Healing PTSD from the inside out.* Wheaton, IL: Quest Books.

Penn, Schoen, & Berland for the American Psychological Association. (2004). *Survey for the American Psychological Association.* Washington, D.C.: Authors.

Porges, S. (2011). *The polyvagal theory: Neurophysiological foundations of emotions, attachment, communication, and self-regulation.* New York: W. W. Norton.

Prins, A., Ouimette, P., Kimerling, R., Cameron, R. P., Hugelshofer, D. S., Shaw-Hegwer, J., . . . Sheikh, J. I. (2003). The primary care PTSD screen (PC–PTSD): Development and operating characteristics. *Primary Care Psychiatry, 9,* 9–14.

Prstojevic, M., Razovic, M., & Wagner, A. (1993). *Sarajevo survival guide.* Sarajevo, Bosnia-Hercegovina: FAMA.

Raskin, N. J., & Rogers, C. R. (2000). Person-centered therapy. In R. J. Corsini & D. Wedding (Eds.), *Current psychotherapies* (pp. 133–167). Belmont, CA: Thomson Wadsworth.

Reisetter, M.; Korcuska, J. S.; Yexley, M., Bonds, D.; Nickels, H., & McHenry, W. (2004). Counselor educators and qualitative research: Affirming a research identity. *Counselor Education and Supervision, 44,* 2–16.

Ricci, R. J., & Clayton, C. A. (2008). Trauma resolution treatment as an adjunct to standard treatment for child molesters. *Journal of EMDR Practice and Research, 2*(1), 41–50.

Rosenzweig, S. (1936). Some implicit common factors in diverse methods of psycho- therapy. *American Journal of Orthopsychiatry, 6*, 412–415.

Ross, C. (2012). *The rape of Eve: The true story behind the three faces of eve.* Richardson, TX: Manitou Communications.

Ross, C. (2013). *Structural dissociation: A proposed modification of the theory.* Richardson, TX: Manitou Communications.

Rothschild, B., & Rand, M. (2006). *Help for the helper: The psychophysiology of compassion fatigue and vicarious trauma.* New York: W. W. Norton.

Santoro, J. (1997). *The angry heart: Overcoming borderline and addictive disorders.* Oakland, CA: New Harbinger Press.

Scaer, R. (2007). *The body bears the burden: Trauma, dissociation, and disease.* New York: Routledge.

Scaer, R. (n.d.). The dissociation capsule, In *TraumaSoma: Articles.* Retrieved from http://www.traumasoma.com/excerpt1.html.

Shapiro, F. (2001). *Eye Movement Desensitization and Reprocessing: Basic principles, protocols, and procedures.* (2nd ed.) New York: The Guilford Press.

Siegel, D. (2008). *The neurobiology of "we": How relationships, the mind, and the brain interact to shape who we are.* Boulder, Co: Sounds True Books.

Siegel, D. (2012). *Pocket guide to interpersonal neurobiology: An integrative handbook of the mind.* New York: W. W. Norton & Co.

Street smarts. (n.d.). *Urban Dictionary.* Retrieved September 24, 2013, from http://www.urbandictionary.com/define.php?term=street+smarts.

van der Hart, O., Brown, P., & van der Kolk, B. (1989). Pierre Janet's treatment of post-traumatic stress. *Journal of Traumatic Stress, 2*(4), 1–11.

van der Kolk, B. A. (1994). The body keeps the score: Memory and the evolving psychobiology of posttraumatic stress. *Harvard Review of Psychiatry, 1*(5), 253–265.

van der Kolk, B. A. (2005). *Developmental trauma disorder: Towards a rational diagnosis for children with complex trauma histories.* Retrieved from http://www.traumacenter.org/products/pdf_files/preprint_dev_trauma_disorder.pdf.

Weintraub, A. (2012). *Yoga skills for therapists: Effective practices for mood management.* New York: W. W. Norton.

Weller, F. (2012). *Entering the healing ground: Grief, ritual and the soul of the world.* Santa Rosa, CA: WisdomBridge Press.

Wilson, J. P., & Thomas, R. B. (2004). *Empathy in the treatment of trauma and PTSD: Brunner-Routledge psychosocial stress series.* New York: Brunner-Routledge.

Worden, J. (2008). *Grief counseling and grief therapy: A handbook for the mental health practitioner.* (3nd ed.) New York: Springer Publishing Company.

Yalom, I. (2001). *The gift of therapy: An open letter to a new generation of therapists and their patients.* London: Piatkus.

Appendix

The "Greatest Hits" List of Positive Beliefs

(Assembled by Jamie Marich, PhD; may be duplicated for use in clinical settings)

Responsibility

I did the best I could.

I do the best I can with what I have.

I did/do my best.

I am not at fault.

I can be trusted.

Safety

I can trust myself.

I can choose who to trust.

I am safe now.

I can create my sense of safety.

I can show my emotions.

Power

I am in control.

I have power now.

I can help myself.

I have a way out.

I have options.

I can get what I want.

I can succeed.

I can stand up for myself.

I can let it out.

Value

I am good enough.

I am a good person.

I am whole.

I am blessed.

I am unique.

I am worthy.

I am significant.

I am important.

I deserve to live.

I deserve only good things.

I am smart.

I can belong.

I am special.

I am a success.

I am beautiful.

My body is sacred.

I can make friends.

It's okay to make mistakes.

I can only please myself.

I cannot please everyone.

Others Not Listed:

217

The "Greatest Hits"
List of Problematic Beliefs

(Assembled by Jamie Marich, PhD; may be duplicated for use in clinical settings)

Responsibility

I should have known better.

I should have done something.

I did something wrong.

I am to blame.

I cannot be trusted.

Safety

I cannot trust myself.

I cannot trust anyone.

I am in danger.

I am not safe.

I cannot show my emotions.

Power

I am not in control.

I am powerless/helpless.

I am weak.

I am trapped.

I have no options.

I cannot get what I want.

I cannot succeed.

I cannot stand up for myself.

I cannot let it out.

Value

I am not good enough.

I am a bad person.

I am permanently damaged.

I am defective.

I am terrible.

I am worthless/inadequate.

I am insignificant.

I am not important.

I deserve to die.

I deserve only bad things.

I am stupid.

I do not belong.

I am different.

I am a failure.

I am ugly.

My body is ugly.

I am alone.

I have to be perfect.

I have to please everyone.

Others Not Listed:

The "Greatest Hits" List of Addiction-Specific Beliefs

(Assembled by Jamie Marich, PhD; may be duplicated for use in clinical settings)

I cannot cope without alcohol.

I cannot cope without drugs.

I cannot cope without cigarettes.

I cannot cope without acting out violently.

I cannot cope without victimizing others.

I cannot cope with emotions without eating.

I cannot live without sex.

Sex is my most important need.

Escaping reality is my most important need.

I cannot survive without a partner/relationship.

I am not capable of dealing with my feelings.

I am not capable of dealing with my life.

I cannot accept/deal with reality.

I am incapable of being social without drugs.

I must victimize others to cope with my past.

I am nothing without my addiction.

I have no identity without my addiction.

I have no identity if I can't act out.

My addiction is my security.

I must use alcohol to cope with my past.

I must use drugs to cope with my past.

I must have sex to cope with my past.

I must eat to cope with my past.

I must have sex to be in control.

I must gamble to be in control.

I must smoke to cope with my past.

I must eat to be in control.

I must use drugs to be in control.

I must drink alcohol to be in
control.

I must smoke cigarettes to be in control.

I must act out violently to be in control.

I must victimize others to be in control.

I am incapable of being social without
alcohol.

I must be in a relationship to be in control.

I must act out violently to cope with
my past.

I am incapable of being social without
cigarettes

Others Not Listed:

Index

Made in the USA
Monee, IL
25 August 2020